WOMEN'S SPIRITUALITY
Power and Grace

MARY FAULKNER

HAMPTON ROADS

Cover design by Barb Fisher
Cover art by Daniel Nevins, *danielnevins.com*
Interior designed by Maureen Forys, Happenstance Type-O-Rama

Hampton Roads Publishing Company, Inc.
Charlottesville, VA 22906
www.hamptonroadspub.com

Library of Congress Cataloging-in-Publication Data is available upon request.

ISBN: 978-1-57174-625-2

Malloy
10 9 8 7 6 5 4 3 2 1
Printed on acid-free paper in the United States of America

CONTENTS

❧ ❧

Part IV: People of the Earth

Part V: Transforming Culture

Part I

❧ ❧

THE MULTI-LEVEL, MULTI-FACETED, COLOSSAL RETHINK

In the multi-level, multi-faceted, colossal Rethink, we catch a brief glimpse of Great Mother. We take a look at our spiritual origins and begin to identify the dual nature of power and grace. We'll shine a light on brilliant new theology and philosophy being written by women that is taking religion and spirituality in a whole new direction. This new work is correcting errors of the past and giving voice to what has been misrepresented or overlooked by religion and by society. Women theologians lend credence to what is being prompted by instinct and intuition—a new logic rising up out of the depths of women's psyches. Looking at our common heritage provides compassion for and understanding of our human journey and helps determine a course of action for the future.

Chapter 1

❧ ❧

TIME BEFORE TIME

Women's spirituality is a work in process. It begins with the realization that women's religious and spiritual heritage is missing more than a few pages. It takes a new look at power—where it comes from and how it's used. It takes a look at new archeological discoveries, ancient cave art, mythology, and scripture, reaching back in time to fill in the blanks in our shared history. As we discover more about the beliefs and practices of our earliest relatives, we begin to get a broader and more balanced understanding of the human story and our place in it.

She's Back!

Sometime in the early 1970s, a woman rolled over, propped herself up on one elbow, and snapped open a window shade of consciousness in women all across the country. Shaking off thousands of years of sleep, she yawned and exclaimed, "I'm back!" Since that time, droves of women have been exploring ancient ruins, mythology, literature, and their collective memory to find out more about "her."

Believing in Goddess as a deity is not required in women's spirituality, but understanding her symbolic and historic significance provides helpful insight into the meaning of women's spiritual quest. The interest she holds for women and the values she represents are at the heart of this spirituality—and offer balance to the history in which we've been steeped.

Who is Goddess? Why is she so important to so many women? Is she real or wishful thinking? Does it matter? To answer these questions, and perhaps to raise a few more, we'll take a look at the most interesting spiritual phenomenon of our time—the return of Great Mother.

Our Humble Beginnings

For a long time, what we knew about pre-history was just an educated guess. Today, it's moved beyond guesswork and made that big leap into accepted scholarship. Thanks to new archeological discoveries, carbon dating, and women's increased professional involvement in interpreting data, information about our early ancestors continues to surface. Now we know that, as long as 700,000 years ago, the ancestors of our ancestors carved images of the Goddess out of stone and painted her image on cave walls. Evidence showing that, from the dawn of prehistory, this Mother figure was the focus of ritual and ceremony is overwhelming. For all but the last 6000 years of our considerably longer story here on earth, "God" was a woman.

Unlike the images of a club-swinging caveman dragging his woman by the hair, our early relatives seem to have existed in peaceful communities in which power was shared between the genders. These early relatives made art, invented technologies, and worshipped a Mother figure. When viewed from this perspective, the world's "great" religions—Hinduism, Buddhism, Judaism, Christianity, and Islam—are the new kids on the block. What this means to us today is that there exists a long history of the female as sacred, and that living peacefully is as much or more a part of our heritage as competition and war.

Rocking the Cradle of Civilization

The hand that rocked the very first cradle of civilization was black.

Our common beginnings go back to southwestern Ethiopia near the Omo River. Just as our physical life began there, so did our spiritual life and our earliest relationships with the sacred. And our first image of the sacred was of the Great Mother.

Migration of modern humans out of Africa began approximately 50,000 years ago. Traveling on foot and by sea, our early ancestors began to move out from their homeland, expanding into Asia, Europe, Australia, and North and South America. They carried

FIGURE 1. *"Mitochondria DNA," the original mother of Africa. (Artist, Noris Binet; courtesy of Martha Leigh Ferrell collection.)*

images of their Great Mother with them. Figurines of the large-breasted, big-bellied, round-hipped women known as "Venuses" have been found along African migration paths throughout Spain, Italy, the Pyrenees, the Dordogne area of France, central and Eastern Europe, and Austria.

Our Spiritual History

We can infer the religious practices and beliefs of our prehistoric relatives from archeological findings. The sub-Saharan region of Africa, rich in rock art, is an archeologist's picnic. The sheer numbers of paintings that are found there create a comprehensive picture of prehistoric society. "Figures dancing, singing, playing musical instruments, engaging in initiation rituals, with body decoration and masks, characterize the art of the entire heterogeneous African continent, according to archeologist Umberto Sansoni" (Lucia Chiavola Birnbaum, *Dark Mother: African Origins and Godmothers* [Authors Choice Press, 2001]).

Images indicate that our ancestors observed the patterns of the seasons, drawing their spiritual images from nature. Vegetation bore fruit in summer, died in winter, and greened again in spring—birth, death, and rebirth were woven into the human psyche and celebrated in religious rites. Since females gave birth, it was assumed that the earth must also be female, as all life flowed from her. "She" was their source of food, water, shelter, and beauty. The earliest feasts and celebrations honored this earth Mother.

Interpretation of burial practices further fills in our family archives. Graves were lined with pine boughs, apparently to offer comfort and warmth to the deceased for the journey—implying the belief that life extended beyond the grave. The body was painted with red ochre, most likely symbolizing the mother's blood that sustained them in the womb. Bodies were arranged in a fetal position and covered with flowers, returning the body to the Great Mother where it could be kept safe inside her body until the time of its rebirth. When a child died, images of the mother's breast were carved on rock and placed over the grave so that the child's spirit would have plenty to eat and not be frightened.

Figures of the Mother consistently show her as fleshy, with large round hips, a big belly, and big breasts. The statues were placed in niches alongside the hearth in the cave—a central place in the home—indicating her importance in the lives of the people. She is often shown pregnant, reflecting life's abundance—not to indicate a fertility cult, but in recognition of our origins in a female body. She was seen as the primary creative force of the cosmos; all life sprang from her womb.

FIGURE 1. *The Venus of Willendorf, an archetypal female figure carved from Upper Paleolithic limestone ca. 25,000 BCE, Europe. (Artist: Susan Faulkner)*

African Origins and NaNa Buluku

Oshun priestess Luisah Teish, writer, performer, and ritualist, describes African cosmology in her book *Jambalaya: The Natural Woman's Book of Personal Charms and Practical Rituals* (HarperCollins, 1985). Here, she tells us how NaNa Buluku, a deity with both male and female aspects, created the world. NaNa Buluku gave birth to twins, a woman called Mawa and a man known as Lisa. Together, they embody the principle of duality, showing how nature is composed of opposites—two aspects that together become the whole. Teish teaches classes in African religion, and tells about the time before colonization when Africans believed in a living universe she calls "continuous creation," a universe that is still in the process of becoming.

The Yoruban people use descriptions like "Author of Day and Night" and "Discerner of Hearts" to describe their deity and its presence to them and to life itself. It was said that the Black Goddess carried a snake in her belly, signifying that her nature contained both female and male—in other words, she was self-fertilizing. Teish believes that it's important to explore female images of God to get our balance back from thousands of years of patriarchy.

"From the minute the priest announced that I was the daughter of Oshun," Teish remembers, "I began to think of myself in a different, more positive way. Oshun is the goddess of love, art, and sensuality. She is a temperamental coquette with much magic up her sleeve. She was the me I hid from the world" (Teish, *Jambalaya*). Teish believes the modern world is out of order and that the oppression of women has been built on an erroneous assumption that the "Most High God is male." She talks about Oshun, Goddess of Love, reflected in the voluptuous curves of the river, in its sweet, life-giving water, and in the beautiful jewel-like stones found there. The people intuitively know she is female. If they observe a certain woman moving as if she carried the flow of the river in her hips, they may call her "Daughter of Oshun."

> *Oshun is brass and parrot feathers in a velvet skin. Oshun is white cowrie shells on black buttocks. Her eyes sparkle in the forest, like sun on the river. She is the wisdom of the forest. She is the wisdom of the river. Where doctors fail, she cures with fresh water. Where medicine fails, she cures with fresh water. She feeds the barren woman with honey, and her dry body swells up like a juicy coconut. Oh, how sweet, how sweet is the touch of a child's hand. (Yoruban chant to Oshun, from Patricia Monaghan's* The Goddess Companion: Daily Meditations on the Feminine Spirit *[Llewellyn, 1999]).*

One Moon, Many Reflections

The Great Mother was represented in many images. The late Marija Gimbutas, author and professor of Archeology at UCLA, identified numerous carvings throughout Europe, recognizing them as different representations of one universal Great Mother—Bee Goddess, Snake Goddess, Mountain Goddess, Mistress of the Animals and more—all in celebration of different aspects of one deity.

Historical data exist showing that these early ancestors grew crops, wove fabric, kept animals, and figured out how the sun, moon, and stars worked. They gathered huge stones and made calendars marking the exact location of summer and winter solstices—the longest and shortest days of the year. They spent their summers hunting and gathering food and their winters in spiritual celebrations and painting on the cave walls.

Interpretation of these artifacts, as well as other archeological findings, led experts to believe our early relatives honored their ancestors. Their pictures indicate that they held all forms of life in sacred partnership. No instruments of war have been found; no wars are depicted in any art; the locations they lived in did not offer protection against invaders.

The images they created are far from crude or simplistic. When assessed against contemporary art using the same standards, they are found to be of significant sophistication and remarkable beauty. Their use of color, composition, and perspective are artful by all standards. Their understanding of the anatomical structure of animals is considered exceptional.

For many years, these drawings were considered only to show the mundane, day-to-day activities of the people. However, when indigenous teachers interpret the paintings, they discover their spiritual significance. What was previously seen simply as a figure standing with arms extended is now identified as a shaman opening portals to the spirit world or in communication with animal spirits. Moreover, these teachers recognize elements of ritual that are still used today.

Beating the Drums of War

Gimbutas conducted major excavations of Neolithic sites in southeastern Europe from the 1960s through the 1980s, unearthing artifacts of daily life as well as objects of ritual and worship, which she documented throughout her career. Introducing an innovative methodology to her discipline, she combined traditional archeological "digging" with her extensive knowledge of linguistics, art, ethnology, and the history of religions. This resulted in a more comprehensive picture of the lives of these early communities than previous exploration had revealed. She essentially reinterpreted pre-history, concluding that, before 4000 BCE, the people of Old Europe (her term) lived harmoniously, worshipping a Mother Goddess figure represented in art as the creator and sustainer of life.

In her book, *The Civilization of the Goddess* (HarperSanFrancisco, 1991), Gimbutas describes essential differences between the old European system she identifies as matriarchal—Goddess- and woman-centered—and patriarchal—god- and male-centered—warrior cultures. She concluded that matriarchal society was peaceful and based in economic equality. Andro-centric (male) warrior cultures invaded Europe about 6000 years ago, she tells us, and imposed their hierarchal rule, creating the male-centered patriarchal system that replaced the earlier societies. This more warlike culture marked the end of Goddess time and the beginning of God time.

The Rise and Fall of the Goddess

Excavation of two civilizations that survived into fairly recent times shows us a good picture of what early matriarchal societies actually looked like and how they functioned. Catal Huyuk, located on the Anatolian plains of what is now Turkey, is one. The other is the Greek island of Crete, considered to be the high point of Goddess civilization, lasting well into patriarchal time to approximately 1700 BCE.

Catal Huyuk—Life on the Anatolian Plains

Catal Huyuk was a Neolithic city established somewhere around 8500 BCE and occupied for over 800 years. Archaeologists have uncovered the remains of twelve different cities on the site.

Religious art and symbols unearthed there support earlier evidence of a peaceful society. It was a spot chosen for its beauty, not for its ability to be defended against attack. In fact, no evidence was discovered that would lead to the conclusion that the people of these cultures were involved in warring.

Burial sites at Catal Huyuk show that the female graves were in a central location; gifts buried with them, as well as the size and position of housing, show a slight preference toward the women. Children were often buried with mothers, but never with fathers, which indicates that lineage was passed through the female line.

The art at Catal Huyuk establishes an important link between the archaic Mother Goddess cultures of the prehistoric world and those of classical times. The Madonna and child, venerated in the religious art of Christian churches and homes all over the modern world, go back in time in an unbroken line to this Mother Goddess imagery. The Great Mother that is so firmly rooted in the psyche of the people of Neolithic times is the Madonna of our psyches as well.

Crete—The Goddess' Last Stand

The Greek island of Crete was the site of the most highly developed civilization of the ancient world. It was also the last to fall. Crete was home to approximately 100,000 inhabitants in its heyday. Its culture, known today as Minoan, originated about 6000 BCE, when Anatolian immigrants arrived from Turkey bringing their sacred goddesses with them. Crete's cultural development, particularly the city of Knossos, encompassed the shift from an independent cave-dwelling society to city life and to the building of modern houses. Dwellings began as one or two rooms and, over time, expanded into complex structures complete with art and indoor plumbing.

The remains of this remarkable society tell a story of great prosperity. Crete was a cultural center known for its art, music, and agriculture. The inhabitants built viaducts, fountains, and irrigation systems to transport water, as well as sanitation systems providing domestic conveniences that put them ahead of all the cultures around them, including those on the mainland of Greece.

For the Minoans, as for their earlier ancestors, religious celebrations expressed a joy of life. Music, art, dance, processions, ban-
quets, and games were all essentially religious ceremonies that were
depicted in art. Male and female enjoyed equal status, as indicated
by their similar style of clothing and their mutual participation in
recreation.

FIGURE 2. *Minoan snake goddess from Knossos, Crete, ca. 1600 BCE.
(Archeological Museum, Herakleion)*

Crete prospered and its later development included large, elaborate multi-leveled palace structures—again with indoor plumbing. Roads and bridges connected the island communities, and Crete became a trading center for exchanging goods with Asia Minor, Egypt, Africa, and the mainland of Greece. Art, pottery and vase-making, fresco painting, sculptured stones, and jewelry were perfected to a high level. Above all was the Goddess, shown with a snake in each of her hands and her arms raised high above her head. She was celebrated in art and dance—loved and respected.

Speculation continues regarding the end of the Minoan culture. According to some archaeologists, the Minoan civilization was weakened as the result of a tsunami (or possibly even a series of these massive waves) pounding the coastline in the late 17th century BCE. However, the goddess culture managed to keep going for another 150 years. The final destruction of the Palace of Knossos came in the mid-15th century BCE, as the Mycenaeans invaded from the Greek mainland, marking the end of the Minoan period.

Western culture is said to have begun on Crete. Religious rituals like the Eleusinian Mysteries, as well as Greek mythology—including tales of Aphrodite, Athena, Demeter, Persephone, Artemis, and Hecate—were incorporated into the Greek pantheon from Crete. Their stories were woven into Greek culture and later into Roman mythology, ultimately becoming part of Western culture. However, each translation of the Goddess took us deeper into patriarchal time, and her story and images began to reflect her diminished place in the culture.

Matriarchies Are Not Patriarchies in Drag

Honor of the Great Mother translated into power and social position for women. Society under the Goddess was called *matriarchal*. Although it is often assumed that a matriarchy is simply a patriarchy in drag, this is not the case. In a matriarchy, men and women share leadership, which is characterized by service rather than privilege. Matriarchal social systems aren't rigidly stratified. Societies under the Goddess were most often *matrilineal*, meaning that property passed through the female side of the family. For differences between matriarchal and patriarchal societies, see Table 1.

TABLE 1. *Differences Between Matriarchy and Patriarchy*

MATRIARCHY	PATRIARCHY
Shared leadership	Male dominance
Equality	Stratified/hierarchical
Cooperative	Competitive
Inner authority	External rule
Spiritual	Religious
Leadership by serving	Leadership as privilege

Now, our story fast-forwards several thousand years. In the next chapter, we'll look at women's spirituality today—what women are doing and why they're doing it.

Chapter 2

✿❦ ❦✿

WHAT IS WOMEN'S SPIRITUALITY?

*I*n order to understand women's spirituality, it helps to think of
it as a verb rather than as a noun, because it's a process rather
than a doctrine. It is a spirituality of questioning and discovering. It
begins at the personal level, becomes political, and then gets practical. It questions many of the traditional understandings about
power and authority, and eventually questions assumptions that
have been made about God.

This spirituality doesn't preach or teach a specific theology or
doctrine and it doesn't send you to the traditional religious sources.
It encourages you to go within—to find your own truth. Leaving
the familiar is scary; we all cling to what we've known. Yet, something is dying and something is asking to be born—it's an ancient
story. Like giving birth, it isn't something you want to do alone.
And all over the country, women are gathering together to explore
spirituality—to discover what they hold sacred and create ways of
celebrating it. *This is a spirituality of possibilities.*

Out, Out Damned Spot!

The desire to explore spirituality comes from a variety of experiences. It may grow out of hope or a dream, or out of a longing that
doesn't go away. It can come out of a growing dissatisfaction, a lack

of fulfillment, anger, or boredom with organized religion. We often interpret this as a sign that something is wrong with us. We try to be better, to shift our caretaking into high gear or shut ourselves down, and yet, no matter how good we are, how well we perform, or how much we accommodate, these feelings refuse to go away; we still feel as if we are in the wrong. Like Lady Macbeth, we can't wash away this longing, nor can all the perfumes of Arabia cover it up. Not because we're guilty, but because we aren't. You can't expunge what isn't there!

"The goal of spiritual practice is full recovery, and the only thing we have to recover from is a fractured sense of self."

–MARIANNE WILLIAMSON (from *A Return to Love: Reflections on the Principles of a Course in Miracles* {HarperCollins, 1992}).

One day, you hear someone talking about feeling the same way you do—and the curtain begins to lift. Women's spirituality acts as a sounding board for questions, thoughts, and feelings, and for exploring those persistent doubts. It's a source of validation. As women discover that many others are asking themselves similar questions, they begin the process of discovering their spirituality, too.

For the Record

The women in this book are asking themselves questions about sexuality, economics, political power, religion, ecology, family structure, community, health, well-being, sickness, death, and life after death. These questions have been floating around since the beginning of time. The difference here lies in whose answers will make it into the record book. Women's spirituality points to the fact that, for thousands of years, the sacred writings of the great religions of the world have been based on men's interpretations of life. They contain valuable teachings, but they are incomplete. The rest of the story is waiting to be written.

Caroline Myss, best-selling author in the fields of medical intuition, spirituality, and human consciousness, calls this search "discovering your sacred contract." "It's your birthright to discover your sacred contract," she claims. "It will guide you to find your divine destiny" (*Sacred Contracts* [Three Rivers Press, 2003]). Moreover, in this process, you are the expert.

How Will I Know If I Am "One of Them"?

Women's spirituality is a spirituality of diversity—a celebration of the feminine and of life in all shapes and forms. As a community, we share some general ideas; how we play them out, however, is each woman's unique statement. The only requirement for membership in this movement is a desire to belong. The following list begins to identify the essence of women's spirituality as we're defining it. These ideas will be explored further and others will surface as you read on—this is just a sample. So, you may be "one of us" if:

- You identify yourself as being more spiritual than religious, although you may be both.
- You are guided by an inner sense of justice more akin to the Golden Rule than to the Ten Commandments.
- You aren't threatened by your own or others' beliefs.
- You sense the sacred in nature as more than just renewal; your soul is fed there.
- You instinctively know the importance of freedom, respect, sharing, concern for the quality of life, and other relational ethics; you don't have to reason your way there.
- You are imaginative and have a sense of adventure, regardless of whether you act on these impulses.
- You intuitively "get" concepts like body, mind, spirit, and the web of life—the interconnection of all things.

The Inevitable Question—What about Men?

Men and women are on similar paths—we are all looking for meaning. However, men and women have different life experiences, and as a result, different questions and answers. A lot of assumptions have been made about women—what we're like, what we want, what we need, what we ought to be like—but our voices have not been heard. For the most part, our wisdom isn't being tapped—our insight isn't reflected in society. I recognize that many men share the same values I'll be describing in this book, but the focus here is going to be on empowering women in finding their voice.

Why Do We Need Women's Spirituality?

Women in the United States, at this moment in time, probably enjoy more freedom of expression, have more choices, and have more access to education, jobs, and money, than has ever been true in any culture throughout recorded history. This leaves many wondering why "certain" people see a problem where others do not. What are these women looking for? Why here? Why now?

Many believe we stand on the brink of a major shift in consciousness. This shift is being fed by women discovering their power and becoming a vital force in shaping the world. Physics has taken us past the world of atoms into quarks and finally to cosmic soup. Science is saying that everything is interrelated. As science and spirituality talk to each other, a "new" view of the world emerges—a view of a spirited universe, a living cosmos constantly in process, unfolding, always becoming. This isn't new—women have known this for a long time. It's what indigenous people know, as well as mystics from many traditions. However, modern culture and mainstream religion have not grasped the concept yet. That's about to change.

The new consciousness is about having a significant relationship with the cosmos as a living system in which the flapping of a butterfly's wing sends a ripple felt by the farthest star. It contrasts sharply with the scientific reductionism that has analyzed, dissected, and categorized creation and the creator, but failed to respect either. Women's spirituality stands in the mystery and realizes we probably will never really understand it all—nor do we need to. In this transformed and transforming relationship with the big *all there is*, the personal is political—each individual's consciousness contributes to the whole.

Is It Religion or Spirituality?

Spirituality is one of the "buzzwords" of our time, yet there isn't an agreed-upon definition of how it differs from religion. The position taken here is that religion has a defined system of beliefs and governed practices. It tends to find its identity in how it is different from other religions and from those who profess no religion. It seeks to define the sacred—to know the unknowable.

Spirituality connects us. It recognizes that we, as human beings, share certain needs, and it calls us to be responsive to them. It's inclusive, incorporating a variety of people, beliefs, and ways of expressing those beliefs, and doesn't seek to control them. Women's spirituality has no problem crossing spiritual or religious lines—it's the ultimate potluck.

In spirituality, you'll recognize universal principles found in Buddhism, Hinduism, Native American teaching, Celtic, Wiccan, and Neo-pagan traditions, Christianity, African/Caribbean practices, Judaism, Jungian psychology, and assorted folklore. Simply put, spirituality can't be bundled into one philosophy, one culture, or one set of beliefs. And it embraces the unknowable—that which cannot be quantified, only sensed and experienced.

Many people think of spirituality as an otherworldly kind of thing, separate from our human nature. Women's spirituality, on the other hand, understands spirituality as intrinsic to our human nature.

Transcending Politics—A Whole New Poetry

It may surprise some readers to know that spirituality has a *political* underbelly and vice versa—politics has a spiritual underbelly. At its best, politics serves to secure and protect innate rights; it stabilizes culture. As a country, we began with the declaration that we are "endowed by our creator with certain inalienable rights." This is our founding statement; it's the spirit of our nation. We all know the story—that our forefathers did not include everyone in that first round of making the vision a reality. With time and effort, however, more were included. Today, our national political vision, which reflects our spiritual understanding of ourselves, remains a vision in the making, and it's women's turn to enter the system fully.

Building a Better Mousetrap

Women know that, without going deeper into the issues that lie at the heart of politics, systems that were meant to protect and stabilize society. Those who create political systems will continue in the same tradition, because their religious beliefs support their decisions. For example, when religion supports supremacy of any one group over another—whether by virtue of ethnicity, gender, or religious affiliation—politics will support it as well. Women, on the other hand, understand that social transformation is the result of spiritual transformation.

Resistance to new ideas follows a law of physics—it's easier to leave something the way it is than to change it. And being disparaging seems to be popular today. We hear more about the failure of new ideas, including women's struggle to improve society, than we do about the successes. Yet, throughout history, women have spearheaded most of the social changes that have moved us toward our political vision—as one people under God, for instance. These women understood society spiritually and politically as a unified force. Women who are attracted to this spirituality are working on a dream in which everyone shares in the vision.

"Set your sights high, the higher the better. Expect the most wonderful things to happen, not in the future but right now. Realize that nothing is too good. Allow absolutely nothing to hamper you or hold you up in any way."

—Eileen Caddy

It's human nature to hang on to what you know, even when it isn't working, until something better comes along. Women have been creating options for a long time—sometimes boldly and sometimes under the radar. This ebb and flow of ideas is often described in waves, but the agenda remains consistent. The goal is always about self-determination and securing political rights that will give all people more opportunity to build a better life—more inclusion, more equality, a place at the decision-making table as a spiritual right.

One Ocean, Many Waves

What is described as the "first wave" of the women's movement emerged during the early 19th and 20th centuries. It focused on the abolition of slavery, universal suffrage, and the right to own property—and it was successful. The second wave occurred in the 1960s and 1970s. Its primary agenda was to secure further rights in society and in the workplace. It focused on equal work for equal pay, rights over our bodies, and child care, and it successfully advanced these causes. During this time, women created a system for questioning the status quo. They wrote women's history and developed women's theology and literary criticism, thus establishing a place for themselves in the academic world. We see the results of this today, as more women than men are attending college.

The third wave began in the 1990s and continues into the present time, as women seek self-definition rather than letting themselves be lumped together and defined by others, even when the *others* are women. You will hear this described as addressing the failures of the previous generations. However, seeking self-definition isn't a failure of the preceding generations; it's the end product. It's what our mothers and grandmothers had in mind when they took to the streets and challenged authority in every social arena.

Today, we speak of globalization—a word that barely existed a generation ago. The multi-level mission of the fourth wave of the women's movement—sometimes called Generation Y—is to affect the transformative level of globalization, birthing us into earth consciousness and a world that shares its resources as a spiritual imperative. Women are taking up this cause in great numbers. Master-blogger and entrepreneur Rebecca Thorman describes today's young woman as a "compassionate alpha," excelling at leadership and displaying strength with community and empathy.

Generation Y's women are strong leaders who have moved past hierarchical leadership models into a strong sense of community and communal leadership. While men and boys continue to base their thinking and reasoning on applying established laws and rules, young women and girls are thinking outside the box and applying creative problem-solving to the issues at hand. Men who may feel threatened by women end up clinging even more closely to "old think." They've bet on the rules and are not willing to look at the issues through new glasses. Winner-take-all politics is off the table, however, and concepts like dependence and subordination are outdated. Women's more relational style uses a team approach and builds alliances.

For the first time in history, the geo-political tables have turned. Today, humans are less at the mercy of their environment than ever before. Indeed, quite the opposite is the case: the environment is at the mercy of humans. Those who dream the common dream believe that our unchecked lust for acquired power has brought us to this perilous position. As we teeter on the brink of tomorrow, we are ripe for transformation.

"Do what you feel in your heart to be right—for you'll be criticized anyway. You'll be 'damned if you do, and damned if you don't.'"

—ELEANOR ROOSEVELT

Transforming Power

Women's spirituality is part of a global transformation and the shift to understanding power as a spiritual right—the indwelling of the sacred. All over the world, indigenous people gather in tribal circles; pilgrims journey to temples, churches, mosques, and monasteries. They come together offering prayers around the clock, paving the way for our imminent transformation. Those who hold the sacred vision of creation pray in many different tongues. Behind the words, however, the thoughts are the same—*thy kingdom come.*

We have sought power in a variety of ways: money, prestige, beauty, strength, academic expertise, religion, ownership, and the list goes on. These pursuits share a common theme—they are all based in the concept of power as something you acquire. As you read this book and explore your thoughts and beliefs, consider a new definition of power—not as something we have to earn or accomplish, but as something we already have. This kind of power is innate. It came pre-installed on our hard drive. *I call it grace.*

Wrapping Things Up

Women's spirituality is a movement of women who are asking questions, exploring their history, getting clear about their beliefs, and finding their voice. It's a process of coming to greater awareness of what you hold sacred, and finding ways to express your spiritual beliefs in the world. There isn't a particular set of religious truths or written rules that define this spirituality; it works from common principles. You can belong to your traditional religion and partake of women's spirituality, too. It exists in the way we approach the sacred, the questions we ask, and what we want to see reflected in the world.

Chapter 3

※ ※

POWER AS GRACE

The idea of power as grace recognizes that the origins of all power are transcendent—that is, God-given, a human right. Because religion developed in a patriarchal time, it embraces particular ideas about God, power, and spirituality—qualities reflective of a male worldview. Women offer a radically new understanding of spirituality as right relationship. How we imagine our relationship with Source informs all our relations—with each other, with nature's creatures, and with the earth itself. When we acknowledge power as grace, all aspects of creation are sacred.

There are two main impediments to making our common cultural dream a reality. Both are antiquated ideas, yet they still draw a crowd. They are the concepts of hierarchy and patriarchy. Hierarchy is an organizational system that ranks people in ascending order from bottom to top, each level having power over those below. Dolly Parton said it best when she declared: "The higher the hair, the closer to God!" The foundational belief of a spiritual hierarchy is that God exists outside of this world and above us. Those at the top of the pyramid are closer to God. They have more power than those below. And since power is a close relative to rights, this has translated over the centuries as those above having more rights than those below.

Hierarchy can be a valuable way of organizing our experience—particularly when leadership is based on service. It allows for quick

23

decision-making and, in the hands of a skilled leader, provides a unifying presence. It is a point around which folks can rally. There have been examples of its success. But we've also all heard the adage that power corrupts and that absolute power does so absolutely. In other words, for the most part, human nature is not well-equipped to handle that kind of power.

Father Knows Best

Patriarchy is, literally, rule by fathers in families, tribes, or kingdoms, and is extended to include political rule by males. In a patriarchy, power is handed down from father to son (usually the eldest son); in marriages, it means that the family, including the wife, is ruled by the husband. Cultures have dealt with this dynamic in many ways—softening the edges and even ignoring the whole thing and moving on to other more satisfactory ways of doing business. However, many haven't. A look at the portraits of those who have presided over the Oval Office, or a peek into the Senate or the House of Representatives or the Supreme Court is enough to show that we have not come off this old dynamic all that much. A look at the leadership in organized religion shows us the same.

When you combine hierarchy with patriarchy, you automatically rule out half the world's population—in this case, the half that would be the most likely to have some new ideas on how to run a railroad. When you consider the leadership of mainstream religion, the Catholic Church has the largest membership worldwide and it doesn't ordain women. Southern Baptists are second in number of followers and, as recently as the year 2000, they restated their position against women's ordination. The Society of Friends ordained women as early as 1800—probably the first modern religion to do so. Although women have been ordained in other Christian denominations in the United States going back almost that far, they represent only a small percentage of the population. Major denominations that have opened their ranks to women have done it so recently that the results, while felt in the immediate sense, have not had time to impact the structure or the system.

When hierarchy is coupled with patriarchy, it consolidates power within certain groups of people and begins to erode social and religious integrity. In other words, it tends to yield to special interest.

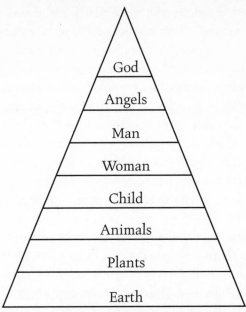

FIGURE 4. *Those occupying each level of the pyramid have power or dominion over those below. The assumption is that those near the top are closer to God than those below.*

Rethinking Power

Both patriarchy and hierarchy entered the cultural mainstream about 6000 years ago, when the world shifted away from matriarchal societies. Most people assume that matriarchies are the opposite of patriarchies—meaning rule by women. However, there is no indication that women were ever the designated leaders of society. Matriarchy is a term given to pre-patriarchal societies by social scientists, usually indicating simply that men were not in charge. What is called matriarchy is actually a model of shared power—apparently an incomprehensible concept to the investigators.

Throughout our history, we have developed a belief in power as something we acquire—and the more you have, the more God-like you become. In this model, power is attributed to whatever the culture values. Strength, beauty, money, age, size, education, and acquisition of territory are some of the ways we establish the pecking order. The term "pecking order" itself hints at how we regard the position—those higher up on the scale peck at the weaker ones below. As stated earlier, power is a close relative of rights, and power over others quickly becomes rights over others. In 6000 years, we've grown used to these ideas; we may even have come to accept them as God-given. However, these ideas are only human constructs—not bad or good in and of themselves, but ripe for a rethink. Power is a spiritual dynamic that, when applied, becomes political. *How you think of power matters.*

Because they have been on the short end of the power equation for most of history, women have a tendency to back away from power—we don't want it and refuse to acknowledge having it. Owning power can be dangerous; safety or security can depend on denying we have it. However, denying our power jeopardizes our authenticity.

A considerable part of women's spirituality focuses on issues of power and authority—where it comes from, who is believed to have it, and how it is used. Power isn't good or bad—only how it's perceived and how it's used. When power is separated from the idea of grace—recognizing sacred presence in another—it quickly becomes about privilege and about rights over others. When it's seen as grace, power is about respect and service.

Power as Grace

Power as grace means we all have the same access to it. One person or one group of people doesn't have more power than any others. On a practical note, it immediately reduces the jockeying for position and run-away competition so present in our culture. It frees us up to do more of what we want to do, and reduces the need to pursue money or prestige when we're really not interested in them, or to buy things we can't afford to impress people, or to work out at the gym endlessly to make our bodies look like someone else thinks they should... and the list goes on.

Mostly, power changes our self-perception. We begin to have a different experience of ourselves—what we can hope for, what we can accomplish. And we begin to have a different relationship with others. And most everyone would agree that reaching out to empower others is spiritually valuable. Understanding power as the indwelling of spirit in self and others creates a radical understanding of relationship. It goes beyond being *connected to* the *all there is,* and becomes about intrinsically *belonging to* the *all there is.* Perhaps only a matter of a couple of words, but a big difference in perception. This radical relationship carries essential values—love, compassion, and justice among others.

God Here, God There, God Everywhere

Power as grace means that God is present here and now. This, as you will find, is a major theme throughout this book. The idea of sacred presence means that the spirit of the creator permeates creation— it's everywhere. Creation is sacred—all of it. Full is full, regardless of the size or shape of the container. Nothing in creation has more God or less God in it than something else. We can't squeeze, cajole, force, or manipulate any more of it out of God or anyone else. There is absolutely no hierarchy in the sacred model of creation.

Maybe There Really Isn't Any "There" There

Gertrude Stein made famous the remark that "There isn't any there, there," referring to her hometown of Oakland, California. Her statement can also help us understand sacred presence. While traditional believers are content to say that God is both "here" and "there," they get very touchy when we talk about God just being "here." And that's what got me wondering—in a seamless universe, *maybe there isn't any there, there.*

When this thought came to me, I took a break from writing and went out to the river to think. I was sitting under a tree, stirring a small bonfire, soaking up some nature, musing on this chapter and the realities of "here" and "there," when I happened to look up into the branches over my head and saw a squirrel. He appeared to be smiling at me. As I looked back, an idea came to my mind that it was time for me to go out on a limb, theologically speaking.

Everyone seems to agree on the idea of God's *omnipresence*. I learned about it a long time ago in the *Baltimore Catechism,* that little brown book that contained all the answers for Catholics.

Question: Where is God?

Answer: God is everywhere.

Omnipresent means just what it says—present everywhere at the same time. You can't have "omni-some places" or "almost-omni." You can't have God present in your soul and not in your big toe, for instance. Or present in you and not me. Or, for that matter, present in church, but not present in the squirrel swinging on branch over my head. God's presence is fully—*here*. So when you read the fine print on omnipresence, know there is no separation between the material world and the spiritual world. It's all really here, now—and there really isn't any there, there.

Be here, now. Isn't that what spiritual teachers have been telling us all along? What if they're right? What if everything is all here now? What if the only thing missing is our ability to realize that fully—and to live it? Isn't this what the mystics in every tradition have been telling us? As they practice being still and going inside, they're able to open more levels of awareness, and they say they will eventually find God.

Paradise Revisited

Much of Western religion teaches us that the separation that resulted in *We the People* and God happened when we committed original sin, were issued our walking papers from the Garden, grabbed a couple of fig leaves, and headed out into the world to seek our fortunes. In the story, "original sin" is symbolized by the image of a snake successfully tempting Eve. Many women believe the choice of this particular image was not accidental. For thousands of years preceding biblical history, women were believed to have gifts of prophecy and vision. It was recognized that they had the ability within themselves to discern "morality" and were the guardians of the beliefs and ethics of the society as priests and spiritual leaders. This power was symbolized in the image of a snake.

In scripture (Genesis 3:1–24), the snake is the means by which Eve commits "original sin." The snake, once the symbol of woman's gift of moral discernment, turns against her. On the psychological and theological levels, this translates to her not being able to trust herself—furthermore, she becomes untrustworthy. She's a temptress who not only sins, but lures her mate into sin as well. (Women point to the fact that Adam does not take responsibility for his actions, but blames Eve.)

Biblical scholars and theologians from all religions are in disagreement over the exact meaning of the creation story and may never completely agree on what it means. However, the common understanding has been woven deeply into our societal fabric and continues to have a major impact on how women are thought of and treated. The story is the basis for male authority. Its impact is unquestionable.

Today, "new" biblical scholarship written by women over the past forty years is beginning to impact our culture. As a result, the beliefs expressed in women's spirituality will become widely accepted as part of mainstream religion. Eve will finally be given her get-out-of-jail-free card and we will look at different ways of understanding power and authority. Women are shaping that new paradigm.

Sarah's Circles and Jacob's Ladder

Psychologist and pioneer in mind/body healing Joan Borysenko uses the image of "climbing Jacob's ladder" to describe men's spirituality. She talks about the male understanding of spirituality existing outside of self and having to be accomplished through certain tasks men must do—things men must ascend or transcend. Culturally, we have come to think of religion and spirituality through this male lens. The fact that women don't always connect to this model—it doesn't match our understanding—is contributing to the current rise in a female model of spirituality. Borysenko draws a distinction between the male image of "climbing Jacob's ladder" and the female image of "walking Sarah's circles" (see figure 5). This image, she contends, is one of women's spirituality. Women find God in the center of the circle that encompasses all of creation. They connect to the sacred by connecting to their own center and to one another. This female model is essentially relational.

The circle is a good way to understand ourselves as women, both spiritually and physically. We're cyclical by nature—consider the rotation of the earth, lunar cycles, our menstral cycles, and how this all works to wire us in a circular pattern (more on circles in chapter 7). Those of us who are living in the new paradigm don't want to take over—we don't want to be at the top of the ladder. We don't think in terms of ladders. We want the circle expanded to include more people, and we want to include the environment. This new model is not about changing the players; it's about a whole new game.

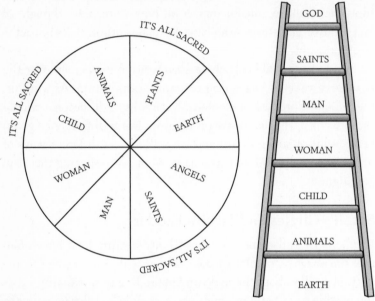

FIGURE 5. *The circle and the ladder. The ladder is hierarchal and has limited interaction among the levels. It also represents tasks that must be accomplished to get to the top. The circle is relational; the various aspects that make up creation touch in the center. Circles represent wholeness; they are not complete without all the parts.*

A New Coalition

Women's spirituality is a gathering of seekers. The tent under which we meet is large. We come from a variety of religions and cultural backgrounds, and we don't all see things the same way. You'll find women who belong to mainstream religion, women who have left that world to explore new spiritual territory, women who have never practiced a formal religion, women of all ages, races, and economic and political backgrounds—sometimes all in one circle. What we share is our commitment to seek our spiritual truth and to find ways to express it in the world. Women's spirituality has been called a new religion, a political movement, and an emerging tradition—and it is some of all of these things.

What we're calling women's spirituality has no "super" structure. No one is in charge and there is no central office, rulebook, or prescribed law. This bothers some who think spirituality is dangerous if left in the hands of "the people." That's probably because they don't realize it's always been located there. We're starting to show our true colors, now.

Women are hard-wired for relationship; with that comes an ethical framework of seeking the common good. We want everyone to have food and shelter; we want all babies to have a good shot at life; we believe in fairness and equality; we understand our dependence on the environment. At the core of this spirituality is the understanding that power is innate—God-given—*grace*. And we refute the idea that true power is acquired through money, position, physical beauty, strength, or political manipulation—even when we're the ones doing it!

Wrapping Things Up

Women's spirituality doesn't challenge God. It challenges specific assumptions that have been made about God. In doing so, it challenges long-standing cultural assumptions about power and authority—who has it, who doesn't, and where it comes from. Women's spirituality considers the possibility of sacred presence here, now, in this world. It believes all authority comes through divine Source—God or Goddess—or by whatever name you may call *grace*.

Chapter 4

BONES, MUSCLE, AND BRAINS

While theology often lacks poetry, it packs clout. It provides the platform for ideas to be recognized by professionals and work their way into the system. New interpretations, new discoveries, and new insights are put to the test of rigorous scholarship to be presented in schools, universities, and seminaries, and they eventually make it to the pulpit. Getting women's theological perspective into the record is important. Theologians are free to agree and disagree with any treatise; but having women's spirituality accepted into academia means it becomes part of the discussion. It has to be reckoned with; it gives us a seat at the big table.

Those who study scripture identify two essential themes—salvation and liberation. Salvation has to do with how we get to heaven; liberation is about our innate freedom as people of God (all people) here on earth. The liberation theme targets political oppression and the need for change, expressed as our ongoing dependence on God's grace. It recognizes that our human constructs carry the potential to be both supportive and oppressive.

Religion was supposed to swing the argument in favor of freedom. However, religion is a human construct, and, as such, it began to reflect civil power—preaching the salvation message to the exclusion of the liberation message and focusing the people on getting to heaven rather than on political analysis. Most people don't read between the lines; they just take their preachers' word for things. Over the centuries, religion got to be seriously out of balance.

Over the last quarter century, women scholars have compiled a body of work that forms the bones and muscle of women's spirituality. They're using their power to make the case for women, as well as for other groups of people who aren't effectively included in the political system. Their studies have given feminist theology a place in colleges and universities throughout the country. Many of these theologians follow the lines established by classical or systematic theology; others are using a new method called *process* or *liberation* theology. This new theology is written from the viewpoint of the people in the pews rather than religious authorities. It calls on religious leaders to be accountable for the fulfillment God's law—a radically transforming concept.

Playing the Social Equality Card

Traditional or systematic theology begins with a question about what "the people of God" are called to do in any given situation. Theologians traditionally search scripture, looking at how it has been applied in the past. Using logic as their tool, they discern what the situation at hand calls for and determine the correct response *for the people.*

Feminist theologians approach the discussion from a different angle. They talk with the people and listen to what they say; then they assess the situation or condition from the perspective of the people as it relates to religious teachings.

Christian theologians work from the understanding that the core teachings of Jesus are based on love of one another, community, and outreach to the less fortunate—God's plan for creation, they call it. They approach theology through that perspective as well. As they read scripture, they apply a theory of social equality to religious leaders—meaning that, if leaders are not actively working for this principle, they are in conflict with the basic teachings of Jesus and Christianity.

Jewish theologians draw on the prophets of the Old Testament. They are looking at errors in translation that have occurred over the years that have resulted in holding women back. They are developing rituals of empowerment for women.

A Variety of Opinions and Approaches

There are a variety of positions within the liberation tradition. Some theologians believe in the sacredness of the Bible as the word of God. They recognize it as our shared religious history and honor its deep spiritual value, but don't believe it is the infallible source that traditionalists and evangelicals believe it to be—and they question many of those interpretations.

They draw on biblical themes of Exodus, Jesus as liberator, and the idea of a God who transcends all imposed limitations, including matters of gender. They turn to scriptural images of Shekhinah and Mary the Mother of God, and Mary Magdalene as faithful disciple.

Christian theologians point to the central place women occupied in Jesus' ministry and the prominent role they played in witnessing his death and resurrection. Women remained with Jesus at the cross, and it is to women that the risen Christ first appeared. Women were the first preachers, directed by the risen Christ to go and tell the others. If this is not a direct ordination, Christian women ask, what could it be? Following are examples of women theologians from a variety of perspectives whose work is widely recognized.

Rosemary Ruether—Eco-Feminism

Rosemary Ruether is a feminist theologian at Garrett Theological Seminary, and author of over three dozen books and numerous papers. She is a pioneer in the eco-feminist movement. Eco-feminism is a term used to identify those who work to stop the abuse of women and the exploitation of the natural world. It focuses its criticism on our culture's domination of nature, seeing racism, classicism, and sexism as aspects of the same oppression—one caused by the belief in *acquired power,* or power over others, and where this kind of thinking has led us.

Eco-feminists aren't all female and they aren't all Christian. They are men and women inside traditional religions practicing as Jews, Hindus, Buddhists, and Christians. They share the idea of transforming religion from the inside. They work to eliminate patriarchy and institute new models of partnering. Ruether combines social activism and religious scholarship in her numerous books, articles, and lectures.

Rita M. Gross—Calling for Shekhinah

Rita M. Gross—scholar, Buddhist practitioner, and teacher—received her Ph.D. from the University of Chicago. She teaches, writes, and publishes in the area of women and religion, using Kabbalah and the mystical tradition of Judaism as the basis of her discussion. She says that *galut,* meaning "exile," is a fundamental part of existence. She claims that the primary cause of exile is the perceived separation of masculine and feminine in God.

She is a breath of power, a pure vision of glory,
a reflection of eternal light, a spotless mirror of goodness.
She is one, but she can do all things.
She remains herself, but renews all things.
Each generation she creates prophets and holy ones,
for she is more beautiful than the sun or the stars,
mightier than the earth itself, and she orders all things well.

–Wisdom 7:25–8:1

While Gross fully realizes that God is neither male nor female, she believes that female images for God must be reintroduced, and she uses female pronouns for God. Just as God has been split in half in Western culture, she observes, the female half of creation is likewise in exile. Gross calls for reparation. Only when the female part of God has been reunited will the world be restored to wholeness.

Spirituality and Inclusion— Speaking a New Language

My first experience with inclusive language happened at Scarritt Graduate School and Vanderbilt Divinity School, where it was more than encouraged—it was required. The use of non-inclusive language in the classroom was corrected. If a student used it in a paper, it resulted in an automatic failing grade. I had no idea how much translating I had been doing and was amazed at the difference it made. Questions like "Is that a *he* as in male or *he* as in everyone" had taken up more time than I realized.

I remember discovering that, although we had been told by our culture that "he" included "she," in fact the word "she" includes "he"—literally. Likewise we were told that the word "man" includes "woman," but actually the word "woman" includes "man." The off-campus world wasn't ready to hear it yet, however, and argued that saying "he and she" would take too long. I remember thinking that 6000 years is probably long enough. Today it has become common to say "he and she," and it takes only a split second and three strikes on the keyboard. Using inclusive language for God can still bring people to their feet. God the Mother is still an image waiting to be recognized—but it will be.

"All religious language is really metaphor. God language does not really tell us about God, but it does tell us a considerable amount about those who use it."

–Rita M. Gross (1979)

Sallie McFague—"Super, Natural Christians"

Sallie McFague, a pioneer in feminist theology, calls for a new face and a new focus for Christianity. The new face is female, and the new focus is the earth. McFague is a professor of theology and former dean of Vanderbilt Divinity School. Her book, *Life Abundant: Rethinking Theology and Economy for a Planet in Peril* (Fortress Press, 2000), urges Christians to redefine their relationships with the natural world—specifically, to realize that they are only part of the bigger scheme of things.

McFague demystifies theology and encourages readers to come up with their own version—it's about becoming conscious of how we live and work. She believes our dominant American worldview is outdated and has resulted in the gross materialism that is threatening the world ecology. She pulls no punches when she says the consumer culture is a market ideology that has become our way of life, our *religion*. She believes we are addicted to a consumer lifestyle, and in denial of its consequences.

McFague cautions that loving the earth isn't enough! People are going to have to make essential economic changes to make a significant difference in the ecological devastation we are currently wreaking on the earth. She points out that, while Americans are 20 percent of the world's population, we use 80 percent of the world's resources as if it were our divine right.

McFague addresses her message to the people rather than to the church hierarchy. By doing so, she is showing us where the real power for change rests. She is taking the liberation model one step further than some of her contemporaries by focusing on the people and bypassing the institutional church.

Thealogy—Frying Other Fish

"Thealogy" is not just theology spelled with an "a." It's a comprehensive study of the religious systems of the Great Mother—a religious symbol that predates written history. Thealogy explores women's knowledge of themselves, as well as their relationship to nature, particularly their intuitive knowledge of the natural world. It does not rely simply on cognitive reasoning as its sole method; it includes numerous disciplines—archeology, history, mythology, and ancient texts—as well as the unified theory of contemporary science.

Mary Daly—Becoming Post-Christian

Mary Daly is one of the first voices to call attention to the conditions inside traditional religion since Elizabeth Cady Stanton spoke out at the end of the 19th century. She urges women to find their own beliefs. In her first book, *The Church and the Second Sex* (Beacon Press, 1968), Daly accuses the church of promoting the idea of women being inferior. She puts responsibility on it for the worldwide oppression of women. Her writings show her gradual movement away from traditional religion, and her ultimate identification of herself as *post-Christian,* claiming: "If God is male, male is God."

Daly's philosophy is highly controversial and challenges even the most ardent feminists. Some praise her for completely breaking old forms and for rewriting not only theology, but also language itself. Others believe that she has gone too far, finding her books difficult to read. This, they claim, reduces her impact, which feminists believe could be significant to their cause. One thing is certain: Daly will most likely continue to stir the waters and provide rich material for theological discussions both inside and outside religion. "There are and will be those who think I have gone overboard," she writes. "Let them rest assured that this assessment is correct, probably beyond their wildest imagination, and that I will continue to do so."

Carol Christ—Goddess Girls Just Gotta Have Fun

Carol Christ was the first woman to receive a Ph.D. in theology from Yale University and is a former professor at Harvard Divinity School and Columbia University. She wrote the first systematic thealogy of the Goddess. Christ believes that the shift from God to Goddess heralds a transformation of Western theology, philosophy, and ethics. She believes it holds the promise of a new world order, pointing to the growing number of women and men who are finding meaning in a new kind of spirituality that's based on the divine being female. She said, "The image of God as male was at once the most obvious and most subtle sexist influence in religion. Nothing aroused the ire of male theologians or churchmen so much as the charge that traditional male language about God is sexist" (*Womanspirit Rising: A Feminist Reader in Religion* [Harper & Row, 1979]).

Alice Walker—Womanist Theology

Much of the feminist theology you've been reading about here has focused on the works of white women. African American women rightly point out that, when the word "woman" is used in our culture, it usually means "white woman." Black women have different experiences of the culture, a different history, and a different agenda. Working from these perspectives, they are creating a new theological category they call Womanist Theology.

When Alice Walker's book *In Search of Our Mothers' Gardens: Womanist Prose* was published in 1983, it gave birth to a new religious symbol that would serve to unlock the door for many black women struggling with liberation. This symbol became the starting point for a new theology called Womanist Theology.

Walker describes a colorful feminist and feminist of color who is "...outrageous, audacious, courageous," and engages in "willful behavior." This behavior is further described as "wanting to know more and in greater depth than is good for one...." (*In Search of Our Mothers' Gardens: Womanist Prose* [Mariner Books, 1984]).

Walker, and black womanist theologians inspired by her image, identifies essential differences between how black women and white women approach the same goal of liberation. Womanist wisdom has been the source of discussion among women in the black community. As their stories are heard, the scope of our perceptions of racism and feminism is broadening, and a better understanding of the dynamics black women face is emerging.

These revolutionaries believe Goddess isn't just a phenomenon occurring in women's lives, but an archetype existing within everyone's psyche. Thealogians, as well as women from every walk of life, believe that the suppression of Mother Goddess imagery, along with the life-affirming values associated with her, have been part of a concerted effort on the part of patriarchal religions to accumulate power. Author Barbara G. Walker points out that, when we are free of the oppressive politics of patriarchal society and free to recognize the divine as an archetypal symbol, our unconscious mind will take us back to the Mother Goddess.

Holism and Black African Roots

The black Christian Church is a community from which African American women and men draw strength. Black churches played a key role in the struggle for freedom during the civil rights movement of the 1960s and 1970s, and continue to be a primary source of empowerment. White feminism is often directed at the church as a patriarchal institution that has contributed to the oppression of women. Black women's experience of church is different in a significant way for many.

The modern-day black Christian church has its roots in African soil, which gives it an essentially different flavor from the white church that came out of Europe. The black church is rooted in a holistic understanding of God's presence in body and soul, here and now.

While the messengers in the African American church have been disproportionately male, their message has been one of liberation. Many black women shy away from the overall white feminist movement because it fails to recognize this basic difference. Black

Christianity is a transformed and transforming church. It concentrates the liberating presence of Jesus Christ and directs it toward the systems and structures of a society steeped in oppressive politics. In so doing, it transforms them.

White feminism builds a powerful case against a patriarchal interpretation of scripture. However, once again, many black women have a different relationship with the Bible. Black Christianity is a prophetic church. The black struggle for equality and freedom is based in the biblical themes of exile and exodus, an image of God as a God of Justice, the words of the prophets, and Jesus as Liberator. Their interpretation of scripture is thus a transformed one and is preached from the pulpit.

bell hooks—An Ethic of Solidarity

Black women endured the oppression of slavery working side by side with black men—they faced a common enemy. They worked together in the fields, and suffered the same consequences under the hands of their tormentors. They faced the continued oppression of racism together and, in their struggle for civil rights, they fought the same war against a common enemy. Black survival has always depended on solidarity. This is different from the experience of most white women, who have had to take a stand against the men of their own culture. Theologian and author bell hooks describes it this way:

> "My life experience has shown me that the two issues [race and gender] were inseparable, that at the moment of my birth, two factors determined my destiny, my having been born black and my having been born female" (Ain't I a Woman: Black Women and Feminism [Sound End Press, 1981]).

Womanist theologians talk about the sexism in black culture between men and women. However, Hooks and others feel that feminist theory tends to drive a wedge into black culture. Black women feel that they are being asked to choose between the issues of race and gender—and sometimes between man and woman. This is a choice that many of them are not willing to make.

Wrapping Things Up

Women's theology approaches scripture and religious tradition from the belief that social equality is God's plan for creation. Women theologians and scholars have found many errors in biblical translation and interpretation that builds a case for this. Some women work for reform from inside their traditions; others have left traditional religion and are discovering new forms of spiritual expression. All are working for the same goal of sounding the spiritual and theological trumpets to work for a better world—*thy kingdom come*. Black Christianity is a prophetic church, based in the words of the prophets. It has already accomplished the spiritual liberation that women's spirituality seeks. The image of Womanist Theology provided a voice for black women to express their experiences and women's spirituality is richer because of it.

Part II

❧ ❧

CELEBRATING GREAT MOTHER

For 200,000 years or more of human history, Mother Earth was the primary religious symbol. The body of a female incorporated the spiritual essence of creation, defining our relations with each other and with the earth itself. Thus our earliest cultures were Goddess cultures. They understood divine presence and the sacredness of life, which they expressed through rituals and ceremonies that followed the cycles and seasons of the year—binding the spiritual with the physical.

Culture is alive; it changes. As the world shifted from the time of the Mother to the time of the Father, changes were felt at every level. Contrary to common understanding, the time of the Mother, or matriarchal culture, is not a reversal of patriarchal culture; it is simply organized according to different values. It wasn't "Girls Rule," as the tee shirt says, but promoted a peaceful partnership between the genders. It promoted female values.

In Part II, we'll examine our origins and how women are creating ceremonies and practices today that connect them back to the Mother—a time of feminine spiritual authority.

Chapter 5

❧ ✦ ❧

SEEKING WHOLENESS—
GODDESS AS ARCHETYPE

*O*ur human spirit won't stay in the box. Life prompts us to grow, expand, and develop more of our innate self. Archetypes help us reach beyond our personal experience and understand ourselves in a deeper, more profound way. In Jungian psychology, archetypes are universal symbols of the human spirit. In matriarchal time, the diversity and complexity of the human spirit of both women and men was celebrated as the archetypal pantheon of goddesses and gods. As patriarchal culture developed, it compressed women's spirit into one archetype—that of procreator. Women came to be valued only for their ability to produce more male children. Likewise, the cultural ideal of God was compressed into a male archetype. This imbalance lies at the core of Western culture. Restoring balance is one of the primary purposes of women's spirituality.

Creation's Blueprints

Archetypes are like psychological templates or inherited memory—spiritual and psychological forces or impulses in the human psyche that contain the basic human instincts that are found in all cultures. Carl Jung described them as the blueprints for creation. They hold the patterns for every created thing—the instructions for being

a human. Jung called this archetypal realm the collective unconscious. He said it was the compilation of all human experience of all
time; it contains everything anyone has ever done or known.

Today, physicists may explain the archetypal realm as the unified field theory of quantum physics. The quantum field is the
energy in which everything exists. It appears to be empty space, but
is pure potential—the raw matter of creativity, Source. This field
is not time- or space-bound—anything that ever was still exists in
the quantum field. Quantum spirituality identifies this intelligent,
ever-creating field of energy as God.

Squeezing through a Crack in Consciousness

In addition to the visions and dreams that Jung described, archetypes are awakened by external sources like music, art, film, and
theater. We may also see a quality in another person that awakens
something inside us. What was a vague idea or longing is reflected
back to us as a reality and it comes alive within us.

On the other hand, when we live in very limiting circumstances,
the very poverty of that experience creates a deep hunger or longing, and an archetype emerges. This may very well be the impe-
tus behind the rise of the Goddess archetype today. It's awakening
specifically to fill a void in human consciousness. In response to
women's untapped potential, "she's" waking us up!

Symbol and Substance—Shelf and Springboard

The Goddess is both the symbol and substance of women's power,
their vulnerability, their sense of belonging, even their legitimacy.
In the original mythology, goddesses did not take a back seat to
the gods. When the world shifted from matriarchy to a patriarchy,
their stories were interpreted through that lens and they began to
reflect patriarchal values—eventually becoming more of a fantasy
than a mythology. It is important to go beneath these patriarchal
interpretations, however, to get to the real substance and dimension of Goddess archetypes and understand the importance of these
images and stories to women's full empowerment.

Without the image of female as primary, women are always other
than, different from, second class. It is not possible to overstate the

absolute importance of recognizing our oneness with the female as divine.

The Goddess archetype speaks to the psychological, political, and spiritual dimensions of women's lives. It refutes the common cultural misidentification of women as inferior and of women's power as dangerous or treacherous. Spiritually, it supports women in their attempt to override thousands of years of conditioning and to trust in themselves and in each other again. In her poem "Transcendental Etude," Adrianne Rich warns, "But there come times—perhaps this is one of them—when we have to take ourselves more seriously or die…" (*The Dream of a Common Language, Poems 1974–1977* [W. W. Norton & Company, 1993]). Goddess is the rock shelf and springboard from which we defy the forces that would hold us back; from here, we take that transcendental leap into new consciousness.

The Essential Imbalance

The killing off of Goddess cultures was gradual, but it soon created imbalance in the world. The only socially "approved" female archetypes in the new paradigm were the roles of wife, mother, and mistress. This remained true up until very recently. Prior to the 1960s, women who pursued careers did so mainly as extensions of mothering or caretaking, becoming "mothers at large." You can still see this reflected in the disproportionate number of women who work as teachers, nurses, social workers, waitresses, and child-care specialists—positions that, for the most part, are not adequately compensated. The statistics are changing with each generation, but the scales are still tipped in favor of males in most high-paying and decision-making positions.

The roles of homemaker and mother, as well as caretaking positions in society, are valuable, and this discussion in no way diminishes them. However, when the entire female psyche is compressed into one or two archetypes, women's potential is limited and society is stripped of vital talent, insight, and wisdom. While women continue to challenge the status quo, we've just scratched the surface when it comes to full expression in all areas of society; we are far from being recognized and appreciated for who we are. And more to the point, we are far from adequately valuing ourselves.

Today, women who enter society as professionals enter a male-constructed world. We operate within systems and traditions that represent the male psyche almost to the exclusion of the female. Female involvement will eventually change how the system functions, but until that happens, women are challenged by working in environments that fail to support them as women. That we continue to excel is a testimony to our creativity, talent, and chutzpah. However, it puts limits on our effectiveness in transforming the systems and structures of society—and it's tiring!

Myth and Legend for $1,000

Besides being a category on Jeopardy, myth and legend are also sources for archetypal patterns. Unfortunately, school textbooks don't include information about pre-patriarchal history. Yet, despite the narrowness of available role models, women continue to expand into new cultural territory. This push is coming to us—as Jung would say—from the archetypal realm.

Jacquelyn Small, psychologist and author, writes in her book *Embodying Spirit: Coming Alive with Meaning and Purpose* (Harper-Collins, 1994) that a culture's artists, writers, visionaries, and philosophers are the ones who often birth a new archetype into consciousness for an entire culture. Women like Harriet Tubman, Sojourner Truth, Georgia O'Keeffe, Amelia Earhart, Eleanor Roosevelt, Madonna, and Venus Williams opened consciousness for today's young women. That is why women's history classes and other attempts to integrate women's accomplishments into mainstream history are so important.

The human soul seeks wholeness. The rise in Goddess awareness described earlier as the collective window shade snapping open in the late 1960s and 1970s signaled the return of the Goddess to the feminine psyche. Women who follow that urging and seriously explore their history are still very much in the minority, but as they talk about their exploration and write about it, they open new doors for other women. Authors Woolger and Woolger, in their best-selling *The Goddess Within: A Guide to the Eternal Myths That Shape Women's Lives* (Fawcett-Columbine, 1987), remind us that, in recognition of the divine nature of our human urges, history's elders dignified archetypes by calling them "the compulsions of the gods and goddesses." Archetypes carry an intense and transformative quality, insisting on and assisting in the full spiritual expression of the human soul.

Jean Bolen—Writing a New Psychology

Jean Shinoda Bolen is another pioneer in reclaiming mythology as a source of archetypal images for women. Her book *Goddessess in Every Woman: A New Psychology for Women* became a national best-seller shortly after being published in 1984. At the time, Bolen was a Jungian analyst and a Clinical Professor of Psychiatry at the University of California, San Francisco. She realized the inherent problem in relying on a psychology that was based exclusively on male models of the psyche. Men and women have different experiences and different psychological processes, she noted, a fact that was not being addressed by what was virtually an all-male profession.

Bolen explores goddess archetypes found in Greek culture, uncovering their essential natures and showing how they continue to inform contemporary culture in multi-dimensional ways. She divides them into three categories: virgin goddesses that represent women's independent nature, mother goddesses that focus on relationship, and transformational goddesses that portray women in the roles of priest or shaman.

Virginity—It's Autonomy, Not Anatomy

The term "virgin" needs to be re-defined for today. In the pre-classical world, the word did not refer to physical virginity, but rather described a psychological state. It represented the part of a woman's psyche that is not relationship-oriented. *It's her autonomy, not her anatomy!* It's the pro-active component in her soul, her indomitable free spirit.

A virgin follows her own rules—not to prove anything or to rebel, but simply because she must live her truth. The virginal archetype can manifest as a desire to accomplish something in the world, or it may lead to a life of quiet contemplation—as long as you are making your own choices and following your own inner map. A woman with this archetype doesn't seek validation from her family, from a man, from her culture, or from any source other than herself; and she doesn't explain or apologize. She is connected to a deep awareness of her natural wholeness.

Next, we'll look at three virgin goddesses of Greek mythology: Artemis, a goddess of nature; Athena, who rules over culture, wisdom, and crafts; and Hestia, keeper of the sacred fires, home, and temple.

Artemis—Girls Gone Wild

Artemis is our pure wild nature. In the old Greek world, her image was that of the virgin forests of the Greek countryside where she lived and danced and ministered to the wild animals. There was a saying, "Where has Artemis not danced?" that referred to her all-pervading presence in the Greek psyche and Greek world. Artemis is depicted as a midwife in both the physical and spiritual senses. She assisted at the birth of the animals, mixing herbal potions for the mother and comforting the newborn. Symbolically, it is she who continually gives birth to nature—ever renewing, always regenerating. In the spiritual sense, she awakens new awareness in us. Without death, there can be no life. True to the duality of Goddess consciousness, it is Artemis whose hand we first feel at birth and her touch that marks us for death.

Symbols of Artemis

Artemis is symbolized by the new moon, which is considered the virginal aspect. She connects with two other goddesses: Selene, of the full moon, and Hecate, the wise woman of the dying moon. The three of them create the trinity of Virgin, Mother, and Wise Woman or Crone. This threesome is an archetype for a woman's life and can be found throughout the old Goddess stories. This archetypal Goddess trinity predates the later Father, Son, and Holy Ghost of Christianity.

Artemis in Today's World

An Artemis woman can be in a relationship, but only if she honors her Artemis needs. If you are the partner of an Artemis woman, take comfort in the fact that she is with you out of choice, not need.

Dame Jane Goodall, British primatologist and anthropologist, is a modern-day expression of Artemis. She is well known for her 45-year study of chimpanzee social and family life in Tanzania in Africa. American zoologist Dian Fossy is another example of a modern-day Artemis. Her 18-year study of the gorilla groups in Rwanda has resulted in saving the species from extinction.

Athena—A Man's Woman

You've heard of a lady's man? Well, Athena is a man's lady. She challenges female stereotypes by being a logical thinker, and by being level-headed. Athena exemplifies wisdom. She operates with clarity and effectiveness as she makes decisions in business and government, and in the military or scientific realms. Athena is the architect of cities and culture; in the patriarchal stories, she protected Athens, which is named for her. She was also patron of the arts—a skilled weaver, and in more ways than one! She was able to weave together two apparently different worlds—the world of business and politics, and the world of arts.

According to fragments of pre-patriarchal references collected by Charlene Spretnek in her book *The Lost Goddesses of Early Greece: A Collection of Pre-Hellenic Myths* (Moon Books, 1992), Athena existed prior to springing fully grown from the head of her father, Zeus. That was, in fact, a later version of an existing story—and one that baffles the imagination.

Athena in Today's World

Today, Athena women can be found at the top of organizations, in politics, education, and scientific laboratories, or heading up community projects. If you are a math whiz, enjoy science, or excel at research or writing papers, you've got Athena skills. If you pride yourself for being objective, logical, moderate, clearminded, physically active, or practical, you are reflecting Athena. If you are the partner of an Athena woman, relax and enjoy her skills. She isn't laying a power trip on you; her nature is authentically that of a CEO.

FIGURE 6. *Athena is the largest indoor statue in the Western world, located in the Parthenon in Nashville, TN. She is the work of artist Alan LeQuire and stands 41 feet 10 inches tall. (Photograph, Gary Layda)*

Hillary Clinton is an example of an Athena woman. Her marriage, even though it made her First Lady of the most powerful nation in the world, did not fully define her. She has a destiny beyond that and has gone on to live it.

Oprah Winfrey is another example of an Athena woman. Her work as a leader and champion of many women's causes, her accomplishments as a remarkable business woman, and her status as one of the richest and most powerful women in the world remain front and center in her life. Her relationship of many years with Stedman Graham is, no doubt, important to her, but remains in the background.

Hestia—Keeping the Home Fires Burning

Hestia is expressed in the image of keeping the home fires burning. Hestia is at the very center of home life, providing illumination and warmth. She has no human form, but is the fire itself—the soul of the family.

Unlike the outwardly directed energy of Artemis or Athena, Hestia's intuitive, sensitive nature flourishes in the quiet spaces and beauty she creates in her home. Hestia women seek stillness and often find that home and homemaking offer the solitude they require. Household chores keep them centered and balanced—in them, they find harmony rather than drudgery.

Hestia in Today's World

In the ancient world, Hestia tended the temple. In contemporary times, she can be found in religious life, particularly in contemplative orders. Outside of the convent or ashram, she may be a respected elder—the unmarried aunt whose detachment can be counted on for wisdom and guidance. She holds the values for the tribe and offers deep spiritual insight. Hestia women do not draw their identity from the home or marriage; they *provide* identity to those realms. If you are the lucky partner of a Hestia woman, you will be blessed with a happy home—but don't expect her to go out and get a job.

In recent history, Rose Kennedy may be considered to embody Hestia. She was the unequivocal matriarchal center of the Kennedy family, quietly inspiring her remarkable clan. At the same time, she was contemplative by nature, holding the family values and attending daily Mass up until she died.

Relational Goddesses—The Softer Side

Three examples of relational goddesses are Hera, Wife and Goddess of Marriage; Demeter, Mother and Goddess of Grain; and Persephone, Daughter and Queen of the Underworld. These three women represent what we have come to accept as traditional roles for women: wife, mother, and daughter. Their core identity and well-being is expressed in their relationships. They bring their identities to this role; they don't draw them from the role.

Hera—"Marry Me and Take Me Away from All This!"

Hera presides over fertility and marriage. While she energizes all aspects of women's lives, she particularly presides over the years of marriage and child-rearing. She does not draw her identity from her husband, but from the marriage itself.

As an example of how the patriarchal stories put women in positions subservient to men, we know Hera only in relationship to Zeus, where she is portrayed as the jealous wife. She is described as wandering the Greek countryside mourning and weeping after her philandering husband. Angry at his infidelities, she directs her rage against the women in his life rather than at him. Yet her pre-patriarchal temple at Olympia, where she is known as Herion, predates that of Zeus by many years. Since the beginning of time, she has presided over the Olympian games and races that were the precursors of the modern Olympics.

Hera in Today's World

Hera's archetype embodies women's desire and instinct to bond as loving and faithful wives, despite the difficulties a marriage may bring. She epitomizes unconditional commitment. She fulfills her destiny through *sacred* marriage. It's marriage itself, not her husband, that is her focus and source of satisfaction. However, as later versions of her story show, her absorption with relationship at the expense of self can bring depression and despair. Partners of a Hera woman can be assured of her faithfulness and loyalty, but should remember that it isn't about them; it's about the marriage.

Princess Diana embodies the later Hera stories. She was married to a powerful man, but, to the dismay of the royal family, she drew her identity from the marriage itself, not from her husband.

Demeter—Archetypal Jewish Mother

Demeter is the definitive mother figure, containing the archetypal form for nurturing and generosity. She was sometimes pictured with bundles of grain in her arms, as it was she who raised the crops and fed the people. She was celebrated every autumn in Greece in agricultural festivals honoring fertility. The intensity of Demeter's relationship with her daughter, Persephone, was so powerful that it formed the basis of the Eleusinian Mysteries that were enacted in Greece for over 2000 years.

In the duality of the Goddess, Demeter embodies both birth and death. She gives birth to all things and welcomes the dead. Her maternal instinct can be called on to assist with pregnancy and child-rearing. Demeter women are depicted in the Madonna-and-child image of Western art. But not all is sweetness and light. It's important to claim Demeter's rage, as well—she empowers the rage a parent feels when a child is threatened.

Demeter in Today's World

Demeter is reflected in the helping professions like nursing, teaching, social work, or counseling. Demeter women are often the matriarchs of their families; they are counted on by everyone to pull the holidays together, as well as organize the annual family reunion. At work, they'll know everyone's birthday, spouses and children's names, and will likely organize the company picnic.

The challenge for a Demeter woman is to respect others' boundaries and their need for autonomy—not to cross the line from mothering to smothering. If you are the partner or child of a Demeter woman, your laundry will always be clean and folded and in your dresser drawer, and your bed made. However, you may have to struggle for your independence. It's hard to get angry with Demeter, but occasionally, you'll have to stand your ground.

An over-the-top version of Demeter is represented by Raymond's mother, Marie, in the television series *Everybody Loves Raymond*.

Persephone—To Hell and Back

Persephone was Demeter's only child. As Kore, the maiden, she represents the new crops growing in the field in spring. Her abduction into the underworld by Hades is a later adaptation of her story. Demeter, grief-stricken over the loss of her beloved daughter, shuts nature down, thus creating winter, until her daughter is returned to her.

Persephone eventually returns to Demeter. However, before leaving the underworld, she eats six pomegranate seeds. Persephone deceived Demeter, telling her that she was forced to eat the seeds when, in fact, she did it willingly. In so doing, the line between her abduction and her willing participation is forever blurred. As a result of this deception, Persephone must return to the underworld for half of every year.

Persephone in Today's World

Persephone represents the struggle for individuation that many women experience. She is both the eternal innocent maiden, compliant and passive, and the Queen of the Underworld. In modern times, she may be seen as coquettish, a people-pleaser, or the eternally lost little girl. She draws power from that role, which belies her innocence.

Counselors and spiritual advisors can use her insight and skills in helping others negotiate their shadow side. Persephone has survived abduction and rape and lived to become master of her fate. She can inspire and assist women in healing from similar wounds. She is the archetype for re-birth and our ability to begin again—she is eternal springtime. Partners of Persephone women may sometimes wonder with whom they teamed up. Persephone archetype can seem inconsistent if you don't remember that she lives with her feet in two different worlds. She is wise beyond her years.

Transformational Goddesses—The Magical Side

The next two goddesses, Aphrodite and Hecate, are transformers. Aphrodite, the Goddess of Love, embodies the creative impulse— the force behind all acts of creation, from art and music to making babies. She charms and beguiles, illuminates and seduces; she keeps the wheel of life turning and reproducing. Hecate, Goddess of Wisdom and Death, is the embodiment and master of all the aspects of woman. She is wise old Hecate, also known as the crone. She has seen it all and done most of it. She has learned life's lessons, and is able to help other women through all their passages. She is the one who takes you through your final gate into the dark and mysterious realm of death as shaman and high priestess. Both Aphrodite and Hecate archetypes are extraordinarily powerful, but are the least understood female roles in today's culture.

Aphrodite—Sex and the Single Woman

Aphrodite has inspired poets, artists, musicians, and lovers. Her singularly fixed goal is to consummate a relationship and create new life. She will do that through physical intercourse, bringing a new child into existence, or through the arts. She is the soul of creativity—an archetypal magician invigorating and charming all in her presence.

Aphrodite pushes the patriarchal buttons. She is passionately and intensely focused on her mission to create new life. In the unrelenting pursuit of her goal, she breaks the rules written by men. She can create intense intimacy and deep compassion with the flutter of her eyelashes—keeping her cool at the same time. She governs women's enjoyment of sexuality and sensuality, but marriage and commitment are not even on her agenda. She falls in love easily and often, but never forever. She gets what she wants, giving pleasure in return, but when she's satisfied, she moves on.

Aphrodite's ultimate transformational power is the power of love itself. She heals by opening our own hearts and connecting us to our deepest selves—our passion, our art. Aphrodite shines her golden light, causing us to fall in love with ourselves, transforming us in the process.

Aphrodite in Today's World

Marilyn Monroe still remains the definitive Aphrodite of our time. She enchanted poets and playwrights, baseball players and presidents. Her white dress, tousled blond curls, red lips, innocence, and sex appeal captured the affection of women as well as men. Her beauty and unique mix of vulnerability and power cast a spell and made us all love her. Ironically, and perhaps true to the Goddess' penchant for paradox, this iconic sex symbol ultimately died alone.

Hecate—Wise Woman and Gatekeeper

Hecate, Goddess of Wisdom and Death, is the old woman of the dark moon. Commanding respect and engendering terror, she guards the passage through which we must all go to reach eternity and, eventually, regeneration. Hecate is sometimes shown wearing a long black robe, holding burning torches. On moonless nights, she roams the earth with a pack of ghostly, baying hounds. She can be found standing at the triple crossroads, where she symbolizes the power of choice and helps women choose wisely.

Hecate in Today's World

In today's culture, Hecate women are the most feared and also the most respected women in the culture. They have come to grips with themselves and with their innate power. Having moved beyond the external beauty of the virgin, and no longer child-bearing like the mother, they have slipped the bonds of patriarchal control. Like the crone of the ancient world, Hecate women are respected for their embodiment of wisdom, and feared for the truth and clarity they bring to any situation.

Hecate is the family's invincible matriarch, or she may sit on the boards of big businesses and charities. Women in our culture embodying Hecate are Eleanor Roosevelt, Maya Angelou, or, in a comedic version, Sophia, the mother on the television series *The Golden Girls*.

Wrapping Things Up

Archetypes are blueprints of universal human characteristics, skills, and talents—our shared memory. They inspire and also assist us in becoming fully human. Western religious tradition compressed all the Goddess archetypes into a monotheistic God who is male. As a result, many women have difficulty finding adequate female images that reflect our innate power. Women's spirituality explores the pre-patriarchal mythological world to find a richer picture of the feminine that expresses women's spirit in a more complete and accurate way than is available in modern society.

Chapter 6

✿❧ ❧✿

REBELS, CIRCLES, AND REFRIGERATOR WISDOM

*A*ncient archetypes continue to speak to women today, but in a language they can understand. They keep us actively involved in our process, prompting us to make changes as necessary for our growth. Women's spirituality is about knowing ourselves through our own longings and experiences, not through the male culture. Spirituality is about trusting our inner promptings and finding our sense of authority. Archetypes are part of the inner dialogue—a mirror and map for discovering who we are. In this chapter, we'll hear from two women who have taken this voyage of discovery, in their own words.

Katherine Fowler and the Rebel

Katherine Fowler, artist and therapist, started drawing and painting at the age of three and discovered the joy of just being—a joy she spent many adult years attempting to recapture. Following college, she had a series of jobs in which she experienced success, but not satisfaction. In her words, "I was unhappy, unfulfilled, lonely and still looking to fill what I refer to as the *hole within*." She went to a therapist and discovered the abuse that had driven her most of her life; she left her office and went home and picked up her brushes. She recalls, "I was able to deal with the remembered, painful, childhood memories and released those deep-seated emotional scars through creativity." Through her painting, she discovered her archetypes and rediscovered the lost joy of her early childhood. Having found herself, she returned to college at Prescott College in Arizona to pursue a Master's degree in Expressive Art Therapy, with the desire to help others in their healing journey.

Fowler isn't a big believer in long-term therapy, particularly in the traditional modalities. She studied yoga, body movement, meditation, energy work, and spirituality, and discovered her archetypal world through voice dialoguing. That's where she began a healing conversation with her body and emotions.

FIGURE 7. Katherine's Rebel, as imaged in meditation and painted by her.

Painting and Dialoguing

Voice dialoguing involves carrying on conversations with archetypal voices embedded deep within our consciousness. Fowler knows from experience that these inner characters hold the secrets of the past and bring insight and wisdom to the present. They also help us create the future. Her primary personal focus has been on three of her archetypes—her Inner Healer, her Rebel, and her Lover. Their portraits hang on the walls of her studio like trusted friends. As a part of her own awakening, she meditated and connected to her archetypal images, painted them, and began a conversation with them through the image that had come from her subconscious mind to the canvas. In these talks, her archetypes told her their stories and each gave her insight into herself.

Katherine describes her Rebel as "a superhero, with hair blowing in the wind. A French revolutionist, very tall, just having accomplished some great feat in battle, compassionate, but intense. This was an ass-kicking, name-taking chick."

I instantly liked her!

Katherine sat with the Rebel for two days before their dialogue began, because her energy was so intense. She described it as comforting, scary, and intense all at the same time—and it made her feel safe. Here is a part of that dialogue.

Artist: *Who are you?*

Rebel: *I stand for Victory. I know truth, love, and light. I am action. I know what must be done. I am confident. I reveal what must come to the surface to be seen, heard, and spoken. I question and seek truth and know what is false. I move forward constantly and am constantly still. I am balanced. I am strong. I am of the night and day integrated into one. I have fought and will fight battles for the truth.*

I have learned what is worth fighting for. I have learned when and what to fight for and against. I know what is mine and what is not. I am power. I am regal. I am a badass. I am fit, and in top condition—physically, mentally, emotionally, and spiritually. I rule my universe with knowing my own truth. I do not shy away from whatever needs to be done. Rest, I am here whenever you need me.

Katherine realized that it was the Rebel who kept her alive during her difficult childhood. She was a combination of her own Welsh and Native American backgrounds. "This Rebel of mine made me feel invincible and vulnerable at the same time." Her transformed Rebel combined with her Inner Healer and Lover to heal her child within.

My Circle of Archetypes—Striking a Balance

After meeting with Katherine, I decided to try an adaptation of her process and perhaps glean a little insight from it. I had met my inner characters through earlier work, and I placed them on a wheel as shown in figure 8.

- Rebel sits across from my Altruist self, protecting me from *altruism*—believing in the system and getting all caught up in work. Rebel is a seeker of justice and reminds me that much of what we take as the real world *isn't*. Altruist keeps Rebel from getting arrested and going to jail—a full time job!

- Parent and Child sit across from each other to stay in good communication, assuring that my basic needs to eat, sleep, and play are met. Child keeps Parent focused internally—making sure it's all about me!

- Wild Woman and Wise Woman work together. Wild Woman is just as her name implies—wild. She takes the shape of a wolf, eagle, bear, wind, rain, tide, raging river, spewing volcano—the forces of nature. Wise Woman translates the information from primal force into words.

- Shaman and Healer work from the subconscious and the origins of creative imagination to assist people in their healing journey. Shaman uses feathers and drums and Healer makes it real—translates it to the pragmatic level.

- Fool and Higher Self seem like a contradiction in terms, but we access Higher Self through the Fool's ability and willingness to begin again, to see things differently, to be vulnerable. Fool is Higher Self's ground—she brings Higher Self into form from the realm of pure spirit.

- Lover and Creator are constantly creating. Every thought, emotion, and action leaves an imprint in the world. Lover makes sure things are brought forward in the spirit of love. And Creator makes sure love is nourished.

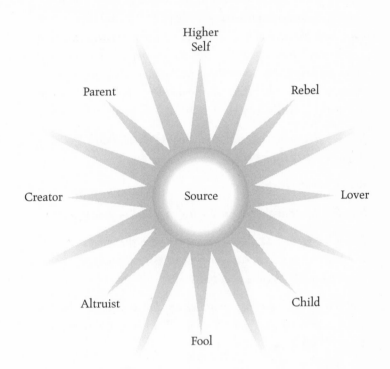

FIGURE 8. *Wheel showing the archetypes in the author's subconscious mind.*

I asked which character would like to speak and I began my usual meditation. It wasn't long before my Rebel showed up. The Rebel is one of my dominant archetypes—and can be both best friend and chief trouble-maker. I'm not an artist like Katherine, so I used a Janice Joplin album cover to put a face on him. Paradoxically, Rebel is male, even though the image I chose was female. I leaned the picture upright against the back of a chair in front of me and began our conversation using some of Katherine's questions and some of my own. Once the Rebel got going, there wouldn't be any chance of following the script. Here's how the conversation went.

Me: *Why do you want to talk with me?*

Rebel: *Because you are willing to see what you see regardless of how others see it. You don't care who hears or doesn't hear, and you don't care what others think. You're a true non-conformist. Just because someone says you need to do something doesn't mean you have to go along with it—but you might if it's a good idea. You are not a team player—in fact, you don't play all that well with others. I really get heated up when it comes to "group think." And I hate those self-help books you used to read—they're just another way of saying you should be one way or another—their way. It was me who got rid of them, you know.*

Me: *I didn't know, but it doesn't surprise me. I didn't "get rid of them," I passed them along.*

Rebel: *Whatever.*

Me: *Talk to me about power. What's your idea of power?*

Rebel: *Power is just power. I get mine from the wind in my face and fast-moving scenery. You need to ask someone else in there about power. Who cares about it? I don't.*

Me: *It feels as if you do. You attack anyone or anything that you feel is encroaching on your freedom. You just got all worked up about the word.*

Rebel: *Okay. I'm willing to say I get a sense of power from being free of power. How does that grab you?*

Me: *Oddly enough, I get it! It's one of those conundrums you're so good at. What strengths and talents do you bring me?*

Rebel: *To resist going with the majority just because it's easy—to seek out and listen to the minority opinion—even the underdog.*

Me: *What opportunities do you bring?*

Rebel: *The chance to be free! That "I've got to save the world" nut job in there [pointing to his head] gets all up in a project and forgets about you. I won't let that happen. I'll hide your appointment book when I think you need time off. I'll forget to return calls; I can even crash a computer! I've got a lot of ways I can get us some time off. I can turn any situation or any person into the enemy. When you see things through my eyes, freedom rules! What are your fears about me?*

Me: *I'm afraid we won't ever belong anywhere. It gets cold and lonely out there all the time. Everything can't be as awful as you think it is. Surely there is some good in the world.*

Rebel: *Yes. The open road! Are you going all Mother Teresa on me? Have you heard the news lately? The world is a mess. There isn't any point. Skate fast, die young! That's my motto. If I had a license plate, I'd have that on it.*

Me: *You sound hopeless. What does that feel like—to be hopeless? To think everything is bad or against you?*

Rebel: *It feels right. Too bad you can't handle it. We come into this world alone and we die alone. May as well get used to it.*

Me: *I can't handle that. It's too isolating. I'm not even sure it's true.*

Rebel: *That's my girl! Don't take anyone else's word for it—even mine. Question authority!*

Me: *The world you live in is free, but it's also an existential black hole! What's the point?*

Rebel: *Now you're cooking on the front burner! I like that existential black hole stuff. Lead me to it!*

Me: *I don't want to become bitter—alienated. The "me against the world" thing gets old. You run over all the other archetypes. You're like a self-fulfilling prophecy!*

Rebel: *Wrong! I'm not like anybody or anything. I am not like a self-fulfilling prophecy—I am one!*

Me: *I need people. I can't buy the hopelessness you live with. I don't even care if I'm making it up—I need to believe in goodness of some sort. What if we are just making it all up anyway? That ought to make you happy—the idea that we're just making everything up. That ought to satisfy your need to be right.*

Rebel: *I like the way you think! I believe we've run ourselves into a nice big blank wall in there. Round and round we go... What inevitable challenges do I bring?*

Me: *I can be okay being different. I am different. But so are other people. We're all unique. I can handle that, but I can't handle the amount of negativity you seem to need to keep your motorcycle charged up. Can you at least open the door a crack and let some sunshine in?*

Rebel: *What's the real question? What are you trying to get to that I stand in the way of?*

Me: *I need to feel a part of something bigger than me—bigger than us. I need to feel that sense of camaraderie others feel. A sense of connection—as if we're all in it together.*

Rebel: *You don't have the neuro-receptors for it. You can't stay with anything long enough for those feelings to ground. I'll drive off into the sunset if you really need me to. You can let your inner groupie or whatever have the spotlight. Just tell me when.*

Me: *Do I hear the voice of altruism? Surely that isn't you talking like that. As if you'll get out of the way to help me.*

Rebel: *It's my shadow side.*

Me: *Wow. Who is your shadow?*

Rebel: *I'm out of here—you figure it out. I'm not the fix-it guy. Call 911 if you need help.*

Me: *Who rides bitch?*

Rebel: *I mentioned her name a while ago and you didn't hear me. Figure it out for yourself. I'm gone.*

Me: *Mother Teresa?*

Rebel: *Yep. And Little Miss Rosary Beads doesn't wear a helmet!*

Me: *So you bring balance to my altruism? You keep me from being overly empathetic?*

Rebel: *Or just pathetic! Mother Teresa, or Beads as I call her, has done nothing to change the system. She practically sleeps with power. She takes government handouts and hobnobs with the pope—now he's a piece of work! If I let Beads up front for long, you'd go way overboard. I'd never see you again—or worse, you'd never see me.*

Me: *She inspires people.*

Rebel: *People need to be inspired like I need a cell phone! By the way, do you know where yours is? Maybe I'll just text you the answer! Or, better yet—I'll post it on my "Spacebook." Or have you de-friended me? What a crock! "Hi everybody. I'm at the grocery store looking at the potato chips. Now I'm in another aisle looking at laundry detergent. Now I'm scratching my butt! Losers!"*

Me: *You seem to be changing the topic. Are you uncomfortable talking about her?*

Rebel: *I'm uncomfortable. Period. Antsy. Ill-tempered. Dissatisfied. Uncaring. A self-centered hedonist. Isn't that what you think?*

Me: *No. I love you. You keep me from losing myself.*

Rebel: *That's it. I'm out of here. Talk to the vapor trail. I'll see you in the funny papers.*

From this dialogue, I came to appreciate the close relationship between my Rebel and my Altruist. I've experienced the conflict of these two parts of me. Now I see them as connected and balancing one another. This will be helpful because, when one or the other takes over, I'll know where to find the antidote quickly. Caring about people or the state of the world or the ecology can overwhelm me. Rebel disconnects me from all that. I can hop on his bike, hit the open road, and forget about everyone and everything. Nothing but the wind and fast-moving scenery; as he says, skate fast and die young!

In reflecting on our conversation, I realized that, not too far into it, Rebel took over the microphone and began asking me the questions. I was surprised to discover that I haven't given him enough credit for the insight and wisdom he brings. I think of him as reactionary—not thoughtful. The direction he took me and his questions were helpful.

Altruistic Self, or Beads, as Rebel calls her, can take over. When she does, I have a difficult time setting boundaries. I can take on way too much. Rebel will not let that happen. He'll pull the wires on Altru*ism* (emphasis on *ism*).

Grounded and Bounded

I work in the alternative or non-traditional healing field. Rebel keeps me from being New Agey! He has no time for the airy-fairy "Rainbow Breath" folks, as he calls them. He can get jaded in his disregard for those he doesn't appreciate. I have to watch him in that sense. But he is a good balance to Beads and whoever else in there makes me reach out to others, sometimes at my own expense. I can definitely stand to learn something from him.

Out of this new-found appreciation of Rebel, I feel less conflicted and less stressed. I am willing to talk more with him before things get so intense inside that I over-correct—jump on the bike and go. I can even consult him before taking on a new project or job. He can smell a potential set-up a mile away—meaning a situation where I'll go past my limits and disregard my own needs to take care of others. In further conversations, Rebel and Beads made a connection. Together, they represent a more mature, yet relentless, seeker of justice. They choose their battles. He still rides a motorcycle and Beads now wears a helmet.

Jane Marzoni—Refrigerator-Magnet Wisdom

Jane Marzoni is a retreat director who is taking time off to be a new grandmother. She talks about the various archetypes that assisted and continue to assist her through her life transitions. This little piece of refrigerator wisdom initiated her into a new awareness of herself.

> *I saw it every morning on the refrigerator door as I got the cream for my morning coffee and countless times throughout the day:* <u>*"Stand in your own space and know that you are there."*</u>

Marzoni talks about standing in every space except "that of my own soul." People, places, and things became the center of her life, anesthetizing the pain of neglecting her own soul through addictions and codependency. She compares this part of her life to being like Persephone: "abducted and taken to the underworld of alcohol and drugs and damaging relationships." And like Persephone, the lines were blurred and confusion reigned. Claiming her feminine power was a rite of passage that plunged her deep into the depths of her unconsciousness—a journey in which she was guided by wise mentors, authors, scholars, activist housewives, and goddesses of myth and fiction.

Out of Touch with Athena

Marzoni describes herself as the daughter of a Southern-born-and-bred mother with only traditional conservative models to draw from. She was molded by the patriarchal Athena archetype, out of touch with her power and unaware of Athena's true power as the Great Mother of Athens—politician, artist, and healer. "My mother couldn't teach what she didn't know." She found new mothers: Marianne Williamson, Jean Shinoda Bolen, Carolyn Myss, Shakti Gawain, and Joan Borysenko all provided solace, guidance, and support in her home schooling. She learned about becoming the woman she longed to be—a discovery that brought her freedom. "As the energy of my feminine mystique erupted, I stood straighter and taller. I stood up not only for me, but claimed solidarity with all women—connection that became an internal force, activating my life purpose."

Marzoni goes on to describe her life with Artemis as she developed Soul Spring retreat center tucked away in the hills of Tennessee:

> I felt myself moving out of Athena and into my Artemis archetype as I wrenched barbed wire from trees and watched them sway in freedom; as I walked the dry creek bed with a freshly shed snake skin around my neck, calling my ancestors for guidance; as I tracked the stars and moon across the seasons of the sky. I finally stood in my own space and I knew I was there.

Her life took another unexpected shift when she found out she was to become a grandmother. She felt the Wise Woman come to life within her and she moved to California to be a part of her granddaughter's life. "It takes a lifetime to live a life," she reflects, "and with the freedom to call my soul my own, I stand in this new space and once again I know that I am here."

Marzoni plans to build Soul Spring West, knowing that, when the time is right, the teacher will appear—from the archetypal world. In the meantime, she is teaching her granddaughter about altars and the wonder of nature.

Wrapping Things Up

Archetypes connect us to deeper parts of self—they help us discover who we are beyond our conditioning. As you identify your archetypes, you often find aspects with opposing characteristics—when seen as complimentary, they offer a more balanced picture of the human condition. Rebel is a good character to bring balance to our desire to help, which can easily cross the line and become pathological. On "his" own, Rebel can be anti-establishment just to make waves. He can engage in dangerous behavior for the thrill of it. When paired with his opposite or complimentary aspect, Rebel brings balance to the caregiver. Rebel has a zero-tolerance policy regarding guilt!

Chapter 7

❦ ❦

CIRCLE WISDOM—MORE THAN πr^2

Women's spirituality is about inner authority and shared power—spiritual qualities that are best represented by a circle. There is a different relationship to the sacred and to one another when the altar is raised and set apart from the people than when it is in the center of the circle. And there is a different spirituality involved in building your own altar than in honoring a traditional religious one. We'll look at these basic concepts—form and space—and how they telegraph important spiritual principles.

The circle is an intrinsically female geometric form—it creates sacred space. It represents the roundness of the female body—hips, breasts, and womb. It reminds us of our very first experience of the world in our mother's round belly. The roundness of the earth itself signifies safety, nurturing, and home. As the earth rotates and moves in a circular path around the sun, it forms our understanding of life in roundness and rotation. The moon, the turning of the seasons, birth, death, and rebirth are ancient circular patterns and feminine images. Our female cycle connects us to life's essentially circular nature and to one another.

"'God is a circle whose circumference is nowhere and whose center is everywhere,' is a Hindu saying, and God as the unbroken circle was an image for the Gnostic communities."

—BARBARA G. WALKER (from *The Woman's Dictionary of Symbols and Sacred Objects* {HarperOne, 1998})

Circles through Time

Early tribal villages were built with round shapes—round hearths, round houses, and round ceremonial circles—that echoed the primal circular pattern. In a circle, all members face each other; all are equal. In a circle, as backs are turned to the "outside" world, the energy is pulled into the center. The circle represents sacred or consecrated space. It offers protection against the world.

Tribal dancing follows circular patterns, as do later folk dances. Prehistoric sites like Stonehenge were built in a circular shape, and King Arthur designed his famous Round Table based on the classic symbol of equality. It showed that all who sat at the table were equal; there was no hierarchical ranking there.

Throughout the ancient world, it was commonly believed that the female form gave birth to the universe. This is a likely conclusion, because all of nature was observed to function in this way. A variation of the circle, the egg, is also an archetypal feminine form that is associated with birthing and with divine origins. It represents the Great Mother, who gave birth to all of creation.

As architecture developed, circles gave birth to domes. Temples like the Pantheon in Rome have survived from ancient time. Domes represented the sky and were often painted blue, with stars in the form of constellations. Romans further developed the art of constructing domes, and they have become one of the primary architectural forms associated with temples, churches, and mosques.

The film *How to Make an American Quilt* showed how a group of women used the old tradition of the quilting circle to celebrate their lives and transmit spiritual lessons. They met to make quilts. At a deeper level, their quilting circle was where they shared their lives, solved problems, and found meaning. The circle became the way they passed important information on to the next generation. If you are interested in exploring your spiritual process through women's spirituality, try drawing a group of friends together and working from the traditional place: a circle.

Meeting in Circles

If you have decided you want to create a circle, begin with one or two other women who are also interested. This can be your learning circle, where you develop your skills and also do some powerful work together. If you plan to increase your circle, you can do it after a time of working together and finding your identity as a group. Starting small can help you make some core decisions about the nature of the circle you're creating.

Some things to decide are:

Will this circle be based on a religious faith or move outside traditional religion?

Will the Goddess be the focus of your circle?

Are you going to explore earth spirituality?

What sources will you draw on?

Design a process for joining the group—a period of time in which the person comes to the circle and observes, maybe some required reading. A formal request and time for members to decide are important before bringing someone new into the group.

Develop a process for leaving the group. It is inevitable that someone will need to leave the group for one reason or another. Having an exit plan helps hold the sacred bond you've created together. The process may be just a simple statement. The point is to recognize it and honor each other's process.

Once established, your core group will guide the rest of the group—hold the form. Other issues on how the circle will function can be group decisions, but for now, core members can determine the vision and the essential nature of the circle.

Shaping the Vision

The core group provides an opportunity to talk about the vision. Ask each woman to share a bit about herself and also what she would like to have happen in the circle. If the visions don't match, it usually becomes clear quickly. Sometimes the vision expands to include a bigger picture, and occasionally someone's goals just don't line up with the vision. How much you want to expand to include someone is up to you—just don't lose sight of what you set out to do.

The following decisions can't all be made up front—especially with a larger group—but it's good to know that, when they do arise, you're right on track. They won't derail your vision. The level of commitment to the group is a defining factor. If the core group has already made a commitment to do deep work, then you probably will need to meet together for a couple of years. I suggest you make a shorter commitment simply to begin exploration. Those who are ready for deeper work will become apparent as time goes on.

As you begin to design the structure, further sorting out will happen. Practical decisions you will be making include the following:

Where will you meet?

How long will the meeting last?

How often will you meet?

What will your topics or focus be?

Will you follow a specific form?

What will your style and tone be?

Will your leadership follow a rotation?

A Bit about "Rules"

Less is more when it comes to rules in spirituality, but you need some. A group needs structure or it will fall apart. Rather than thinking about rules, think "commitment" or "design."

Design is a group process. Part of the design can include a time set aside for evaluation and redesign. Nothing needs to be cast in stone; but as you form your structure, you may want to write down the vision and the core elements—even if you write them in pencil. It may be a good idea to have a copy for each person. Establish a time to review the process and make the changes you feel will work better.

Things that may help you are:

Have time frames for sharing and a way of letting people know when they are getting close to the limit. It's easy to get caught up in our stories and an established time frame helps to guide the process.

Decide on when the group begins and ends, and try to keep reasonably on schedule. Timing is a subtle way to create safety. If we know the boundaries and they are respected, it's easier to trust the circle.

Learn how to listen to each other without interrupting or commenting.

Agree on a statement of confidentiality.

Avoid projecting your feelings onto other members. It is okay to ask someone how she feels, but don't make any assumptions. Freedom to have an emotional response without everyone getting into it creates safety.

Don't "fix" members. Make it a rule from the beginning that, if anyone needs anything—even a drink of water, an extra pillow, a pat on the back, or a group hug—she will ask for it.

Respect the inner knowing process. Other than brief readings that can be the source for reflection, avoid bringing books, quotations, and other outside references into the circle. This is a function of design. A reading that fits the focus of the ritual can be predetermined.

Empower your leader by allowing her to guide the group through the process, keeping you on track.

Troubleshooting

There will be times when you need to resolve conflict in the group. This is okay! Just find a good process for conflict-resolution and work through it. Very good things can happen.

Keep things fair. If one person begins to dominate the meeting with long stories, needs too much attention, or always has a problem, deal with it as a group. It won't go away on its own.

Avoid telling people what you think or even know is the right answer. This circle is about each one of you learning how to find your own answers.

Here's a partial list of statements that will keep you tuned in, and also out of the way, while you encourage a person to find her inner knowing:

"You have the answer."

"Stay with it, you'll get it."

"As creative as you are, I know you'll have a really great solution when the time is right."

"Relax—the answer will surface."

"You know what you need to know when you need to know it."

"What would the answer be if you could imagine it?"

All of these statements work well any time you are listening to someone express a difficult situation. They indicate that you are paying attention, but don't invade a person's emotional space.

Adding to the Circle

When you begin to invite others, find out if they are interested in the same focus as the group. Your circle is more than a social gathering; you'll be doing some deep spiritual work together. Make your list carefully. Think about whom you want in the circle. It isn't necessarily appropriate to invite just anybody. And you should definitely not invite people you don't want but think you should include. For example, if you have decided that you want to explore the Goddess and your best friend finds that idea threatening, maybe you don't need to have her there. Robin Deen Carnes and Sally Craig give this advice:

> *Choose only psychologically stable people. You aren't creating a therapy group, so you don't want to have to be dealing with people's unprocessed emotional "stuff" all the time. This isn't a judgment but common sense* (Sacred Circles: A Guide to Creating Your Own Women's Spirituality Group [HarperSanFrancisco, 1998])

You probably want people who are doing some other kind of spiritual work, but it doesn't matter if the faith journeys are different. In fact, diversity gives your group depth. Spirituality is about locating common ground—coming together from different perspectives creates a bigger picture. I suggest a trial time, during which members can get to know a potential new member. Find out if they're interested in what you are offering, and also if you are interested in what they bring. Only then invite them to the membership meeting. Remember, you aren't necessarily forming friendships outside the group, just membership within the group. Despite all the suggestions, it's still a creative process. You'll have to learn as you go.

The Inner Circle—Women's Altars

An altar is a reflection of your deepest self. It is a place of power in your home. Meeting in circle generally happens around an altar laid for that specific purpose—it becomes a spiritual center point for a ceremony.

Mirrors of the Soul

The tradition of building home altars and creating ceremonies goes back to the beginning of time and remains central to the expression of women's spirituality today. While formal altars and religious ceremonies follow prescribed rules, home altars and ceremonies are unique spiritual expressions of a woman's deepest self. In her book *Beautiful Necessity: The Art and Meaning of Women's Altars* (Thames & Hudson, 1999), Kay Turner describes home altars as "...existing at the point of intersection between art and religion where the sacred is apprehended in a woman's imagined relationship with the Divine." She goes on to say, "They are wedded to a creative impulse."

A simple and attractive arrangement using a plant, a shell, a candle, a beautiful rock, a photograph, and whatever else attracts you can be an altar. Don't worry about what is sacred and what isn't when you build your altar; it's all sacred. Just follow your intuition

FIGURE 9. An altar celebrating the winter solstice (December 21–23).

and see what ends up there. It will surprise you and teach you something new about yourself.

Cultural Memories and Golden Calves

Two questions that touch the absolute heart of women's spirituality often arise when you build your altar. First: By whose authority do you build the altar? Second: To whom are you building it? Most of us are familiar with the story of Moses and how he dealt with his followers who were building altars. For those of you who aren't familiar, here's the story.

Moses went up on Mount Sinai to pray, leaving his people for forty days and forty nights—which translates to a long time. His followers began to worry, wondering if he would return. These people were from the Goddess culture. Not surprisingly, in his absence, they reverted back to the rituals and ceremonies that had sustained them for thousands of years. They built an altar and placed a golden calf on it—a symbol of their former deity. They made offerings and they danced—according to their tradition. When Moses returned, he was furious. Taking the tablets of stone containing God's freshly inscribed law, he threw them on the ground and broke them. He tore the altar down and burned it, ground the remaining fragments into powder, scattered them on water, and forced the Israelites to drink it (Exodus 24:18).

The moral of this story has been reinforced through time and telling, filtering down through the ages—but usually without placing it in its cultural context, which puts it in a different light. The issue of altars has been layered with many rules and restrictions that have served to accentuate their power and, at the same time, made them seem untouchable—particularly for women. It's no wonder we hesitate when thinking of building one.

New Rules!

Unlike traditional religious altars, home altars or women's altars have no one to whom they must answer. Tradition itself backs the authority. Women seem to know naturally how to honor the sacred. You can build an altar to honor anyone or anything that's important to you: a grandmother, a favorite saint, Mary, Artemis, Jesus, or anyone or anything you want to celebrate. Altars express devotion, offer protection, and provide a place to pray and meditate. Your altar is your sacred space. It's where you are in charge—it becomes the focal point for ceremonies and rituals you create.

The Legacy—Grandmothers, Mothers, and Daughters

Altars are a female legacy often passed from grandmother to mother to daughter. Dolores is a young woman attorney of Latin descent who built an altar to celebrate her pregnancy. She called her mother a short time ago to announce the arrival of a grandchild, and her mother's first response was: "Have you built your altar?" She was pleased to be able to answer, "Yes." In fact, Dolores told me, she wouldn't even have made the phone call if she hadn't already built it.

Dolores grew up in a family where home altars were common. Dolores' mother, aunts, and grandmothers all had home altars, sometimes several going at the same time. Here is a look at Dolores' altar, and how she will be using it.

"Relationship with the Divine is a working relationship. Many women say that asking for healing and returning thanks is a labor that they perform joyously at their altars."

–KAY TURNER (from *Beautiful Necessity: The Art and Meaning of Women's Altars*)

Dolores placed her altar on the mantle of the fireplace of her old Victorian apartment in San Francisco. The central piece is a statue of the Lady of Guadalupe. Across the Lady's belly is stretched a blue band, showing her pregnancy. There is a bible, a rosary, and a small blanket arranged around the Virgin. Dolores bought a book she will use as a journal to record her thoughts and feelings for the new child. She lights a candle, sits down by the window, and begins a letter to her baby.

My Little Darling,

Today your arrival was confirmed. I suspected it for several weeks, and now we know for sure. Your father and I are thrilled beyond belief. Soon, I will be telling the family and they will be eagerly

*awaiting your arrival, too. But for now, I want to spend a little
time, just you and me, getting to know each other.*

*I can't exactly feel you, but my breasts are very aware you are there.
They began to ache about two weeks ago and that is how I first sus-
pected you had made it from the other side. How was your journey?
I get the feeling there will be lots of milk for you—not to worry.*

*Today I am lighting a red candle for us. It seems to honor the blood
that did not come this month. And red is the color of love. You must
know that you are much loved. Each morning you and I will sit
here and have our little talk. I will write things down in your book
so you can read all about your auspicious beginnings.*

*We are under the protection of The Lady, and she knows all about
these things. I am going to place this book on the altar now, and go
eat some breakfast. You must have a hearty appetite, because I am
hungry all the time. Welcome to your new home, little one.*

Love,
Mother

A Bear, a Cross, and a Stone

Women in all the traditions are reconnecting to this bit of their
sacred history. Pam, a Lutheran woman who lives in Chicago, began
building her home altar after attending a workshop held at her
church. Her altar is on the coffee table in the living room of her
suburban home. She has placed a picture of her mother in the center, and around it are various tokens that remind her of their relationship: a cookbook, signifying times they spent together in the
kitchen; her grandmother's pearls, connecting her to an important
ancestor; seed packages, as they share a love of gardening; a small
stuffed bear that speaks of Pam's position as the child; shells they
gathered together last summer when spending time at the beach.

Pam attached ribbons to her mother's picture, weaving them
throughout the objects on the altar. They represent what she calls
the strands of DNA that connect her and her mother. There is also a
cross, the Christian symbol of death, and a glass butterfly to represent her belief in the resurrection and the after-life. Between these

two objects is a large stone. The stone represents the rolling back of the stone at the tomb, signifying Christ's resurrection, but it has also come to represent the heaviness in her heart.

Pam's mother is fighting cancer. The outcome does not look good and the family has begun to gather. Her mother's favorite prayer book is opened to the Psalms, and Pam reads one every night before going to bed. Glass containers hold candles that burn twenty-four hours a day. Pam keeps fresh flowers near her mother's bed at the hospital, removing one from the arrangement to keep on the altar at home—again, symbolizing their connection. Pam's intention is to acknowledge her gratitude for the strong bond she feels with her mother, as well as with the women who came before them. Her intention is to ask for God's help in releasing her mother and for the strength to deal with the loss.

After her mother's death, Pam was sitting at her altar when she realized she was staring at the stone she had placed there. Sometimes she held it in her hand while she meditated. It was speaking to her spirit—conveying a new insight. Rather than symbolizing her mother's continued life in eternity, it now symbolized what she must overcome within herself so that she could experience her own resurrection—her life after her mother's death.

Pam asked a couple of her friends to accompany her to the nearby river to witness a ceremony she felt she must do. She held the rock as she spoke about her grief as well as her regrets. All relationships are complex; perhaps none is more complicated than that of mother and daughter. There were aspects of Pam's relationship with her mother that had been difficult for her, and some of the problems between them remained unresolved. She spoke of her willingness to let go, allowing the transformation to happen.

With the support of her friends, Pam dropped the stone into the water and watched it sink to the bottom. She said she physically felt the release in her heart, as if the stone had been lodged there and was now gone. In telling her story, Pam said that she continued to miss her mom and mourned her passing, but something had shifted. At the same time that she felt loss, she also felt her mom's presence, "almost as if she were right here," Pam said. She now laughs about the disagreements between them, recognizing their differences, but no longer feeling threatened by them. She described her overall feeling as "a deep sense of freedom." She said, "I'm still her child, but I'm not the little girl. I'm a woman with my own ideas. I know my mom wants me to get on with my life, and do it in the way I know is best. I can feel it!"

Allowing the Symbols to Speak

When you decide to build an altar, the gathering process can begin with no clear intention of what you're attempting to symbolize. That part of your mind already knows and will guide the process. At other times, you may know the purpose and gather things that represent your intention. In either case, there is a time when the altar takes over and begins directing the process. Artists and writers often tell how the piece on which they are working takes control of the creative process. They feel as if something bigger or greater than themselves is coming into form through them. They talk about not being aware of why they used a certain color or created a particular shape, or where a certain phrase came from. When this happens, the artist has let go with the conscious mind and is creating from the depth of the unconscious—from instinct or intuition.

Often, during the process of gathering things for your altar, you'll find you're attracted to something that doesn't have a clear relationship to the big picture. The women I talked with all described how this or that "insisted" on being part of the altar, even though they didn't know why, as it didn't seem to "fit." The beginning altar-builder may scorn such lack of logic and choose to maintain control of the gathering process. When this happens, you are probably missing some of the intuitive "stuff," but in the long run, the altar will still bring your intention or desire into form. It will express for you what you are intending to say. Often, much to your surprise, it will say it better than you thought you could.

Home Away From Home

Many of you have no doubt seen St. Christopher medals for cars, and also magnetized statues for the dashboard. One woman who is on the road a lot for business keeps an altar in her car. She has rocks, feathers, and stones, along with a picture of her husband and children mounted with silly putty to a piece of slate. There is also a small candle. She doesn't light it, but likes the aesthetic effect and finds it also brings in the element fire. Her altar keeps her from being lonely and feeling separated when she is far from home.

Honoring Tradition

While there aren't any hard and fast rules around women's altars, there are traditions to be honored. For example, when you take a stone from the ground, do it with consciousness. According to my teacher, Buck Ghosthorse, stones are the oldest living nation and the keepers of great wisdom. They live in family groups. When you want to use a stone for an altar, ask its permission. It's customary to leave a tobacco offering in its place.

Springtime in Alaska—Pussy Willows, Pine Boughs, and Dog Biscuits

Valerie and her grandmother began looking for signs of spring to bring to an altar honoring the equinox. It was the 21st of March in Alaska, and signs of spring were not easy to come by. However, on the way home from the store one morning, they spotted a large eagle roosting in the top of a tree near the house. Robins are the traditional harbingers of spring "down South" in the "lower forty-eight," but in the far North, eagles scream its return.

Inspired by the eagle's message, Valerie and her grandmother set out to find something to put on the altar that would remind them that spring was coming. Not too far down the road, they found that shoots of wild pussy willow had sprouted despite the snow and their small white buds were beginning to open. They brought some home and put them in a vase, adding some pine branches to show that, while spring was coming, winter still ruled the day. As in all forms of artistic expression, it's the contrast of light and dark, like and unlike, that most engages our imagination. Altars work from the same principle. They're the place where things that, on the surface, appear to have no relationship come together, causing a new and deeper understanding of creation's interrelatedness to emerge. We can find God in new and surprising ways. This is why this Alaskan spring altar ended up with both pussy willows and pine branches.

FIGURE 10. *Looking for signs of spring for a spring equinox altar in Alaska.*

It's a long way to Alaska, and visits with family and friends there are rarer than we'd like them to be. So we cram as much into each one of them as possible, and everything we do together tends to take on mythological proportions. This visit, we made batches and batches of home-baked dog biscuits. Our plan was to deliver them to several of the neighbors as a good-will gesture. They came to symbolize the relationship between grandchild, daughter, and grandmother, and good neighboring. Valerie's desire is to become a veterinarian, so she included them on her altar. But she also placed them there just because we thought they should be there!

The Sacred and Secular—Finney's Sacred Foot Rest

We've spoken in great detail about how women don't make a big distinction between the practical matters of everyday living and the sacred world of the hereafter. And we mean it! Here is an example of what that principle looks like in action.

My friend Finney died a few years ago. I remember her in many ways, and one of my most vivid memories is of her ever-present always-changing altar. As you entered her home, you encountered a coffee table in the middle of the room that served as her altar. It functioned in all the ways we have just been talking about: making a statement about who she was and what symbol system she honored, as the focal point in ceremonies, as her personal altar, and as a foot rest!

Finney's altar was always in a constant state of flux and flow. At one point, in the center, there was a pottery candelabrum in the form of circle of people holding hands. At another, there was a bowl containing small slivers of dried of ash, thorns from a tree in her yard, and oak twigs also from her yard. These symbolized her exploration into Celtic shamanism. Finney admitted to being a bit too goal-oriented and wanted to learn how to "hang out in the mystery of things, and be comfortable there." She felt that, since mystery is the domain of the shaman and she was of Celtic descent, it just might work.

A bowl of colorful rocks sat in the center, because she liked to see the light bounce off them. There were some dried rose petals left over from a ceremony "because they look pretty." She added one more function to her altar that we haven't explored. It served as a great place to prop her feet up when reading, grounding both her and the altar in the practicalities of everyday life. Finney was not given to sanctimony and would have been the first to remind you never to confuse sacred with sanctimonious. Women's spirituality is reverent, but not stuffy. It's a chance to let your hair down and have some fun with your spiritual side. God probably gets bored with too much bowing and scraping!

From the description of Finney's altar, you can see that the objects you choose are very personal. Liking the way something looks, smells, tastes, sounds, or feels is enough reason to put it on your altar. Likewise, not liking something for any of these reasons is just cause for its removal. Somehow, women are able to close the gap between the everyday "stuff" and what is usually considered sacred. Finney's sacred foot rest illustrates that point beautifully.

Women use the words *connection* and *relationship* again and again when describing spirituality. Altars are where these important spiritual concepts come to life. There, past, present, and future converge "now." At the altar, a woman can acknowledge the divine spiritual network that allows her to call on Sophia of the Hebrew scripture, along with Hestia, Goddess of the Hearth; the Virgin Mary, or her counterpart, Yemaya of the Seven African Powers; as well as the Ahpo Wi Chapi known by the Lakota people as Morning Star, or Maka known as Mother Earth. All can be called with one breath.

Wrapping Things Up

Women's circles are the traditional space for women's ceremonies; they create and sustain spiritual energy, shared power, and a sense of inner authority. It is customary to place an altar in the center of the circle while doing ceremony. Women's altars have been around since before the dawn of history and they continue to exist in all cultures all over the world. A woman is the final authority in all aspects of her home altar. The altar you create has specific meaning to you; it imparts new revelations and symbolizes the things you hold most valuable. Regardless of your spiritual tradition, you can represent your spiritual values with an altar. Whether you speak to Artemis, Yahweh, Buddha, Waken Tonka, Christ, Allah, or nature itself, the building of your altar reflects what is nearest and dearest to you. It's the personal expression of your spirit.

Chapter 8

CEREMONIES AND RITUALS

Meeting in circle, building altars, and creating rituals of transformation are the triple-play of women's spirituality. Rituals use symbols and engage our spiritual imaginations to facilitate a shift in consciousness. Like circles and the building of altars, women's ceremonies and rituals belong to a long tradition. As with all parts of women's spirituality, you can participate in ceremonies and still belong to your faith tradition. Rather than trying to change anything outside of yourself, these ceremonies help you celebrate life and gain insight. They can create the focus and generate the energy to help you make a change in consciousness or behavior when you see you need one. Ceremonies honor the presence of the sacred within us and within the circle.

Between You and Your Higher Power

A short and sweet ceremony popular in twelve-step recovery communities involves writing a worry on a scrap of paper and putting it in your God box—a box or container assigned for this purpose. For example, having trouble making ends meet is a situation to which most of us can relate. While dropping a note in the box will probably not result in God leaving you a check, I know of many cases where people have let go of the worry and gained insight into the situation that ultimately resulted in solving their problem. The point is that the ritual jumped them out of their worry brain, where nothing new can happen, and into their imagination, which allowed for some new thinking.

Rituals and ceremonies in women's spirituality are opportunities to move beyond your conditioned mind and get to some new brain cells. They bring insight or new perspective that often leads to a creative solution. Ceremonies allow you to enter the realm of synchronicity—coincidences that may be more than pure chance.

Let's go back to the God box and the money ritual, for example. Sometime after putting her request in the box, one woman found herself thinking of a friend she hadn't thought of in a long time. She decided to call and found that her friend was thinking of her, too. In the course of the conversation, her friend mentioned that her neighbor was looking for a house-sitter to take care of plants and watch the house for a year. The friend introduced her and she got the job. Some may call this a coincidence and others may consider it synchronicity. You can consider it spirituality in action!

Rituals—Putting the Magic in Imagination

According to right-and-left-brain theory, cognitive rational thinking happens in the left hemisphere of the brain. Imagination occurs in the right hemisphere. Both are necessary functions for healthy balanced thinking. New ideas originate in the right hemisphere. They are telegraphed to the left hemisphere through the *corpus callosum* to be analyzed. Then you make a decision as to whether you'll add the thought to the system, modify it, act on it, or reject it. The two hemispheres work together to add new information into our thought process—updating the system and allowing us to grow and develop intellectually. Without access to the right brain, we are stuck reinforcing the "same ole same ole" and unable to open to new possibilities. Without access to the left brain, we would have a plethora of new ideas, but no way of sorting through them or carrying them out. Without the right hemisphere, thinking becomes rigid; without the left hemisphere, we are unstable. Thus, whole-brain thinking is a healthy balanced system—a partnership.

Ceremonies are a structured way of engaging our spiritual imaginations. They allow the thinking mind to stay on board, but take a backseat while we have a new experience. Later, the thinking mind has something fresh to think about. We may notice our thoughts have been energized with insight and have gained perspective—we're filled with new ideas; we have been transformed.

Transforming rituals engage higher levels of consciousness, or what can be considered god consciousness or divine presence within. All major religions refer to this phenomenon, although they use different terms to describe it. It's been referred to as Christ consciousness, observer mind, Buddha consciousness, awakened mind, wise mind, among other labels. These phrases all describe a heightened state of awareness in which we are able to experience things from a perspective larger than our own. In that time and space, our psychic boundaries expand and we experience belonging to the universe—usually described as Oneness. This is how we gain a new perspective.

1. Unconscious mind: contains instincts and deeper memories that are not readily recalled to consciousness, yet influence the subconscious and conscious mind.

2. Subconscious mind: that which lies below the surface—contains memories, hopes, dreams, and expectations that we can easily call to conscious mind.

3. Conscious mind: the awake state of awareness.

4. Higher consciousness or wise mind: relates to the fourth dimension identified with time/space principles of physics. It connects us with the quantum field—the archetypal realm.

Wise mind, as we are calling it, connects us to the accumulated wisdom of the ages. It's where we go in meditation. We return with an understanding that hasn't been generated out of our past experience, but has tapped into a greater source of knowing. This state is also accessed through shamanic practices like drumming, chanting, ecstatic dance, fasting, and ceremony. Women's ceremonies provide a structured experience of communication with wise mind.

What a Ritual Isn't

We have already talked a bit about what women's spirituality is *not* about, which should clear up any worries about what may be going on during a ritual. Rituals aren't about doing bad things to chickens, hexing your old school principal, or extracting additional child support. There's a general rule that always bears repeating— something to keep in mind when you approach a ceremony: *Do not participate when you don't know the people and aren't clear about the purpose.* This isn't just a spiritual principle by any means; the same rule can be applied to getting into poker games or the back seat of a Chevy as well. It's just common sense.

The Character of Ritual and Ceremony

If you are new to the idea of creating ceremonies, it's helpful to find someone with experience to help get you started. You can also check the resources listed at the back of this book. There are a lot of factors to consider and it can seem intimidating to the beginner, so it helps to have a guide. As you practice, you'll learn how imagery and symbols evoke the imagination, and you will master the art. You can begin by letting go of any worry that you'll do something terribly wrong.

Sustaining Creative Chaos without Going over the Top

Effective rituals have both form and spontaneity. Form quiets the mind and allows participants to relax; it keeps things from feeling chaotic or weird. Form does not imply that things are locked down. A good ritual contains spaces for meditation, activity, and creativity. The balance of form and spontaneity allows transformation to happen. "Allow" is a key word in this process. You can't make transformation happen. It is grace—a gift from your higher power. Ritual sets the stage and your willingness to engage allows Spirit to do its work.

Time

Two hours is an average time for a ritual. You can do effective work in less time and sometimes it takes longer, depending on how many participants and the intention of the ritual. In the altered state of consciousness, it's hard to keep up with time, but if a ritual goes on too long, people get exhausted. Timing is part of the art. Sensing when to pause and when to move things along is intuitive. You gain confidence through practice.

Leading a Ritual

Leading a ritual is a creative and intuitive process. You have to allow yourself time to learn. The leader keeps track of time and pays attention to what's going on in the circle, but doesn't control the dynamics. Leading a ritual is considered working with the energy of the circle.

Purpose

It helps to approach ceremony with an intention or focus; it provides a reference point. The essence of ritual and ceremony is to learn something about yourself—to gain insight. A ritual doesn't fix other people, but it can change your interpretation of another person and your reaction to that person. In turn, the person's reaction to you may well change. You can ask for insight into your part in a relationship, something at work, a health situation—anything about which you seek clarification or deeper understanding.

Space

Generally, people in a ritual sit in a circle, either on the floor with cushions or in chairs. Take the phone off the hook, and ask guests to turn off beepers and buzzers. Put a "Do not disturb" sign on the door.

Group Size

You may want to begin with two or three others while you practice your skills and eventually grow your circle to around seven.

Setting the Stage—Ambiance Counts

You want to create an atmosphere of comfort in which to relax. Low lighting, meditation music, candles and incense, drumming, or chanting help quiet the mind and relax the body. Imagination awakens as you create the altar. Figure 11 provides a flow chart for creating a ceremony.

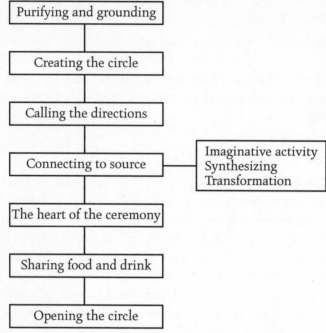

FIGURE 11. *Ceremony flow chart*

Purifying

Ceremonies begin with a purification to release the tension and worry of the day and to focus in on the present time and the process. Sage, cedar, or sweet grass, or a mixture of all three is a way of purifying before a ceremony. You can buy these ingredients in a health-food store or New Age bookstore, along with a container like a shell to hold the herbs. Light a few pieces of the mixture and "wash" your hands and face in the smoke, then brush it over yourself.

You can use a leafy branch or a pine bough to sweep your energy field. Do this as if you were brushing off your clothes, only brush the energy field around your body. A salt-water solution in a bowl can be passed around and guests can dip their fingers or sprinkle it over themselves. The simplest purification is through breath. Taking six deep belly breaths and letting things go in the exhalation clears the mind.

Grounding

Be here, now! Grounding gets you focused in the here and now. It allows you to expand your consciousness without losing a sense of reality—getting too airy-fairy. Grounding creates balance between the right and left brain hemispheres. It allows the ceremony to be more intense, and for you to open to more insight.

Here is a grounding meditation you can use to open your rituals. As you go through this exercise, pause after each image and give the group time to reflect.

> *Beginning with six or more deep belly breaths. Close your eyes or soften your gaze. Imagine you have roots coming out of your spine like a tree (pause). Imagine them going down through the floor into the ground beneath you (pause). Feel the coolness of the soil (pause). Feel the roots going through the layers of the earth (pause). Feel the texture of the topsoil... the rocks... the temperature. Notice how the roots find their way through the cracks and crevices to go deeper, and deeper, and deeper (pause). Finding their way deep into the earth (pause). Take a deep breath and release anything you don't need right now. Breathe it out. Do it again. Again. When you're ready, let your mind come back into the circle, allowing yourself to adjust. Come back slowly and open your eyes when you are ready.*
>
> *Leader: continue repeating the last line until everyone's eyes are open and they come out of the altered state.*

Creating the Circle

The circle establishes an energy boundary between the participants and the "rest of the world." Your circle creates a sanctuary where the ordinary world does not intrude—it helps you temporarily let go of your critical mind. You can do this by meditating in silence for a few minutes, or by having everyone imagine a circle of light around the group, or by honoring the four directions, as shown in the following example. Discourage members from coming and going while the circle is in process to hold the energy. Staying focused in the circle makes a difference in the work—it creates power.

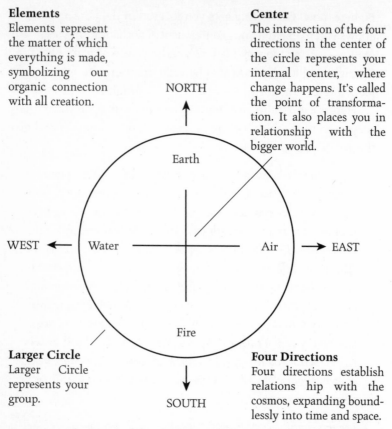

Elements
Elements represent the matter of which everything is made, symbolizing our organic connection with all creation.

Center
The intersection of the four directions in the center of the circle represents your internal center, where change happens. It's called the point of transformation. It also places you in relationship with the bigger world.

NORTH

Earth

WEST ← Water ——— Air → EAST

Fire

Larger Circle
Larger Circle represents your group.

SOUTH

Four Directions
Four directions establish relations hip with the cosmos, expanding boundlessly into time and space.

FIGURE 12. *The diagram shows the energetic dynamics of an altar when used for a ceremony or celebration. The energies meet in the center and provide an internal focus. They reach out into space to connect participants to an expanded awareness as well.*

Calling the Directions

This ceremony honors the four directions according to an ancient Celtic pattern. Remember, however, that different traditions assign the elements to different directions. The four directions are energetic lines that intersect in the center of the circle. They also extend out into space, connecting the circle to the cosmos. Spirituality honors paradox. In the ritual, you always look at opposites. You notice what it feels like to bring the focus into yourself as center of the universe. And you feel what it is like to expand out into the far reaches of outer space and what it means to be in relationship with the universe or all that is.

The directions create the circle and provide a focus for meditation. Ask the group to close their eyes and imagine moving through the day and the seasons as the images indicate, while you lead them through the process. Ask participants to feel the connections in their body. Read slowly and pause after each image, allowing time for the connections to be made.

The purpose is to be imaginative so that the directions "speak" to you, and to allow yourself to feel the characteristics of each one. Enter the "play" as if it were a play, and play! Ritual is rooted in theater—the shaman heals by engaging our active imagination. Table 2 gives a poetic interpretation of the energies of the cosmos. (Read across each line from left to right.)

TABLE 2. *Correspondences for the Four Directions*

Direction	Element	Time	Location	Season	Symbol
East	Air	Morning	Mind	Spring	Feather or incense
South	Fire	Noon	Will	Summer	Candle
West	Water	Evening	Emotion	Fall	Water or shells
North	Earth	Night	Body	Winter	Rocks or bones

Air is breath, the intake of spirit (inspiration) and clear thinking. It brings ideas and energizes new beginnings—it also governs communication. Energetically, it's connected with the morning when things are new and fresh, and to the new moon. It's symbolized by birds and other flying creatures (dragonflies, butterflies). It can be represented on the altar by a feather or by burning incense.

Fire is passion. It energizes our will and personal power. It will strengthen weak will or correct willfulness. It resonates with the solar plexus. Energetically, it is connected to noon or the full moon, whose light is bright. Its time of year is summer. It governs truth, full engagement, and full disclosure. It's represented on the altar by a candle.

West is the realm of emotion—not surface emotion, but the deep feelings that connect us as a human species—longing, joy, fear, grief, forgiveness, or love. It resonates in our hearts. Its time of day is evening and its season is autumn. It is represented on the altar by water or things from the sea like shells.

North is the earth realm. It's the body of the mother where new creations gestate. It is where things are taken when they die and where they await regeneration. It's symbolized as a cave or a tree. Its time is midnight on moonless nights; its season is winter. It embodies mystery and offers comfort at times when we're confused or unsure of what's coming next by acknowledging that such times, although uncomfortable, have a particular spirituality. It's a place to bring your disappointments and broken dreams while you wait for something new to come of them. The North is the most difficult for most people to understand, but it can be a place of great comfort. It's represented on the altar by a stone, bone, or piece of wood—something earthy.

Invocation—Connecting to Source

Each woman is asked to connect with her Source. If you are Goddess gals, you can choose a representation of her that suits the season or the focus of the ritual (see next chapter). As you read more about ritual and ceremony and how the wheel of the year and the energy of the cycles of the moon operate, you begin to weave intricate patterns into your ceremonies.

The Heart of the Ceremony

Shhhhhhhhhhhh! A word or two about silence. We don't use it enough! Most of us are bombarded with sounds all day. Silence is a good way of moving from one part of the ritual to another; it gives people time to become aware of their feelings and to just be. The tendency is to fill up all the space in your ceremony with words, but try it another way. Less is more. Try calling for a moment of silence after each person speaks or following a reading or an exercise. This allows the subconscious mind to percolate and helps quell the desire to comment on everything from the surface level. It thus deepens the experience.

Imaginative Activity—Using Kindergarten Mind

The leader will have prepared a process connected with the season of the year. The purpose of the experience is to engage the imagination. The activity should not be heady or require thinking. It works best to think like a kindergarten teacher when you design your process. Old familiar rituals like arranging fall leaves or planting seeds in a milk carton really work well. The easier and simpler the exercise, the deeper it will go!

You don't have to have an activity. You can build a ritual around self-reflection or meditation. However, an activity helps stimulate the imagination; it acts symbolically on the mind. It provides a platform from which to reflect.

A spring ritual I attended recently used flowers and other greenery gathered from the yard and field to make a crown. We used inexpensive wire from the flower shop, lace, scraps of material, and net. We worked outside on the patio, talking and laughing. Rituals don't have to be "serious" to be spiritual. In fact, laughter is a sign you have gotten out of your linear mind and engaged your imagination. Later, when you start connecting the ritual to life, you'll go much deeper. But, again, the spirit of women's rituals can be light, knowing they go deep when they need to.

Synthesis

When we finished the outdoor activity described above, we went back inside into our circle. The leader asked us to take a few minutes of reflection to discover what it was that we were signifying by the crowns we had each made. We meditated for three to five minutes before going around the circle and talking about what we were crowning in ourselves. It is amazing how such an apparently simple exercise can evoke such deep responses.

Transformation

One woman in the ceremony above declared herself the "Queen of the Arts." She was struggling to create an identity for herself as a professional artist. As she crowned herself, we all bowed in recognition of her new status. Another woman declared herself "Queen for a Day." She has been overworking, and realized how exhausted she was. She also realized she had been taking herself far too seriously. As she crowned herself, we draped a scarf over her shoulders and gave her a yardstick to hold. Someone asked what she was going to declare as Queen for the Day. She declared next Saturday to be a complete day off for her. She was going to stay in bed all day and read, order pizza, and take naps. This represented a complete change in her weekend routine; she usually used Saturday to catch up on every aspect of her life, from housecleaning to gardening to grocery shopping and more. Another woman was in remission from a bout with cancer. She used the ceremony as a way of reclaiming her power following surgery and chemotherapy—a time when her life felt out of control and powerlessness prevailed.

These women were making significant changes in their lives imaginatively and creatively. Changes made like this go to the subconscious mind, where they take root and have the best chance of actually bringing you the transformation you are looking for. Wise mind speaks the language of image. Deep structural change happens when we change the image. In this case, the image of queen represented a transformed sense of self. It lent authority to the decisions being made. As the image changes, self-perception changes, actions change, and the impression we project into the world changes.

Sharing Food and Drink

Some type of refreshment is traditional—it helps participants get grounded again after the ceremony and builds community. How you handle this is up to you. Some groups keep it simple, with herbal tea and cookies; others make a covered-dish dinner affair out of it.

Opening the Circle

A ritual needs a formal way of closing. One way is to be silent for a few minutes and have the leader go back through the elements, thanking them for their presence and presents.

We thank the earth for providing our home, for our food, and for our health.

We thank the water for quenching our thirst and for meaningful moments with friends.

We thank the fire for brightness and warmth, and for illumination both outside of ourselves and inside.

We thank the air for the breath of life, and for inspiration and the chance to begin again.

We thank each other for the gift of friendship.

Some form of the following prayer had been used for hundreds of years and is still widely used in women's circles today.

May the circle be open but unbroken. May the peace of the Goddess go in our hearts. Merry meet, merry part, and merry meet again.

Wrapping Things Up

Women's rituals and ceremonies are contemporary versions of ancient ceremonies. A ritual has structure balanced with spontaneity, and creates an experience that brings spiritual insight as well as practical solutions to real-life situations. The circle is not a place for dogma; however, women's rituals serve to reinforce principles like respect for the earth, equality, and respect for individuals' beliefs. There is a lot involved in leading a ritual. It takes time to get all the parts coordinated and running smoothly, but it's also interesting. Avoid getting too serious or trying to be perfect. Rather, keep it light. The ceremony itself will take you deep when you need to go deep.

Chapter 9

❧ ❧

NATURE'S THEMES—
SEASONS AND REASONS

Women's ceremonies honor the innate spirituality of life's everyday events; they bring insight and strength to our lives. Nature provides universal patterns that can be the source of deep spiritual wisdom. The phases of the moon impart spiritual teachings; as it moves through its lunar cycle, it can provide the focus for your ritual. The Wheel of the Year is the basis for the spiritual celebrations of many earth religions and is the foundation for the liturgical calendar used by traditional religions today. Easter, for example, is determined by the moon and the spring equinox. Festivals of light, including Hanukkah and Christmas, go on all over the world and correspond to darkness and the winter equinox. You can follow the seasons in your rituals, drawing your spiritual lessons throughout the year.

That Ol' Devil Moon in the Sky

In ancient cultures, the moon took precedence over the sun in its importance in people's imagination. The Egyptians called the moon the "Mother of the Universe" because of its connection to women's cycles. In Upper Egypt, where the moon was the "Eternal Great Mother," they honored her by calling the region the

"Land of the Moon." The Sioux Indians called her "The Eternal One." Ancient calendars were based on the moon rather than the sun, and the moon still governs the planting and harvesting times in many agricultural cultures—including in our own *Farmer's Almanac.*

The moon is an ancient feminine form that has always captured the imagination. It seems to have the power to make us pay attention, even to walk outside in winter and watch it rise over the city. The moon has inspired songwriters, lovers, and just about everyone who has ever been out underneath it. The moon's gravitational pull doesn't just affect the oceans; it pulls every body of water—including us. Our bodies are over ¾ water and we feel the moon's pull as well. Its 28-day cycle matches ours. And moonlight is—well, it's just plain beautiful. If the moon is your thing, here are some ways you can use it to create a reflection for a ritual.

Lunar Reflections

Women have used the three phases of the moon as a symbol of their life cycles since the beginning of time. The new moon reflects life as a young woman, or maiden. The full moon symbolizes fruition and the fullness of the reproductive years. As the moon wanes, we are put in touch with our own aging process, which is associated with wisdom. As the moon completely disappears and the sky looks dark and empty, we contemplate death. As the new moon appears again in the sky, we are shown the ongoing cycles of nature and that our own rebirth is inevitable. The moon was one of the first spiritual symbols that told people of the cyclical and regenerative journey of the spirit.

Symbols don't relate to linear time. For example, the waning moon doesn't just mean aging in the physical sense; it could represent an idea or a project that is aging. Its energetic patterns relate to psychological and spiritual principles—supporting our day-to-day lives. Before you start to work with the moon, it may be interesting to spend a month keeping track with its different phases, letting them work with you, noticing how each phase affects you physically and emotionally. Table 3 shows characteristics symbolized by each phase of the moon.

New Moon on the Rise

The new moon reminds us of how we are continuously renewed or reborn. If you are meeting under a new moon, you can use this energy to set an intention or energize a new project. You can ask for insight into a situation you're facing. Or you can just use this opportunity to reflect on your innate ability to begin again—to pick up and start over when things fall apart. The energy of the new moon draws things to you.

Full Moon Madness!

The full moon reminds us of wholeness, magnificence, and richness. It is the mother's belly full with new life. You can use the full moon as the focus for your ceremony to recognize the fullness of your life and to offer gratitude. You can also use it to wish for something in your life. Sometimes, the full moon evokes a celebration and inspires us to just go out and dance under it—or sleep under it, if you want to go totally mad.

Waning Moon

The energy of the waning moon takes things away. You can use it to help get rid of a bad habit, a bad attitude, or anything else you're through with. As the moon wanes through the rest of the cycle, it will take the object of your intention away. Find a symbol to represent it and put it on the altar, or leave it out in the moonlight.

The Dark Side of the Moon

The dark moon is a good opportunity to work on your shadow side. Use it to identify hidden aspects of yourself you'd rather not see and definitely don't want anyone else to know about. Be brave and name them in the circle. Give your shadow to the dark moon and ask the new moon that's coming soon to bring illumination. Everyone has a shadow side—the principle of duality tells us that everything contains its own opposite. If you don't acknowledge your potential dark side, it can unconsciously influence your decisions—even take over without your knowing it. In acknowledging your shadow, you don't make it go away—but in owning it, you become whole. There's a little good and a little bad in each of us. You have a choice in which part you want to express. But to exercise that choice, you have to know your own darkness.

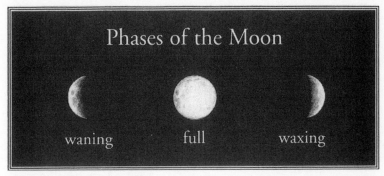

FIGURE 13. Phases of the moon.

TABLE 3. Characteristics Symbolized by the Phases of the Moon

Phase	Time	Characteristic	Emotion	Aspect
New	Morning	New beginnings	Hope	Maiden
Full	Noon	Fruition	Gratitude	Mother
Waning	Evening	Takes away	Surrender	Old woman
Dark	Night	Creative void	Mystery	Death

Moon Struck

A moon ceremony hopefully will include going outside and being under the moon's light for at least part of the evening. You can celebrate moonrise with drumming or dancing outside. However, you can always do a moon ceremony right in your living room.

Moon Meditation Ceremony

In this sample moon meditation ritual, each person has a new white candle (they can bring them, or you can provide them). Put the candles on the altar or in the center of the circle. Ask everyone to lean back, get comfortable, and prepare to go on an inner journey. To stimulate the imagination, suggest that each woman create a magical way of traveling to the moon through space—a magic carpet, on the wing of a giant bird, or perhaps in a more traditional spacecraft. Remember to pause after each suggestion.

Imagine what the temperature on the moon is like.

How does the moon feel to your feet?

Are there any noises up there?

What can you see when you look up?

What can you see when you look down?

Find a comfortable place to sit on the moon, and sit quietly for a few minutes.

Depending on the phase of the moon you're under, ask the group if there are areas in their lives that are full. (Remember to pause after each question to allow time for reflection.) Are they enjoying the fullness? Are there areas of life that lack fullness? What are they? They don't have to do anything about this right now; just recognize the feelings and ask spirit to handle them.

Is there something they have been secretly wishing for? Something they haven't dared talk about? Are they willing to have it in their lives? Are they willing to wish for it now?

Work slowly, allowing time for answers to surface in people's minds. Open-ended questions like these can begin an inner process that continues for a long time. When leading these experiences, the less you say the better. The process should be simple. If there is too much talking, or if it gets complicated, the thinking mind takes over and that gets in the way of insight. Leave it to the participants to fill in the blanks.

At the end of the meditation, have participants spend a few minutes with journals making any notations to be explored later. Or have a few art supplies ready for them to record the images they saw. If your group is too big to accommodate sharing in a reasonable time frame, break into pairs or small groups of three and take turns. Each woman's sharing generally sparks more insight in others. It may be a good idea to limit or eliminate feedback. It's good practice to keep the attention on the person who is sharing. You can imagine how it can get if everyone takes each comment and runs with it.

As you go around the circle, ask participants to talk about one thing they learned, rather than going through the details of the meditation. For example, if fullness was the focus, each woman can talk about specific things about which she is feeling grateful or fulfilled. The interplay of unbridled imagination and form is important to ritual. You want to allow the imagination to run free during the meditation and focus during the interpretation, as mentioned in chapter 9. Have each person light a candle as she shares, and place the candles in the center of the circle to symbolize the full moon. It's quite magical as the room fills with light and the hopes and dreams of the group.

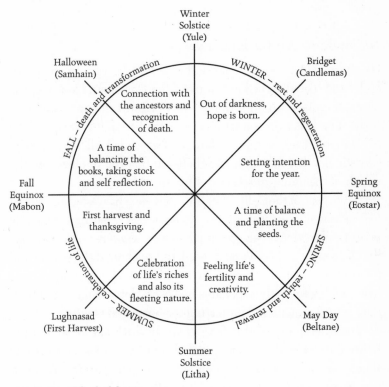

FIGURE 14. *Wheel of the Year.*

Observing the changing seasons feeds our imaginations; it both triggers and reflects our spiritual process. Honoring the earth's seasons is a practice shared by many traditions. Jewish feasts were based on the organic spirituality that was already implanted deep in the hearts and minds of the people. Christianity followed many of these feasts, as well as those contributed by the Celts and the Germanic people of Europe. They all combined to form the basis of the liturgical calendar followed by many Christian denominations. The Wheel of the Year as it is celebrated today is a composite of organic feasts—a timeless and universal spiritual map.

Mother Nature's seasonal feasts and festivals form the basis for the earth calendar. The year begins and ends at Halloween—paradoxically, it is both the time of death and the time of rebirth. You don't have to wait to start at the beginning—begin where you are. Rather than just lasting one day, the holidays create a spiritual focus for each six-week season.

Halloween—All Hallows' Eve

Halloween (October 31) marks the end of the year in the earth cycle, and likewise the beginning of the New Year. However, the new cannot be born until the old dies. Halloween honors death. It is the time when the ancestors are remembered. It corresponds to All Hallows' Eve, the night before the feast called All Saints Day in Christianity. On this night, it is believed that the veil between the worlds of the living and dead is thinnest.

In the time of the Celts, after the crops were harvested and stored for the long winter, cooking fires in homes were extinguished. The priests met in sacred oak groves where the new ceremonial fire was lit. The people gathered and danced and celebrated the season and the coming darkness. Each family took embers home to light their new cooking fire—thus its flame had been blessed and would have the additional quality of protecting the home and family.

The spirituality of this feast is about death and regeneration. Reflections for Halloween may include sharing stories with a friend about someone you have known who has died. As you talk about this person, notice how he or she is still alive in your life. What would you ask this person if he or she were here now? Is there something you want to say to this person? This is a good time to be more conscious of your life. Write your epitaph and you will see what you would most like to be remembered for. Are you being true to this ideal?

A Long Winter's Nap

The winter solstice (December 20–23) honors the darkest night and, at the same time, the moment when the light begins its return. Despair and hope sit side by side at this time. The winter solstice honors the birth of the infant sun, bringing light into the darkness of the world. From now on, the nights will grow shorter, but you will experience darkness for at least three more months. Winter's task is self-care, and themes for this holiday include ways you can rest and regenerate.

Questions for reflection are: What renews you? What are the fears that arise at this time of year? From where do you draw your hope? Activities for a ritual to nourish the body, mind, and spirit include making bath salts, essential oils, or scented candles. Things to consider as you go into the winter may include a book exchange, or a soup exchange. Plan to get together once a week for dinner and a movie. Reminder: Use lots of candles or colored holiday lights.

Candlemas—The Feast of Bridget

The feast of the Celtic goddess Bridget (February 2) occurs midway through the winter. It celebrates the return of the light, which by this time has become more apparent. Metaphorically, it reminds you that the infant sun that was "born" at the winter solstice is now six weeks old and its presence is becoming more obvious. It also relates to quickening or the first movement a mother feels during pregnancy. The days are growing longer, lifting the spirit. You can even begin to look at seed catalogs and plan your garden.

The spiritual theme of Candlemas is planting a new virtue—a quality you may like to develop in yourself. Topics for reflection are: What spiritual seed are you planting this year? What do you hope to cultivate within yourself? What gets stirred up inside of you as you till the field? What are some weeds (old ways of thinking) that will have to go? A planting ritual using small milk cartons for flowerpots is fun. As you place your seeds in the dirt, you are symbolically planting your spiritual garden.

Candlemas is also known as the Festival of Lights and celebrates Bridget of Kildare, the Celtic goddess of fire, the hearth, fields, poetry, and childbirth. She also gives blessings to women who are about to marry. Women still invoke her name on their wedding days when they are referred to as "bride." According to legend, Bridget visited and blessed homes on this day. If the sun was seen on this day, winter was over; if it hid behind the clouds, winter would stay a while longer. This old tradition is still with us in the form of Groundhog Day, when it is said that the groundhog comes out of his den and, if he sees his shadow, goes back in again for six more weeks. Many of the old feast days have translated into modern times and still carry some of their original meaning. It seems that we all look forward to spring in one way or another.

It's a Spring Thing!

The spring equinox (March 20–23) celebrates the earth coming back to life! It is a joyful time, as promise and possibility in the form of new green shoots push their way up through the soil. Spiritually, it is the time to check on the intention you planted at the Bridget ritual. Is there anything holding you back? Anything you need to "push through" in order to grow into the person you want to be?

Spring's spiritual theme is rebirth. Reflection questions include: What is coming alive within you? Is it getting enough water and sunshine to grow? Is there anything blocking it from sprouting? If so, you can ask for help in clearing your path. Is there anything you can do to help your spirit feel more joyful? Make paper chains and bind your wrists together. Say out loud what it is that you are breaking through in your life, and then break the chains and free yourself!

That Lusty Month of May!

May Day (April 30 or May 1) celebrates creativity, love, and fertility; it honors the dance of life. The fields are sown, the birds are tweeting, and the bees are buzzing! You know the rest! In times past, couples made love in the fields to encourage the crops to grow. (At least that was their story!)

May Day's spiritual principle is fecundity. Questions for reflection are: What is your relationship with your creativity? Are you giving attention to your creative urges? Are you giving your creative side enough time to just "be"? What attitude are you cultivating? Is there something keeping you from seeing your current situation creatively? Do you want to change that attitude? Suggestion: Sleep outside on the ground on this night.

May was a month of sexual freedom in Europe up into the 16th century. Wedding vows were suspended, and couples were free to enjoy a sexual romp with whomever they wanted—for one night. The elders believed that it relieved sexual tension and made fidelity throughout the other eleven months of the year workable.

"Summertime, and the Living Is Easy!"

The summer solstice (June 20–23) is the longest day of the year. You have planted your spiritual seeds and they are growing. This is a time for celebration. We are reminded that tonight begins the loss of light that will take us back into the darkness. Even in its fullness, life is fleeting. Grab the moment and celebrate!

The spiritual principle for summer is to take time to enjoy your life. Here are some questions for reflection: Are you too busy to enjoy life as it passes? If you weren't too busy, what would you like to do today for fun? Do you resist the natural rhythms, holding on to people, ideas, attitudes, or behaviors, rather than letting life move through you? This is a time for opening your arms wide and accepting the fullness of life, and celebrating the richness. Go on a picnic!

"Much of religion has lost its sense of celebration because it disconnected itself from the lives of the people and from the earth itself. Yet everything we are and everything we celebrate has a direct connection to the earth and to her cycles and season."

–JANET MARINE (1935–), poet, artist, and wise woman

Lughnasad—First Harvest

Lughnasad (August 1) celebrates the first cutting of the fields. It corresponds to Thanksgiving, as a time of gathering, sharing food, and giving thanks. If you have been attentive, the garden is producing and the fields are ready to be reaped. Share the bounty with friends.

The spiritual principle of this holiday is gratitude. Questions for reflection are: What feeds your soul? What are the things for which you are the most grateful? Take a drive through the countryside and see the fields at their fullest. Look at the bales of hay stacked there like huge loaves of bread. Visit your local farmers' market and bring home fresh fruits and vegetables for a meal with friends—and don't forget to include fresh flowers. As you eat the food, you are partaking of its life force. In the spirit of Lughnasad, the corn king dies so that the people may live.

Become aware of the gifts the earth gives.

Wrapping Things Up

Nature provides a pattern for spiritual celebrations. These ancient themes have been woven into our psyche for 100,000 years and more. When spirituality is connected to nature through the cycles and seasons, it has life. Earth rituals are inclusive of all beliefs, and don't conflict with traditional religious services. In fact, our religious celebrations were taken from the earth calendar. For example, Passover and Easter coincide with the spring equinox and themes of renewal; Christmas and Hanukkah coincide with the winter solstice and themes of darkness and light. Earth rituals build a sense of connection between spirituality and life. They connect us to wise mind and bring creative solutions to life's challenges.

Chapter 10

❦ ❧

AWAKENING WOMAN POWER

Women have created rituals since the beginning of time to mark passages and to assist them in life's journey. We don't know the details of these ceremonies, but women's lives follow a universal pattern; we are woven together through our cycles.

Women today are tapping into this rich spiritual reserve to mark important events, to garner support and strength to deal with life's adversities, and to celebrate the "good stuff." The ancient themes of maiden, mother, and wise woman have long represented passages in women's lives. Today, a new archetype has emerged to help women recognize their accomplishments. Make way for the queen!

It's a Girl Thing!

In a patriarchal culture, nothing is more surrounded by fear, more laden with taboos, or more infused with forbidden power than a woman's menstrual period. It has been upheld as sacred by some and as the rationale for banishment from the altar and the boardroom by others. Roman philosopher Pliny, writing in the 1st century CE, stated that menstrual blood could do everything from blighting crops to rusting iron and bronze. While Pliny isn't currently on the New York Times best-seller list, his influence, along with many others throughout history who have voiced similar fears, has helped shape Western culture. Its impact continues to be felt.

On the other extreme, author, researcher, and noted feminist Barbara G. Walker tells us that menstrual blood was once considered "sacred red wine" in Greece, and that the menstrual blood of Mother Goddess was holy for its healing properties. The Norse god Thor was reputed to have reached the land of enlightenment and eternal life by bathing in a river of menstrual blood flowing from the primal mothers who once ruled the ancient world. Egyptian pharaohs became divine by drinking the blood of Isis, and Celtic kings assured their immortality by ingesting the "red mead" of Mab, the fairy Queen. Tribal people believed menstrual blood contained the soul of future generations, which was one reason why they had matrilineal societies.

Cyclical Isn't Pathological

Somewhere between these two extremes is the simple fact that women have menstrual cycles. Since the half of the world that doesn't have them has pretty much organized itself around not having them, we still struggle with honoring the fluctuating energy of our cyclical nature—and with neither denying it nor falling victim to it.

The female body and all its reproductive functions were honored in matriarchal society. In some cultures, women who were menstruating were excused from their usual duties and gathered together to rest and regenerate. It was considered a sacred time, a time of power and of psychic abilities. Their advice was sought regarding tribal decisions. Separation from the tribe was a bonus, not a banishment.

As the world shifted from matriarchal to patriarchal values, the power associated with women's blood posed a serious threat to cultures built on the idea of male power. Menstrual blood came to be considered dangerous and unclean—the source of tremendous fear. Menstrual taboos were established by Hebrew scripture and became part of the religious heritage of Christian writers and theologians as well.

In some Jewish and Islamic traditions today, women are forbidden to pray during their menses. In Christianity, the restriction on women's ordination as priests and ministers is based on menstrual taboos. It's clear to see that this old idea has not died; it continues to play a part in the structure of Western religion and in the larger world culture as well.

The truth is that women do experience highs and lows during their cycles. We have a time of production and a time of regeneration. If we organized the world according to our energy cycles, everyone would work for two weeks and spend two weeks on the couch reading trashy novels and eating chocolate—or trout fishing, or doing whatever renews your body and soul. Some women want to be left alone; for others, sex with their partner relieves the tension, and is relaxing and energizing. The point is to be aware of your body and honor what it's telling you.

Living in a linear culture, in which being productive 24/7 is highly rated, is stressful for everyone—and it's particularly stressful for women. However, if we want to make it in the "real" world, we are told we have to "man" up. That requires denying our true feelings and getting the work done. *We can do it,* as the woman on the icon reminds us, but we pay a price in increased pre-menstrual stress (PMS). And that often means that everyone around us pays the price as well! There are many factors involved in PMS, but forcing yourself to keep going when your body and psyche are screaming at you to stop makes everything harder to deal with. They don't call it kick-butt-and-take-names day for nothing!

The question remains whether this completely natural function that lies at the core of womanhood can be reclaimed from thousands of years of negative interpretation—much of which women have absorbed and truly believe about themselves. In this chapter, we'll hear in their own words from women who have taken back their power by creating rituals for themselves and their daughters. Often, all the participants—mothers, daughters, and grandmothers—are transformed in the process.

Breaking Menstrual Taboos

As they redefine themselves spiritually, women face the task of unpacking thousands of years of cultural baggage surrounding their natural processes. They do this for themselves and to help provide the next generation with a better experience of becoming a woman than most of them had. Some of the essential questions women ask regarding their coming of age include:

How did you first hear about menstrual periods?

What happened the day you first got yours?

How did you feel about the experience?

What reaction did the people in your family have?

How could it have been handled better?

What advice have you got for mothers and daughters today?

Sylvia Takes It On

Sylvia decided to break the menstrual taboo in her family by inviting her daughter and her friends, along with a few of her own friends for moral support, for a weekend getaway at a cabin the woods. She told them to come with their questions about sex and that no topic would be off limits—and that there would be lots of junk food. What teenager could resist such an offer? They all knew in advance what the topic would be, but no one knew the impact it would have.

The first night was filled with food, music, and dancing. Saturday was spent on the lake, enjoying the water and fresh air. Saturday-night dinner was cooked outside and was followed by time sitting around a campfire. It was well after dark before the subject of the weekend came up, and nature provided the moment. One of the girls, Cynthia, started her period, and it took off from there. Sylvia brought out pillows and a quilt and made a comfortable place for Cynthia on the chaise lounge. Diane began talking about what the ideal situation might be like if women were supported and honored during this time.

Drawing on stories she had heard about Native American moon lodges, Diane talked about how a woman's body follows the cycles of the moon and has times of great creativity and times of regeneration. She talked about the importance of being aware of your body and following its energy. Pretty soon, everyone was really into it, telling stories and asking questions. They decided to create a ritual in which Cynthia would be honored, with her consent.

Cynthia passed on the herbal tea, preferring a cold drink instead. A couple of the girls began brushing and braiding her hair. Two of the women began rubbing her feet. They talked about taking time out to rest, at least during the first day or two of their cycles. One of the women suggested keeping a dream journal, as several had talked about the vivid dreams that accompany their periods. They talked about mild exercise and yoga postures that help relieve menstrual tension.

During the evening, menstrual taboos were set straight, and every area of sex and sexuality was explored. The night ended with the girls grabbing their sleeping bags and forming a dream circle around the fire. Sylvia believes the girls benefited from hearing what the women had to say. She and her daughter have declared the first day of their cycles Goddess Day! If they want to take time off from school or work, they can. The choice is up to them. The main thing is that the girls were given some positive attitudes about their cycles and how their bodies work. And they learned that they have choices. If they feel like taking a day off, they don't have to see it as being dysfunctional; they can do it because it's a good idea. And they have women with whom they can openly talk about sex.

FIGURE 15. Two women enjoying a self-proclaimed Goddess Day on the beach.

The girls decided to meet each full moon for a slumber party reenactment of what they are now calling Goddess Day. Within three months, those who had periods were on the same cycle. They were able to welcome the others into the circle when their time came.

Motherhood—More Than a Hallmark Moment

Becoming a mother is acknowledged through baby showers, visits from friends, and gifts. None of this really addresses the spirituality of motherhood, and doesn't primarily focus on the woman as the central figure in what is probably the most important relationship in our collective human story. From conception to birth, motherhood is pretty much ignored in traditional religion. Most women agree that the situation deserves a blessing. Today, women meet and talk about how to create a spirituality that honors this very important event.

Noris Binet, author, seminar leader, and teacher, notes in her book *Women on the Inner Journey* (Nashville, 1994):

> *Woman is the seed containing the potential for the growth of new life. Her feminine nature is cyclic, corresponding to the cycles of the moon. The intuitive power within her grows toward fulfillment from the beginning of the cycle until ovulation, then wanes toward introspection from ovulation to menstruation. In this intimate process, shared by every woman, no matter what her color, she gives to herself the opportunity to be born again.*

Honoring Pregnancy

Three months into Caroline's pregnancy, she and her husband, Frank, made their announcement. They invited family and friends for a dinner at which they shared their good news. In addition to the traditional declaration, they asked Caroline's grandmother to bless the new mother and child. They had spoken with her in advance to make sure she was comfortable with the request. Caroline's grandmother was honored. She offered her blessing and presented Caroline with a beautiful shawl to wear over her shoulders during her pregnancy. Others volunteered to bring dinner to the house and make sure that Frank took a night out when he felt he needed it.

The focus stayed on the couple during the pregnancy, as well as on the new baby.

Honoring the Difficult Times, Too

Not all pregnancies end with a joyful birth. Miscarriages, abortions, and stillbirths have a lasting effect on a woman's entire being. Women's spirituality supports a woman having control over her body. Regardless of whether an individual agrees or disagrees with the decision being made, women's spirituality reaches beyond judgment to offer support.

What happens when the pregnancy terminates prematurely? Miscarriages may be acknowledged by those most intimately involved, but not with ritual that identifies the loss at the spiritual level. A woman is often left to grieve alone. While her mate may be supportive, it usually takes the experience of another woman to understand the significance a miscarriage can have.

A woman's choice to have an abortion is often complicated and fraught with difficult emotions. Having the support of a circle of trusted friends offers her a chance to accept the responsibility of the choice she has made without fear of being judged. It affirms her authority and acknowledges the dimension of her decision. Such a ceremony heals emotional scars and feelings of guilt that can last a lifetime.

Placing Your Child with Another

Although the process of giving a child up for adoption is not as secretive as it once was, it is not always talked about openly. Women who have faced this very difficult situation often go through it alone or with a few close friends, but it is not recognized with the sensitivity that it requires.

A ceremony can bring support and spiritual understanding to the mother and child, as well as to all who will be involved in raising the child. Whether or not the mother and child will be together, there is an emotional and spiritual relationship that continues between the two of them throughout their lives. Having a process by which this relationship is recognized brings meaning and peace to a potentially devastating situation.

Not Your Mama's Menopause

Many women are active in the world into their sixties and seventies—well past menopause. These can be the most productive and satisfying times in life, and many women don't feel they are ready to step into the role of wise women. A new archetype is emerging in women's psyche to fill in this gap between mother and crone—the Queen. We began experiencing "her" in rituals several years ago, as women shared that they felt energized and creative as their monthly periods stopped. They talked about going back to school, developing an art form, starting new projects and businesses—they had a new-found confidence. It was definitely not your mama's menopause, but a flowering of consciousness—an archetypal event. Donna Henes, urban shaman, speaker, and author, was the first to describe this new archetype in her book, *The Queen of Myself* (Monarch, 2005).

Putting the Pause in Menopause

In celebrating this time in your life, consider putting the pause in menopause. Take time out to experience yourself. Go on a retreat if possible, or at least take time away to reflect on life. This is the time to accept yourself as you are, not to look at what you need to "fix" or develop. Queen does not dwell on what she has failed to do, but only on what she has done—and, by her own proclamation, she declares herself *perfect enough*. Only you have the power to do this—to come to self-acceptance. There is freedom in taking yourself as you are. From then on, you do what you want to do because you want to do it, not to please anyone or to make yourself feel worthy. You are worthy.

If you have not healed from the wounds of the past that keep you from your Queen self, talk to somebody—a therapist, a wise person you know, or a spiritual counselor. The ultimate power you are seeking is inside you. You have the ability to forgive yourself and love yourself, and to let yourself off the hook. Sometimes, it just comes down to making new rules—and queens are good at ruling! Refuse to believe in anything but your perfection—with all your flaws, you are the perfect you! Come up with some new self-talk and make it happen.

You Are the Boss of You!

Queen has four essential realms over which she rules: mental, physical, emotional, and spiritual. Here's how it works.

Mental: Queen is liberator and warrior. She offers freedom from the bondage of old rules. She has ruled against her disempowering thoughts and stepped into the light. She speaks truth and possesses crystal-clear insight.

Physical: Queen brings a new kind of fruitfulness. She births us into our true selves. She supports us in letting go of the responsibilities or burdens of the past and offers us independence. She demands that we take care of ourselves—proper nourishment and rest. She is the complete integration of spirit and body.

Emotional: Queen has emotional freedom, authenticity, and openness. She trusts her emotions and isn't ruled by them. Her powers of intuition are sharp. She loves openly and wisely— not suffering fools gladly.

Spiritual: Queen is a spiritual transformer and she is aware of her gifts. She is healer and teacher, not necessarily by action, but simply by her presence. She has a transformed relationship to herself and loves herself as she would love a new-born baby. She has outgrown guilt.

Queens don't ever:

Apologize for things they didn't do.

Over-explain themselves.

Downplay their accomplishments.

Preface statements with: I might be wrong, but…

Answer questions they don't want to answer.

Have a problem saying "no."

Feel guilty.

Add yours to the list.

FIGURE 16A. *Women making a mask to be used in a crowning ceremony celebrating the Queen.*

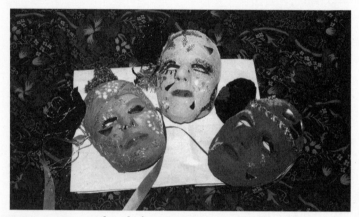

FIGURE 16B. *Decorated masks for a crowning ceremony.*

Crone—Not for the Faint of Heart

In the film version of Fanny Flagg's book *Fried Green Tomatoes*, the culture got a whole new image of what it meant to be a menopausal woman. When the character played by Kathy Bates is "aced" out of a parking place by two young girls who laugh about her for being so slow, she responds with: "Yes, but I am richer and have more insurance than you do." Then she rear-ends their car. It seems that every woman of a certain age can relate to hormonal rage!

Fully embracing your aging process is not for the faint of heart. The old crone is the image of wise woman. It's up to each woman to declare when to accept this part of her life. When you are ready, there are teachers and mentors who will guide the process. Jo C. Searles, retired professor of English and Women's Studies at Penn State, ignores the cultural baggage that has attached to our ideas on aging and goes for the power of it. She lectures on the old crone, Hecate, in workshops she calls "Rise Up and Call Her Name." She also mentors women who are making this transition—she calls them Baby Crones.

The Revenge of the Wise Woman

"I had met the Wise Crone, and She was me," Searles declares. "No more would I apologize for my responses or my age." She continues to say:

> I owned them; they owned me. Finally. Acknowledgement of and recognition for my own experience, my "wise blood," the ability, based on years of cyclical events, to separate shit from sincerity, secular from sacred. With that, Goddess surfaced, and hallelujah came Old Woman. Not just "older"; OLD. The Triple Goddess is triple, not double. To be complete, She must contain the Crone, whose function is not to bring only death, but to continue the cycle into transformation and rebirth. Yes, She is ancient. Yes, She is wrinkled. But on her, wrinkles look great. Spider Mother spins in a frenzy, silver hair flying in the wind. Kali the Destroyer dances Her skull-adorned way through the flux of death and life, equally ecstatic about both. And Destroyer Medusa grimaces dangerously at those who would deny Her wisdom and power. (Jo C. Searles, "New Wrinkles in Old Skins," Of a Like Mind, XIV: 3,25, Re-Formed Congregation of the Goddess International)

Elsewhere, Searles advises her contemporaries:

> We women in our 60s and 70s are now in foreign territory. We're on the cutting edge, with the state of the art, taking risks and having adventures. We're where few women have gone before, exploring a wizened, gray landscape long despised and neglected by our culture at least until now, when more and more souls will of necessity follow our lead, death being the only alternative. (Unpublished papers.)

Stepping into Power—Wise Woman Ceremony

Today women are meeting together, claiming the power of their wisdom, and creating a new identity for themselves through a ritual they call "croning," or Wise Woman ceremony. They are claiming the spiritual wisdom that is acquired only through a lifelong process of gathering experience. These rituals can be extravagant or simple. One group rented a villa in Italy for a month; another group had a night on the town at the local pizza parlor.

The key ingredients of these ceremonies are gathering together with other women, celebrating your transition, and having it witnessed by friends. Taking time to really acknowledge and appreciate yourself and hear it from others is important. How you do that is your creative statement. The point is not to be squashed by the cultural idea of age, but to have your own experience of it. As we accept ourselves through all our phases, new conduits of consciousness open, our psychic gifts increase, and we discover who we are at a deep and satisfying level. Besides that, it beats the alternative, as Searles pointed out.

Wrapping Things Up

Spiritual rituals and ceremonies marking women's lives have been part of the human story from the beginning of time. Western culture is basically built on a menstrual taboo. Today, women are reclaiming their right to be women by transforming negative images from the culture into images that support us in claiming our innate power. Our bodies follow a uniquely feminine pattern—different from that of the dominant culture, but not dysfunctional. Whether we change society isn't the point. Rituals and ceremonies celebrate our lives. They put us in touch with our female spirit. *They let us know that we matter.* The rest will take care of itself.

In the next chapter, you'll hear about some of our foremothers. Their dedication to improving women's lives is amazing. We all owe a debt of gratitude to these women for our place in society today. As we work to make the dream of equality a reality, we walk in their footprints.

Part III

❧ ❧

BREAKING BARRIERS AND
CROSSING LINES

Women's spirituality is one of caring, inclusion, and fairness. As you look back over our history as a nation, you will find that it was women who powered the social, political, and educational changes—not from a self-serving perspective, but by broadening the American dream to include all people. Now, as then, women bring an understanding of right relationship as primary to their lives and their professions. They understand that, for our religious and political vision to be accomplished, the vulnerable must be cared for and the earth that sustains us all must be respected. Women have always understood this sense of justice as a spiritual imperative.

Part III looks at history and how our foremothers overcame huge barriers to make powerful changes in the world. They leave a rich legacy that women continue to draw on today.

Chapter 11

ON THE SHOULDERS OF GIANTS

The women's movement of the 1960s and 1970s went a long way toward recovering our unsung heroes of the past, shining a light on women's important political and religious contributions—even getting their accomplishments into the history books. Hopefully, tomorrow's daughters won't have to dig quite as deep to find themselves as previous generations have had to do.

In following their faith and answering God's call, these women overcame enormous blocks, spearheading important social and political changes that are now part of our national heritage. This chapter presents the stories of six women whose lives and work have been absolutely essential in bringing justice to our American society. They worked from a spiritual and ethical base. This is only a broad-brush depiction of women's history; there are hundreds more women who deserve to be mentioned. I urge you to use this as the beginning of a much larger study.

Freedom and Justice for All

Two movements dominate the social/political/religious landscape in the 1800s—the abolition of slavery and women's suffrage. Four women leaders, two black and two white, saw how these issues were linked, and their lives intersected at this crucial time in history. The understanding, passion, and tenacity of these women have yet to be matched—they are the giants.

Sojourner Truth—"A'n't I a Woman?"

Born in 1797, Isabella Bett was the second youngest of the twelve children of Elizabeth and James Bett. She was born a slave. She would never learn to read or write; yet she would become a great orator and one of the most powerful women of her time. Her childhood was spent on the New York farm of a wealthy Dutchman, and her first language was Dutch. At age nine, she was sold to an English-speaking family in Kingston, New York. Later, she was sold twice more, ending up in the hands of John Dumont of New Paltz, New York. Despite the cruel treatment she received from him, he was unable to break her strong spirit.

Bett married and gave birth to five children. When the state of New York began freeing slaves within its jurisdiction, her owner promised to release her. The proposed date was July 4, 1826. Three months past that date, when she realized Dumont was not going to keep his word, she set out on foot, carrying her youngest child in her arms. Bett found refuge with a family who kept her safe until her liberation was secured. However, in the meantime, one of her children had been sold into slavery in Alabama, despite the New York law banning this traffic.

Bett's first act as a free woman was to recover her son, which she accomplished with the help of her Quaker friends. She brought him home, only to discover that he had suffered permanent injury from beatings received at the hands of his slave master. More than ever, Bett was firmly resolved to do everything she could to abolish the evil of slavery. As she was soon to discover, it was all about power. Author and scholar bell hooks describes the problem:

> Women's liberationists, white and black, will always be at odds with one another as long as our ideal of liberation is based on having the power, which men have. For that power denies unity, denies common connections, and is inherently divisive. (Bell Hooks, Ain't I a Woman [South End Press, 1981])

Bett took the name Sojourner because she traveled around the countryside; she added Truth to signify the word of God she preached. In her travels, she heard about the women's rights movement and attended the first National Women's Rights Convention in 1850 in Worcester, MA. There she met and became closely associated with Lucretia Mott, Elizabeth Cady Stanton, Susan B. Anthony, and other leaders in the rising movement.

Later, in 1851 at the Women's Rights Convention in Akron, Ohio, Sojourner became angry with white male ministers who denied women's claim to equal rights. When white women in the audience failed to challenge them, she spoke up. She specifically responded to one man's charge that females were helpless and needed to be looked after by men by pulling up her sleeve to show her powerful arm and asking her famous question: "A'n't I a woman?"

> Look at me! Look at my arm! I have ploughed, and planted, and gathered into barns, and no man could head me! And a'n't I a woman? I could work as much and eat as much as a man—when I could get it—and bear de lash a well! And a'n't I a woman? I have borne thirteen chilern and seen 'em mos' all sold off to slavery, and when I cried out with my mother's grief, none but Jesus heard me! And a'n't I a woman? (Illona Linthwaite, ed., Ain't I Woman: A Book of Women's Poetry from Around the World [Wing Books, 1993])

Truth settled in Battle Creek, Michigan, gathered her family around her, and continued her work for abolition. During the Civil War, she was invited to Washington, D.C. by President Lincoln. She remained there throughout the war, assisting with integration by teaching and helping freed slaves find jobs.

After the war, Truth turned her efforts toward women's rights. Referring to the wording of the proposed 14th and 15th Amendments, Truth strongly maintained that, if women were not given the same rights, they would end up being subjugated to black men. For the next thirty years, she traveled the country speaking out against slavery and advocating for women's causes. She became a leading figure in all four of the major reform movements of her time: abolition, women's rights, women's suffrage, and temperance. Sojourner Truth died on November 26, 1883 in Battle Creek, Michigan. She remains one of history's most auspicious freedom fighters.

Harriet Tubman—In the Tradition of Moses

Harriet Tubman's grandparents came to America from Africa in chains. She lived to escape slavery and worked to eradicate it. She conducted numerous daring rescue missions on the Underground Railroad, served as a spy in the Civil War, and was also a nurse. Ultimately, she became a leader in the causes of women's rights and social reform. Tubman epitomizes the indomitable spirit of her people and of women.

Tubman was born on a plantation in Maryland in 1820. As a young woman, she heard rumors that she and others might be sold south, and she boldly made her break for freedom. She had no sooner reached her destination in Philadelphia than she set out to rescue others. In a series of daring missions, she brought her family north. Over the next decade, she made over fifteen trips back south, leading 300 slaves to freedom. Indeed, her life epitomizes the words of Eleanor Roosevelt:

> *I gain strength, courage, and confidence by every experience in which I must stop and look fear in the face—I say to myself, I've lived through this and can take the next thing that comes along. We must do the things we think we cannot do.*

Tubman's daring exploits, sharp ingenuity, and fierce determination earned her notoriety, but didn't deter her from her mission. She devised codes and communicated instructions to her escapees by song. Grateful survivors tell of the depth of her commitment as she held a gun to their heads and gave them the choices of dying right there on the spot, going back in slavery—or getting up and continuing! One story tells of a close encounter with one of her former owners in a railway station where she was transporting fellow slaves. Fearing he would recognize her, she upset several crates of chickens and escaped in a cloud of feathers. She continually outsmarted her would-be captors. In their frustration, they put the hefty reward of $40,000 on her head, yet they still failed to catch her.

During the Civil War, Tubman went to Beaufort, South Carolina, where she nursed wounded soldiers, taught skills to newly freed slaves, and served as a spy and scout, leading reconnaissance missions behind enemy lines to gather information for Union raids. After the war, she went home and devoted the rest of her life to helping others. She cared for her aging parents, raised funds for schools, helped destitute orphans, and founded a home for dispossessed blacks.

Tubman saw racial liberation and women's rights as parts of a whole. She supported the movement for women's suffrage and served as a delegate to the first national convention of the Federation of Afro-American Women in 1896. She was the guest of honor at the New England Women's Suffrage Association in 1897. This remarkable woman died at her home in Auburn, New York on March 10, 1913 at the age of 93. In 1886, Sarah Bradford had given Tubman the title by which she is still remembered—the Moses of Her People.

The Gospel According to Stanton

Elizabeth Cady Stanton was born on November 12, 1815 in New York, on the other side of the tracks from her two contemporaries, Truth and Tubman. She was a pioneer feminist, theologian, author, and lecturer who shared the spirit of liberation with them. Stanton and her contemporary Lucretia Mott had met years earlier in London, where they attempted to attend an anti-slavery conference and were refused admission because of being female. Their subsequent discussions on the nature of oppression led to the first women's rights convention in the country, held at the Wesleyan Methodist Chapel in Seneca Falls, New York in 1848.

Stanton became one of the most radical feminists of her day, going further than anyone had before in declaring women's rights and publicly demanding suffrage for women. She soon met Susan B. Anthony and the two became allies. For the next fifty years, they fought together for women's rights.

In 1898, Stanton published *The Woman's Bible,* a translation and critique of scripture specifically aimed at exposing its contradictions regarding women's place in creation. She hoped to inspire women to question theological teachings that held them in subservience. When she published the first volume, it outraged even the most ardent feminists, who considered it sacrilegious and feared it would damage their cause. The clergy, not surprisingly, declared it a work of Satan. Then, as now, controversy works wonders in the marketplace, however, and her book became a best-seller. It was the topic of the day, and her intention of urging women to think about theology succeeded.

> *From the inauguration of the movement for woman's emancipation the Bible has been used to hold her in the "divinely ordained sphere," prescribed in the Old and New Testaments. The canon and civil law; church and state; priests and legislators; all political parties and religious denominations have alike taught that woman was made after man. Creeds, codes, Scriptures and statutes are all based on this idea. The fashions, forms, ceremonies and customs of society, church ordinances and discipline all grow out of this idea.* (Elizabeth Cady Stanton, The Woman's Bible [1895])

Stanton urged women to reject anything that held them back and to question any religious or political doctrines they interpreted to be harmful to women. She died in New York City on October 26, 1902 at the age of 87. She remained a rebel and leader to the end.

Susan B. Anthony Gets the Vote

Susan Brownell Anthony was born on February 15, 1820 in Adams, Massachusetts. As a young woman, she joined the temperance movement, founding the Woman's New York State Temperance Society. Like her contemporaries Truth, Tubman, and Stanton, Anthony was also active in the abolitionist movement.

"I should like to see our young people face with enjoyment the fact that they are going to have to go along uncharted paths. I should like them to be filled with confidence at meeting new challenges. Whether or not they have made the world they live in, the young must learn to be at home in it, to be familiar with it. They must understand its history, its peoples, their customs and ideas and problems and aspirations….the world cannot be understood from a single point of view."

—ELEANOR ROOSEVELT

It was the women's movement, however, that caught most of Anthony's attention, and she became one of the most famous women's rights activists of the 19th century. She met Elizabeth Cady Stanton in 1850, and they joined forces, becoming an impressive force for action and change. Anthony worked to secure an expansion of the Married Woman's Property Act in New York and petitioned the United States Congress for women's suffrage.

The two women did not abandon the abolitionist cause, however. During the Civil War, they formed the National Woman's Loyal League to gather signatures for a petition insisting on the emancipation of all slaves in the United States. Lincoln's Emancipation Proclamation, on the other hand, freed slaves only in the states that were at war with the Union. Both Anthony and Stanton opposed the 14th and 15th Amendments because the language was worded to exclude women from gaining the vote. By withdrawing support from black male suffrage, Anthony and Stanton positioned themselves in the same camp as black abolitionist and feminist Sojourner Truth, who likewise questioned the wisdom of the amendments. However, a 20-year split in the movement resulted from their action, and it is still the basis of disagreement between black and white women today.

Anthony founded the National Women Suffrage Association. She owned and operated the *Revolution,* a women's rights newspaper, and was president of the national American Woman Suffrage Association. The 19th Amendment, guaranteeing women's right to vote, is often referred to as the Susan B. Anthony Amendment. Anthony died in her home in Rochester, New York on March 13, 1906. In 1979, when her likeness appeared on a dollar coin, she became the first woman to be honored on United States currency.

Building Social Systems

The women you have just read about fought to establish basic rights guaranteed by the United States Constitution and the Bill of Rights. They paved the way for women of the next century to build social systems that leveled the playing field for women and minorities. The next two women you'll read about established educational facilities for women and secured women's rights to control their bodies.

Mary McLeod Bethune—Educating the Spirit

On July 10, 1875 in Mayesville, South Carolina, Patsy and Samuel McLeod, both former slaves, gave birth to the fifteenth of their seventeen children. Their daughter, Mary McLeod Bethune, would become one of the most influential women of the 20th century. They quickly recognized her extraordinary intelligence, and she began her education at the Mayesville Presbyterian Mission for Negroes. From there, Bethune earned a scholarship to continue her studies at Scotia Seminary for Negro Girls in Concord, North Carolina, graduating at the top of her class.

"The future belongs to those who believe in the beauty of their dreams," Eleanor Roosevelt would write. And Bethune had a dream of going to Africa as a missionary. When this dream was denied—ironically, because of her race—she made the decision to go back home and work with blacks. She began teaching, and gathered experience in her field for the next nine years. In 1904, she opened her own school, the Daytona Normal and Industrial Institute for girls. With Bethune's hand at the helm all the way, the school's enrollment quickly grew from five to 300 students.

Bethune was a skilled executive; she excelled at bringing together diverse segments of society. She garnered support from other black leaders, wealthy and influential white women, Proctor and Gamble Manufacturing Company, and the Methodist Church to assure her school's development. Her school later merged with the co-educational Cookman Institute of Jacksonville, Florida, and became an accredited junior college. Bethune-Cookman College went on to become a four-year institution, awarding its first Bachelor of Science degrees in Education in 1943.

Again, it was Roosevelt who articulated Bethune's credo: "Do not stop thinking of life as an adventure. You have no security unless you live bravely, excitingly, imaginatively; unless you can choose a challenge rather than competence." In addition to her contributions as an educator, Bethune became the president of the National Association of Colored Women, the most prestigious position in the country for a black woman. Feeling the association's vision was too small, she went on to found the National Council of Negro Women (NCNW), an organization she headed for the next fourteen years. By the time she stepped down, there were twenty-two national professional and occupational groups under the NCNW's wing. The organization created a powerful lobby, speaking out against lynching and job discrimination, and in support of public housing and social welfare programs.

During World War II, Bethune continued her fight for equality, focusing her efforts on the newly developed Women's Army Auxiliary Corps (WAAC), assuring the acceptance of black women into its ranks. She went on to persuade World War II Army officials to designate nearly 10 percent of the places in the WAAC's first officer-candidate class for black Americans. In 1945, Bethune became an assistant to the Secretary of War, helping in the selection of prospective female officers in the renamed Women's Army Corps (WAC).

President Roosevelt and First Lady Eleanor Roosevelt placed Bethune in the position of unofficial advisor on race relations. She organized more than 100 individual black advisors into what was unofficially called the Black Cabinet—a group officially known as the Federal Council on Negro Affairs. She presided over two historic national black conferences held in Washington, in which recommendations were made on government policies. As a special representative of the State Department in 1943, Bethune was invited to attend the conference that established the United Nations. She remained in the capacity of advisor on race issues for Presidents Truman and Eisenhower.

Throughout her career, Bethune held a bold vision, and she thought comprehensively. She always saw how pieces fit together, how organizations are formed, and how power is built. In her later years, she established the Mary McLeod Bethune Foundation, which promotes an international movement with the purpose of uniting people behind a set of universal values. She received a Medal of Honor and Merit from Haiti and the Star of Africa Award from Liberia. Bethune died in her home in Daytona Beach, Florida on May 18, 1955 at the age of 81. She was one of the most influential women of her time.

Margaret Sanger—Rebel with a Cause

It would be difficult to imagine how our lives as women would be today without Margaret Sanger's important contribution. She was born Margaret Higgins in Corning, New York on September 14, 1879, one of the eleven children of Irish Americans Anne Purcell and Michael Higgins. Her mother was a devout Catholic.

Despite the poverty of her early life, Sanger was able to get through two years of college before lack of financing forced her to drop out and take a teaching position. Shortly afterward, her mother died and Sanger returned home to take care of the younger children, while pursuing further training in nursing. She married at age twenty-three and had three children. The marriage ended in divorce. She remarried later, but kept her first husband's name—Sanger.

"We are not interested in the possibilities of defeat."

–QUEEN VICTORIA (1819–1901)

Sanger worked as a home nurse, serving the poorest of New York City. Every day, she witnessed the ravages of unlimited childbearing that many of the women endured. Too many pregnancies, doctors withholding birth control, and the carnage of self-induced abortions drove Sanger to her life's work—getting birth control information into the hands of women. She felt that her work in nursing was merely putting a bandage on a much bigger wound. Believing that, if women were ever going to achieve any degree of autonomy, they must gain control over reproduction, Sanger left her nursing career to enter the world of social change.

Sanger began dispensing birth-control information in her publication, *The Woman Rebel,* in violation of the law, which referred to it as "obscene" and "indecent." She was soon arrested. She escaped to Europe, but not before circulating 100,000 copies of her guidelines for contraceptive use. She came home to New York the following year to stand trial. However, after the sudden death of her daughter, the public demanded sympathy for Sanger; the court responded by dropping the charges.

Sanger forged ahead, opening America's first birth-control clinic in Brooklyn, New York in 1917, only to be arrested again. This time, she received no sympathy from the court, and served thirty days in a workhouse for violating obscenity laws.

However, the Superior Court of New York had opened the door a crack in a decision that included a specific exemption for physicians prescribing contraceptive devices for married women to protect them from diseases. Sanger slipped through the crack by reframing birth control as a medical issue. She founded the American Birth

Control League (ABCL) in 1921 and the National Committee on Federal Legislation for Birth Control in 1931.

The United States Supreme Court eventually held that the law could not interfere with public health by banning the mailing of contraceptive information and materials to medical doctors. However, many state courts weakened this ruling by limiting its application to currently existing cases and patients in danger of dying. In so doing, the courts refused to protect the rights of clinics. It wasn't until 1972 that the distribution of birth-control information and devices became formally settled constitutional law.

In 1923, with the help of a female physician, the opening that began as a tiny crack swung wide open as women entered the first birth-control clinic in the United States with a doctor on duty. It was called the Birth Control Research Bureau and was located in New York City. Sanger's work took on a global dimension when she organized the World Population Conference in Geneva and the International Contraception Conference in Zurich, focusing her efforts on women in India and Japan.

Sanger died on September 6, 1966 in Tucson, Arizona, having secured women's rights to family planning.

Wrapping Things Up

Women address issues of social injustice through the lens of spiritual and religious principles. The women of the abolition and suffrage movements fought on two fronts. They were dedicated to creating a better society for all people. After basic rights were secured, they turned their energies toward building educational systems and the right for women to control their bodies. Today, women who continue to work for justice and human rights do so from this awesome platform—standing on the shoulders of giants.

Chapter 12

❦ ❧

OUR JEWISH ROOTS

*J*udaism is one of the oldest continuing religions. Its origin among the nomadic tribes in the Fertile Crescent of the Middle East goes back to the dawn of the second millennium BCE, as Yahwists emerged from the Hebrew tribes to become the Jewish nation. This new religion was based on the idea of a monolithic God—one embedded deep in the history of the people. The founding fathers of Judaism were the great patriarchs Abraham, Isaac, and Moses.

During much of this time, the goddess Asherah was believed to be the wife of Yahweh—his partner in creation. She was known as God-the-Mother, patron of healing throughout the Middle East. She was associated with the image of a tree—the Tree of Life— and a snake was her sacred totem. Moses and Aaron carried Asherah "poles" as a symbol of power. Her snake and staff later became the caduceus, the symbol of medical doctors. Temples to her stood beside Yahweh's altar as late as 400 or 500 BCE, at which time they were destroyed and most references to Asherah were removed from Hebrew scripture.

Although Asherah, also known as Anath and Astarte, was officially removed from Judaism, she continued to live through the Mystery religions of the Hellenistic period. Egyptians and Syrians reenacted a sacred drama telling of the rebirth of the sun through the virgin Astarte on winter solstice. Her symbol appears in the

Kabbalah as the Tree of Life and references to her as Sophia remain in some translations of the scriptures.

Woman as divine mother and healer is an ancient and enduring theme. We see this archetypal figure again in Christianity as the Virgin Mary giving birth to the Son of God (Sun of God) at winter solstice. Her presence was further preserved in the symbol of the Holy Ghost, pictured as a dove emanating seven rays of light—an image that went back to primitive manifestations of the Goddess.

Kabbalah and Western Mysticism

The Kabbalah is a book of teachings whose exact origins are not known. It was handed down through the ages by oral tradition, thus making the exact lineage of the teachings difficult to determine. It's part of a larger mystical tradition found in many different cultures. It contains core teachings about the nature of existence, our deep purpose, and where we go when we complete our current incarnations.

The Kabbalah gained popularity within women's spirituality because it draws on traditions of the ancient world, some of which are based on Goddess images. It draws on ancient Egyptian Mysteries, Pythagorean mathematics, the work of Plato and Aristotle, Eastern Paganism, Greek philosophy, astrology, Goddess spirituality, and Gnosticism. In other words, it draws on almost the entire body of philosophical and religious thinking developed throughout history. It was written down sometime after 70 CE, hidden in a cave, and not rediscovered until the Middle Ages. The Kabbalah offers a contemporary teaching with deep historic roots and supports a worldview different from mainstream Western thought.

The Tree of Life

The Kabbalah uses the Tree of Life as the symbolic framework for ten basic spiritual lessons that address the "cosmic picture," referring to our questions about the meaning of the universe. These lessons provide guidance for our everyday life.

The Tree of Life (connecting with Asherah's symbol) shows the highly interactive composition of creation. Everything we do resonates throughout and affects the entire universe—up to and including the creator. Divine presence is everywhere, touching and affecting all.

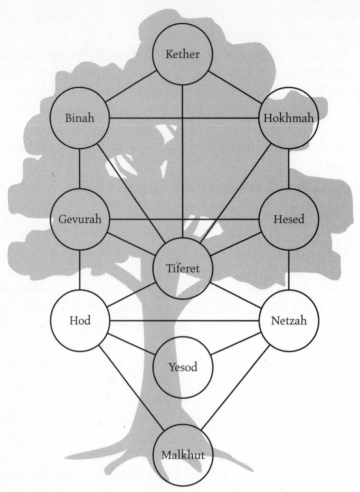

FIGURE 17. *The Tree of Life, showing the names of the teachings. The Kabbalah balances feminine and masculine images as complementary aspects of divine.*

The ten spiritual qualities and activities of the divine as described in the Tree of Life are as follows:

1. Kether—Crown

2. Hokhmah—Wisdom

3. Binah—Intuition and understanding

4. Hesed—Divine mercy and love

5. Gevurah—Judgment and strength

6. Tiferet—Beauty and glory

7. Netzah—Victory and power

8. Hod—Majesty

9. Yesod—Foundation

10. Malkhut—the Kingdom (the Divine Shekhinah, the feminine indwelling of the Divine)

Wise Old Sophia

One of the greatest rewards reaped by scholars in recent years is the recovery of the Wisdom tradition of Hebrew literature. No one knows who actually wrote the Book of Wisdom. It has been attributed to Solomon, a generic image representing a typical wise man of Israel who instructed the people through his discourse. While many have heard of the wisdom of Solomon, few know it refers to the wisdom of Sophia—a female aspect of God. Wisdom material was originally written in Greek about 400 BCE for the Jewish people of Egypt. It belongs to the Greek Septuagint, the text of the Old Testament used universally throughout the early Christian church.

Although she is not as well-known as other characters and stories in the Old Testament, Susan Cole, Marian Ronan, and Hal Taussig, authors of *Wisdom's Feast: Sophia in Study and Celebration* (Sheed & Ward, 1996) tell us: "There are more pages in the Hebrew scriptures about Sophia than about Abraham, Isaac, Jacob, Solomon, Isaiah, Sarah, Miriam, Adam, or Noah." Much of the material is found in the Roman Catholic version of the Bible, and in Ecclesiasticus, Baruch, and Wisdom—texts that originated in the Hebrew tradition. Here, the authors of *Wisdom's Feast* interpret Proverbs' text describing Sophia's role in creation:

> *When God set the heavens in place I was present,*
> *When God drew a ring on the surface of the deep,*
> *When God fixed the clouds above,*
> *When God assigned the sea its limits,*
> *When God established the foundations of the earth,*
> *I was by God's side, a master craftswoman,*
> *Delighting God day after day, ever at play by God's side,*
> *At play everywhere in God's domain,*
> *Delighting to be with the children of humanity.*
>
> *Proverbs 8:27–31*

Sophia is God's female side—God's spirit inspiring creation and taking pleasure in it. Mysterious and allusive, she is as integral to the creative process as breath is to life. She is the *ruah* of Yahweh, the breath of God, going forth creating, enlivening, inspiring, and maintaining life.

> *I came forth from the mouth of the Most High,*
> *And I covered the earth like mist.*
> *I had my tent in the heights,*
> *And my throne in a pillar of cloud.*
> *Alone I encircled the vault of the sky,*
> *And I walked on the bottom of the sea.*
>
> *Ecclesiasticus 24:3–5*

At the time that Sophia entered the religious texts, pre-patriarchal images of the divine feminine still existed in the cultural imagination. She appears both as Creator and the created—intimately assisting God one minute and giving God directions the next. The writers of scripture deferred to God, but spiritual imagination transcends politics, and her presence offers balance to the all male God.

Wisdom's Feast's authors point out the importance of restoring Sophia's image within the context of traditional religion and scripture:

> *If the goddess becomes a strange, exotic figure, substantially lacking in historical context, if she is perceived as a mythic, romantic figure appealing primarily to alienated white middle-class women, she will be of little use in the struggle to develop a new consciousness of connectedness. We must find a way to mainstream the goddess into the universe within which women are actually living their lives. Or perhaps it is simply a question of recognizing that she has been there all along.*

Sacred Literature

Judaism gave the world the Hebrew bible, with its rich spiritual history. Dates for the written text vary from 1500 BCE to the fourth century BCE. Throughout this long period of time, the stories were transmitted largely by oral tradition—passing from generation to generation and place to place. The Hebrew bible stands by itself as a religious text for Jews and also is foundational to understanding Christianity and the Islamic faith.

The Talmud is a collection of ancient Jewish writings that makes up the basis of Jewish religious law. The word Talmud derives from the Hebrew root *l-m-d* ("study" or "teach"). In Judaism, the law represents God's loving care for the people. Jewish scholars study the Talmud in its original form and reflect on its meaning, carefully respecting tradition and also applying the teaching to life in the current context. This ongoing process of discernment continues today.

The Culture Wars

The religion of Judaism and Hebrew scripture came into being in the midst of the woman-centered cultures of the Middle East. Much of Jewish history recorded in the scripture tells of the Israelites' struggle with the Canaanite people, and specifically how God intervened on behalf of the Israelites. Today, we would say that the rising monotheistic religion was in the throes of a culture war with the Goddess societies. Bits and pieces of ancient Middle Eastern mythology were woven into the Hebrew stories and can be found in scripture and other sacred texts. Lilith is one such story that slipped between the cracks and won't seem to go away.

Lilith—Goddess in Exile or Succubus on the Prowl?

Lilith is a woman of questionable reputation. References to her in scripture are sketchy and their meanings are unclear, leaving much to the imagination. She belongs to the mythology of the Middle East that developed as an oral tradition over thousands of years and spanning vast regions, making it difficult to know for certain what the original stories were meant to portray.

Lilith has been described as demon and as goddess—Eve's shadow side and Eve's feminine side. She is said to have preceded Eve as the defiant first Mrs. Adam, leaving after refusing to submit to him—specifically to lay under him for sex. She has been used as a tool of patriarchy and to justify male ascendancy—as in: "Wives, obey your husbands or get out of town." Likewise, she has been used by feminists as a tool of liberation—as in: "I will not submit to your authority just because you're a man (and I get the kids and the house)."

Fragmented references to a character in both Arabic and Jewish mythology with a name similar to Lilith portray a succubus—a demon-woman who hunts men, seduces them, and drains their life with a kiss. Vague references to her or a similar character occur in Jewish scripture in Isaiah 34:14 or 34:15, depending on the version and translation. The story of Lilith as Adam's first wife is traced back to the 8th century CE in Jewish folklore and gained ground during the Middle Ages.

Lilith lurks in the shadows of women's religious history as a mysterious and powerful presence—haunting the minds of biblical commentators and those who comb through ancient texts looking for names that have l's and i's and th's in them. Since men have had the pen for the last 6000 years, Lilith seems to personify the deep fear they have of women, particularly their unbridled sexuality.

Whether the Lilith archetype is real or not, and whether she represents women's independent spirit or woman as evil demon, will continue to be debated. Mythology is a body of stories, ideals, beliefs, and history passed down over the ages. A whole lot depends on who is telling the story and what they believe is true or reinforcing of the reality they are constructing. We do this as families, towns, and nations—we sustain our identity as individuals and as a people through our stories. Women's spirituality is offering its own version of existing stories and adding new ones to the cultural mix.

Mythology is real in that it *really* transmits ideals, and cultures *really* live by them—even go to war over them. However, it isn't necessarily true in the factual sense as we have come to understand fact—as in the likelihood that Lilith has a social security number, DNA, or fingerprints.

Our Shared Stories

Jews, Christians, and Muslims all draw from the same scriptural source. It is the interpretation of scripture, as well as what it emphasizes, that differs among the three religions. Further differences are found among groups within each religion. All are challenged, however, by their common disregard for women and women's stories. While women's stories are told, they universally are told from a man's perspective. Women of all faith traditions are now asking questions of scripture—about what is written as well as how it is interpreted. Here, we'll look at a few stories that belong to women's spiritual legacy to see how they might have been told if seen through women's eyes.

Sarah's Dilemma

While Eve is the mother of the human race, Sarah is the mother of our Judeo-Christian religious culture. She is the wife of the first patriarch, Abraham. Much rested on her ability to produce a son—an heir to the lineage.

When she was in her nineties, God tells Sarah that she will bear a child. Sarah doesn't see how this can happen, and she takes the next best action—she gives her slave, Hagar, to Abraham in hopes that she can produce an heir for him. Hagar bears Abraham a son, called Ishmael. But God comes through for Sarah and she gives birth to Abraham's son, Isaac. We are told that Sarah sends Hagar and Ishmael away to assure her son's place in the family line.

Women point out that we know Sarah as a loving wife and mother, and as a woman of faith. They ask how likely is it that she would send Hagar and her child away to die in the dangerous conditions outside Abraham's camp. African-American "womanists" connect with Hagar's vulnerability as slave and also as a single mother on her own raising a child. They see her as a survivor, not a victim. In the Genesis 22:3–12 story, God tells Abraham: "Take your son Isaac whom you love, and go to the land of Moriah. And there offer him for a burnt offering on one of the mountains, which I will tell you of." Abraham obeys and prepares to sacrifice Isaac. After displaying his faith in God the Father to the point of sacrificing his son, God sends an angel to intervene. God then speaks to Abraham through the angel, saying, "Do not lay your hand on the lad or do anything to him; for now I know that you fear God, seeing you have not withheld your son, your only son, from me." The message is usually interpreted as test of faith—meaning we need to trust God completely and not rely on our own reasoning and ourselves.

Jewish and Christian women raise questions about the wisdom of going against reasoning and instinct—both are considered to be God-given. They question how Sarah might have felt about Abraham's willingness to sacrifice their child. How would she have interpreted God's request? What might she have said to God? What might she have said to her husband? Muslim women side with Hagar, believing it was Ishmael, not Isaac, whom Abraham was told to sacrifice. They give Ishmael and Abraham credit for rebuilding the holy city of Mecca; they celebrate the story of Hagar and Ishmael in sacred pilgrimage, or hajj.

The Book of Ruth

The story of Ruth begins with a woman and her two daughters-in-law—all of whom have recently been widowed. They stand together in the midst of a patriarchal society stripped of their material resources and facing famine. They are at risk of being attacked as well as of starving. Naomi, the mother-in-law, kisses each of the young women and sends them home with her praises and blessings to continue their lives. "Go back, both of you to your mother's homes" (Ruth 1:8). Concerned for their safety, she knows they'll be better off at home with their own mothers. One of the women leaves and the other, Ruth, stays, voicing her familiar declaration:

> Do not ask me to go back and desert you. Where you go I will go, and where you stay, I will stay. Your people will be my people, and your God, my God. Where you die, I will die, and there I will be buried. I swear a solemn oath before the Lord your God: nothing but death shall divide us. (Ruth 1:16–18)

This passionate declaration speaks to devotion that is beyond politics or religion—it is heartfelt. Let's look at the scene from a woman's perspective.

Naomi sends the young women to their mothers' homes rather than their fathers'—oddly significant in the patriarchal context in which they lived. Women were the possession of the husband; they didn't own property or rule the house. Perhaps these women and others like them never yielded their sense of connection to the mother consciousness—never gave up their rights, other than at a surface level—in order to survive. On their own and away from the men, they spoke freely; every woman knows we speak differently when men are present. The young woman, Ruth, swears her undying love and devotion to her mother-in-law. It is an oath sworn by a *woman* to a *woman*. They have come into relationship because of marriage, but their love, at this point, has no bearing on the men.

Ruth begins by saying: "Do not ask me to go back and desert you." It is about them and the spirituality of sisterhood—mother and daughter bonding—superseding religion, law, marriage vows, or patriarchy. Ruth makes a choice to stay with Naomi rather than go home, and Naomi acquiesces. They aren't sure what will happen to them, but they're in it together. How seldom we see women portrayed as loyal to each other!

Naomi and Ruth go to Naomi's home together. Ruth is noticed by Boaz, a man with resources. Naomi encourages Ruth in that direction. Ruth and Boaz marry and have a son called Obed. Naomi cares for the child, who grows up to be the grandfather of King David. The political and religious significance of the story can be debated forever, but the example of female love and devotion is beyond debate. Today, the passage from Ruth (1:16–17) is often recited along with marriage vows, reflecting a woman leaving her home and joining the husband's clan. It is a beautiful declaration of love; however, not entirely true to its context.

Deborah and Jael—Brave Warrior and Courageous Assassin

In Judges 4 and 5, we have the story of two women who, through their courage and faithfulness, pull the Israelites out of the ditch and greatly influence history.

Deborah, a prophet, looked out over the highlands of Israel and saw armed bands preying on Israelite peasants. Caravans were being attacked and driven off the roads—her people were being killed. She rose to the occasion, marshaled troops and a general, and went to war against overwhelming odds. As the defeated leader of the marauding bands, Sisera, retreated, he stumbled on the tent of Jael, a female warrior who was part of Deborah's force. He demanded something to drink. Jael extended him hospitality and invited him inside the shelter. Handing him a cup of milk with one hand, she drives a tent spike through his head with the other. In doing so, she makes good the prophesy: "…the Lord will sell Sisera into the hand of a woman." (Judges 4:8–9)

Deborah's story is told twice. The poetic version, "Song of Deborah," is believed to be the earlier account and shows Deborah as a powerful warrior and leader in her own right:

> The peasantry prospered in Israel
> they grew fat on plunder
> because you arose, Deborah
> arose as a mother in Israel. (Judges 5:7)

Jael's bravery and ingenuity is also celebrated:

> He asked water and she gave him milk
> she brought him curds in a lordly bowl.
> She put her hand to the tent peg
> and her right hand to the workmen's mallet;
> she struck Sisera a blow
> she crushed his head
> she shattered and pierced his temple.
> He sank, he fell
> he lay still at her feet. (Judges 5:25–27)

In the later prose account, both women are shown in lesser roles. Deborah stands on the sidelines while the spotlight is shined on the general. Jael is shown to be manipulative rather than brave. In her book *Warrior, Dancer, Seductress, Queen: Women in Judges and Biblical Israel* (Doubleday, 1998), Susan Ackerman, Professor of Religion and of Women's and Gender Studies at Dartmouth College, proposes that Deborah may be adopted from Canaanite stories. She says imagery in the poetic version of Deborah's story is more reflective of the indigenous cultures than the developing Hebrew literature: "The earth trembled; heaven quaked; the clouds streamed down in torrents. Mountains shook…." (Judges 5:4–5) Later, this account describes "images of stars falling from their courses and rushing floods." (Judges 5: 20–21)

Portraying women as warriors would be a familiar image in Canaanite culture. The differences in the two versions appear to be attempts at rewriting history to reflect the diminishing role of women in the advancing patriarchal culture.

Wrapping Things Up

Judaism came into being in the midst of the Goddess cultures of the Middle East. Its written texts reflect a culture war with these earlier societies that lasted for thousands of years. The goddess Asherah, commonly believed to be God's partner and co-creator, was not completely done away with until 400 or 500 BCE. She continues to surface through symbols. Scripture was written with an agenda. It was the account of the formation of the Jewish people and their faith in God, and how the story of God intervened on their behalf. It is likewise a history of the suppression and/or annihilation of the Canaanite people—a Goddess-centered culture in the Middle East. Jewish scholars continue to update the sacred literature in an ongoing process, making it speak to life today.

In the next chapter, we'll hear from contemporary Jewish women and how they are changing the face of Judaism and improving women's lives today.

Chapter 13

❧ ❧

JEWISH WOMEN TODAY

*H*istory has shown that the rights of women in traditional Judaism were much greater than they were in the rest of Western civilization until recent time. Women could buy, sell, and own property, and hold their own contracts long before these rights were granted to women in America. In the mid-1800s, Judaism began a gradual inclusion of women in all aspects of education and worship. However, it would be more than 100 years before a woman rabbi was ordained.

The Ordination Story

There are branches within Judaism that are different expressions of the one Jewish religion; they are not to be confused with denominations. Their beliefs differ—as suggested by their names: reformed or progressive, traditional, and conservative—only as distinct understandings of the same basic truths.

Reformed Judaism, the most recent expression of the faith, is adapted to Western culture. In 1972, the reformed branch of Judaism ordained Sally Jane Priesand as the first female rabbi in the United States (more about Rabbi Preisand appears later in this chapter). Traditional Judaism, often further identified as Reconstructionist, ordained its first female rabbi, Sandy Eisenberg Sasso, in 1974. Conservative Judaism, which rose out of 19th-century Germany, ordained Amy Eilberg in 1985. Orthodox Judaism, which dates back to the days of the Talmud (second to fifth centuries) does not ordain women.

Rabbi Regina Jonas, however, holds the position of the first female ordained rabbi worldwide. After studying at the Academy for the Science of Judaism in Berlin, she graduated in 1930 as an Academic Teacher of Religion and successfully challenged Jewish tradition. Like many women before her, history almost forgot Jonas. In 1991, researcher and lecturer Katerina von Kellenbach discovered a document signed by Rabbi Max Dienemann, head of the Liberal Rabbis Association in the city of Offenbach, ordaining Jonas to serve as a rabbi in Jewish communities in Germany. It was dated December 25, 1935.

Jonas served in Jewish social agencies and, later, in the capacity of pulpit rabbi, filling in for male counterparts who were being arrested and deported or killed by the Nazis. In 1942, Jonas was also arrested and, in 1944, she was murdered in Auschwitz. Thanks to the efforts of Kellenbach, this amazing woman was given the recognition she deserved as Judaism's first woman rabbi and an important piece of women's spiritual history was reclaimed.

The presence of women as religious leaders has begun to change the face of Judaism by addressing errors in scriptural translation and creating new rituals and ceremonies that allow females greater participation. With this increased presence of women comes an increased emphasis on social justice and world peace.

Love of the Law and the Law of Love

Reformed Jews understand revelation as a continuing process and believe the Torah contains not only the history of a people, but also their hope. Today, Jewish scholars are working to redefine scripture, removing the accumulation of cultural bias. They believe we must work out God's law in our social interactions, and that effort continues. Most agree that humans were created as androgynous—containing both genders—and were later separated into male and female, each an equal part of the whole. Differences between the genders are reflected in various religious practices or in demands made on men but not women. This is said to be out of respect for women's highly developed spirituality, not because they aren't worthy. Today, thanks to the efforts of feminists, women are gaining ground in the struggle for equality in all aspects of religious life.

Women are working to further bridge divisions within their faith communities and within themselves as well. They have challenged their men and their religious heritage by reinterpreting scripture and transforming rituals and prayers using a feminist perspective, as well as through art and literature. Such challenges come with a price tag, however, bringing painful feelings of betrayal and alienation. Yet the pain of not acting on their deep beliefs compels these reformers forward. They do it for their daughters, for themselves, and to honor the women who came before them.

Plaskow's Midrash

Judith Plaskow was born in 1947. She is professor of Religious Studies at Manhattan College in New York and lectures widely on feminist theology, particularly Jewish feminist theology. In 1979, Plaskow co-edited (with Carol Christ) *Womanspirit Rising: A Feminist Reader in Religion*, which has become a classic anthology of the writings of contemporary feminist theologians. Plaskow is known for shaking up complacent attitudes, a practice she enjoys. She encourages women to reflect critically on both political and religious traditions in the hope of creating more just social and religious institutions in the future.

Plaskow draws on the classical model of Jewish religious reflection called a Midrash. Midrash is the process of questioning gaps or contradictions in biblical texts, in an effort to correct injustices. In her book *Standing Again at Sinai: Judaism from a Feminist Perspective*, (HarperCollins, 1991), Plaskow states that the Torah and Jewish history itself sanction the marginalization of women; this must be redressed, she insists, by redefining its content to include material on women's experiences.

> *Jewish feminists, in other words, must reclaim Torah as our own. We must render visible the presence, experience, and deeds of women erased in traditional sources. We must tell the stories of women's encounters with God and capture the texture of their*

religious experience. We must expand the notion of Torah to encompass not just the five books of Moses and traditional Jewish learning, but women's words, teachings, and actions hitherto unseen. To expand Torah, we must reconstruct Jewish history to include the history of women, and in doing so alter the shape of Jewish memory.

Plaskow is the first Jewish feminist to identify herself as a theologian. She created a distinctively Jewish theology that is true to classic Jewish structure and categories, yet that recognizes the feminist theologies of other religions. Plaskow is considered one of the most significant constructive theologians of the 20th century.

Phyllis Trible—Texts of Terror

Most readers approach problematic scripture with the realization that it reflects ancient times rather than as a recipe for living today. However, they also know that these stories have been used to justify the mistreatment of women and violence against others. They want these disparities addressed more rigorously by the experts. Phyllis Trible, scholar of Hebrew scripture, is one of many who are calling for correction in these biblical texts.

Trible cites the stories of rape, murder, and dismemberment of women, calling them "texts of terror." She asks that these anonymous women be remembered in prayer today. She talks about the concubine in Judges 19:1–20:7. In this story, a man traveling with his concubine passes the night in a strange town. Men of the town surround the house demanding that the stranger be sent outside so they can rape him. Rather, the stranger pushes his concubine through the door and the men rape her all night. In the morning, she falls dead on the doorstep. Her "husband" retrieves her body and cuts it into twelve parts, which he divides among the tribes of Israel to provoke war.

Trible connects these stories with women today who are the victims of domestic abuse and other violent crimes. Unless these stories are theologized for modern times, she points out, regardless of how incorrect they may be, they are used by the less informed to support misogynistic beliefs and behavior. She urges us to remember these women and grieve for them.

Judy Chicago—Mother of Feminist Art

Artist Judy Chicago was born Judy Cohen on July 20, 1939. A descendant of twenty-three generations of rabbis, Chicago was educated at the Art Institute of Chicago and at UCLA, where she earned a Master's degree in 1964. The Jewish spirit of *tikkun*, the healing of the world, provides the driving force for her art, in which she explores questions of gender and power.

Chicago makes her theological statement through her legendary art project, *The Dinner Party*, which celebrates women's contributions to Western civilization. The concept began percolating in the 1960s after she began researching women's history when she realized that women's contributions to society were belittled or missing. Chicago believes women's endeavors have been intentionally written out of the record because of their significance. Not only does the culture suffer from this loss, she claims, but, as has been pointed out by others, it results in the loss of any platform on which women can stand. As Gerda Lerner, feminist, author, and historian at the University of Wisconsin in Madison points out:

"Men develop ideas and systems of explanations by absorbing past knowledge and critiquing and superseding it. Women, ignorant of their own history {do} not know what women before them had thought and taught. So generation after generation, they {struggle} for insights others had already had before them {resulting in} the constant reinventing of the wheel."

–GERDA LERNER (*The Creation of Feminist Consciousness* {Oxford Press, 1994})

Chicago documents women's specific contributions through her massive project, *The Dinner Party*, a multimedia rendering consisting of three banquet tables forming a triangle, elaborately and beautifully decorated with thirty-nine place settings. Each setting includes ceramics, china, painting, and needlework commemorating a woman of historic importance. The table stands on a tile floor marked with the names of an additional 999 women.

Chicago turned to myth, literature, history, and popular entertainment to compile her guest list. She incorporates traditionally "domestic" art in the work and the model for the project brought hundreds of volunteers together honoring women's sense of community. *The Dinner Party* reads like a Who's Who of feminist history, taking us from Primordial Goddess to Georgia O'Keeffe.

Wing I—Prehistory to the Roman Empire: Primordial Goddess, fertility goddess, Ishtar, Kali, snake goddess, Sophia, Amazons, Hatshepsut, Judith, Sappho, Aspasia, Boudicca, Hypatia.

Wing II—Beginnings of Christianity to Reformation: Marcella, Saint Bridget, Theodora of Byzantium, Hrosvitha, Trotula of Salerno, Eleanor of Aquitaine, Hildegard von Bingen, Petronilla de Meath, Christine de Pisan, Isabella d'Este, Elizabeth I of England, Artemisia Gentileschi, Anna van Schurman.

Wing III—From the American Revolution to the Women's Revolution: Anne Hutchinson, Sacajawea, Caroline Herschel, Mary Wollstonecraft, Sojourner Truth, Susan B. Anthony, Elizabeth Blackwell, Emily Dickinson, Ethel Smyth, Margaret Sanger, Natalie Barney, Virginia Woolfe, Georgia O'Keeffe.

The Dinner Party premiered in San Francisco's Museum of Modern Art on March 14, 1979. Over the next ten years, the exhibition visited fourteen institutions. The project, having been viewed by more than a million people, is now permanently housed in the Brooklyn Museum in Brooklyn, New York.

Chicago's *Dinner Party* created a new art form that is intrinsically feminine, earning her the unofficial position of the mother of feminist art. Chicago is a prolific artist, author, and lecturer. A complete list of her work is available at her website, which is listed in the resources at the back of this book.

Rachel Adler—"Mother" of Modern Jewish Feminism

Rachel Adler was born Ruthelyn Rubin in Chicago, Illinois on July 2, 1943. She is associate professor of Modern Jewish Thought and Judaism and Gender at the University of Southern California and the Hebrew Union College Rabbinical School, Los Angeles campus. Adler, originally an orthodox Jew, now considers herself as belonging to the reform movement. As a pioneering feminist theologian, she integrated feminist perspectives into Jewish texts, becoming instrumental in the renewal of Jewish law and ethics. Her accomplishments have been widely recognized, making her a leader among Jewish and non-Jewish scholars alike.

Adler spoke out against the existing interpretations of cleansing rituals for women and the anti-female climate they engendered. Her position grew increasingly feminist and she eventually wrote that, "purity and impurity do not constitute a cycle through which all members of society pass, as I argued in my [1972] essay. Instead, impurity and purity define a class system in which the most impure people are women" ("In Your Blood, Live: Re-visions of a Theology of Purity," in *Tikkun* 8: 1 [January/February, 1993]). Her statement marked her movement from orthodox to reformed Jew.

Adler developed a new theoretical approach to Jewish law, proposing that its primary function was to be regenerative rather than authoritarian—a mode in which the law functions to enforce current rules. According to the regenerative principle, the function of the law is to promote and protect the highest ideals of the community. Accordingly, legislation and judgments must work to enact the messianic goal—the ongoing creation of a more just world—a principle that Adler maintained lay at the heart of Judaism. The messianic goal requires that each generation of Jews further the cause, working toward the realization of messianic justice.

Adler further applied the regenerative principle by challenging the language used to describe marriage—specifically the *acquisition* of a wife by her husband, which clearly does not describe an equal partnership and is therefore in violation of Jewish law. She proposed basing marriage on the covenant principle, whereby partners promise love and devotion to one another as permanent partners. The principle of a covenant, she believes, more truly sanctifies the bonds of true marriage.

Rachel Adler is considered one of the "mothers" of modern Jewish feminism. Her work moved women's concerns from the shadows to the forefront of today's Jewish life and scholarship. She is one of the most significant Jewish theologians of the modern era.

Marcia Falk—The Poetic Touch

Marcia Falk, born in 1946 on Long Island, New York, attended both public and Hebrew schools throughout the week; on the weekends, she attended the Art Students' League, where her passion for poetry and art was nurtured. She earned a B.A. in Philosophy from Brandeis University and a Ph.D. in English and Comparative Literature from Stanford. She is a Fulbright Scholar and has done post-doctoral work in the Bible and Hebrew Literature at Hebrew University in Jerusalem. She taught at colleges and universities for the next fifteen years and, in the 1980s, began writing prayers that are used in prayer books and feminist rituals. Her creed is simple:

> Let us restore Shekhinah to her place in Israel and throughout the world and let us infuse all places with her presence. (from The Book of Blessings: New Jewish Prayers for Daily Life, the Sabbath, and the New Moon Festival [Harper Collins, 1996])

In 1996, Falk released her innovative prayer book, *The Book of Blessings*. And in 2004, she published *The Song of Songs: Love Lyrics from the Bible* (Brandeis University Press, 2004). Following is a sample from this book:

> Poem 24
> Turning to him, who meets me with desire—
> Come, love, let us go out to the open fields
> And spend our night lying where the henna blooms,
> Rising early to leave for the near vineyards
> Where the vines flower, opening tender buds,
> And the pomegranate boughs unfold their blossoms.
> There among blossom and vine I will give you my love,
> Musk of the violet mandrakes spilled upon us...
> And returning, finding our doorways piled with fruits,
> The best of the new-picked and the long-stored,
> My love, I will give you all I have saved for you.
> (The Song of Songs 7:11–14)

Marcia Falk lives in Berkeley, California, where she divides her time between writing, painting, and lecturing. She also leads congregations in services and rituals from *The Book of Blessings*.

Sally J. Preisand—Pioneer, Trail Blazer, and Role Model

In the 1920s, the Jewish reform movement ruled that there was nothing in Jewish law forbidding women from becoming rabbis—a break with tradition that took fifty years to reach fruition. In the

1960s, the American Jewish community was debating the idea of women rabbis—a debate that led to Sally J. Preisand's ordination in 1972.

Priesand, born in 1946, was the first woman in this country to earn seminary ordination. (Several women, including Paula Ackerman, served Jewish communities in the United States in a rabbinical capacity before Priesand, but were never formally ordained.) She effectively opened the doors to rabbinate study for 1000 women and impacted the lives of countless more.

"Dare to dream, and if you dream, dream big."

–Hadassah founder, Henrietta Szold (1860–1945)

Preisand did not set out to become a pioneer; she just wanted to be a rabbi. Despite the attention of the press and celebration among feminists, she soon discovered that synagogues were less than welcoming to the idea of hiring the first woman rabbi. She took a variety of positions before finding her spiritual home in the Monmouth Reform Temple in Tinton Falls, New Jersey, where she served for the next twenty-five years. After three decades in the rabbinate, Priesand retired in 2006.

On April 23, 2009, she received the prestigious Elizabeth Blackwell Award, given by Hobart and William Smith Colleges (Geneva, New York) to a woman whose life exemplifies outstanding service to humanity. In 2010, in honor of its 125th anniversary, *Good Housekeeping Magazine* named her one of 125 women who changed our lives and our world.

Gloria Steinem—Feminist Icon

No look at the women's progressive movement would be complete without paying tribute to Gloria Steinem. Born on March 25, 1934 in Toledo, Ohio, Steinem is considered the leading icon of American feminism. She comes by her revolutionary spirit naturally, as the granddaughter of Pauline Steinem, 1908 delegate to the International Council of Women and president of the Ohio Woman's Suffrage Association. When asked why she was a feminist, Gloria

Steinem replied: "If you're a woman, it's the only alternative to being a masochist."

Steinem gained fame in the 1960s, when she secretly entered the "Playboy bunny" world as an undercover reporter. Her journalistic coup earned her an invitation to become a contributing editor for *New York* magazine when it was founded in 1968. Here, she began her column, "The City Politic." She entered the women's rights movement, and her involvement has become legendary. In 1972, the revolutionary magazine *Ms* hit newsstands with Steinem as a founding editor. The magazine was published for twenty years before it closed down for a brief time in December 1989. It reopened in July 1990 with Steinem as an advising editor.

Wrapping Things Up

Jewish women theologians and scholars have won a place at the grown-ups' table for women's spirituality. They are correcting many of the errors in biblical translations and interpretations that have been used for thousands of years to keep women out of leadership positions in religion. They draw on classic themes within their religion in challenging tradition and law, and they effect change through art and political discourse as well. They encourage all women to engage the scripture, to become a voice, and to fill in women's missing stories.

Chapter 14

❧❧❧

CHRISTIANITY—THE BACK-STORY

Christianity began as a small sect within Judaism. The group was expelled by Jewish leaders in an attempt to tighten their ranks following the destruction of the temple in Jerusalem by the Romans in 70 CE. Biblical history shows that Jesus was a charismatic leader—he inspired his followers by his words and actions, but didn't create dogma or form a religion. And he clearly challenged the traditional role of women in society.

Women were central to Jesus' ministry. They were present in the intimate gatherings of his followers and in the public arenas as well. This was against the cultural norm of the time in which these events were happening. His radical teaching and growing popularity caught the attention of the authorities. He was arrested on charges of sedition and his trial resulted in a death sentence. He was crucified according to Roman tradition. Accounts say women remained at the foot of the cross until Jesus' death, and it was to women that the risen Christ first appeared, ordering them to tell the others. Women and many men see this as a direct ordination.

Followers met in homes and women continued to take an active role in spreading the teachings of their founder, working side by side with the men. As commonly happens with charismatic communities like the one formed around the teachings of Jesus, once the leader is gone, the mission tends to drift off course. Shortly after his death, Jesus' followers reverted back to the societal norm—meaning they pushed women into the background.

Nothing about Christ's ministry was written down during Jesus' lifetime. Twenty years after his death, Paul—who was not part of these early experiences, but was inspired by them—began a series of instructional letters that would eventually form the basis of Church policy and New Testament scripture. Some stories were accepted into the new scripture; others were left out. Stories of women like Mary Magdalene, Priscilla, Aquila, Mary, and Martha, and early Christian martyrs like Perpetua, Agatha, Agnes, and Lucy tell of the strong faith and bravery shown by women in the early years of Christianity—yet many of these stories were not included.

Today, scholars rightly point out that this editing process was done by men, thus women's roles were greatly reduced and even written out of the text—leaving only a few references to their ministry. As women seek full empowerment in the Church, they point to scriptural references that show women's integral involvement in the early church. These stories validate and energize the cause for women's full inclusion.

Theotokos—A Theological Loophole

A young Jewish woman called Mary was the mother of Jesus; she was impregnated by the Holy Spirit. Like her son, she was a Jew. She occupies a pivotal place in religious history, connecting Judaism and Christianity—and connecting the ancient Goddess traditions with Western religion.

Mary's story developed in the cultures of the Near East, North Africa, Greece, Turkey, and the mixed cultures of Rome, where the Goddess was still very much alive in the minds and hearts of the people. For them, it would be impossible—and illogical—to have a "Father God" without a "Mother God." Moreover, the female deity was almost always more powerful than the male, who often appeared as her son and/or consort. The Mother Goddess carried with her the means of creation—her body, which was symbolized as the earth—and the means to care for creation through the sustaining qualities found in nature's abundance.

The stories of Mary interacted with the Goddess culture and she took on the legendary status of the Great Mother. Images of Madonna and Child have captured the imagination of artists throughout history. Even today, the church identifies itself as Holy Mother Church, embodying the characteristics that were once incorporated in the image of Mother Goddess.

Church fathers were concerned about Mary's rising status and called a council at Ephesus to address the matter and to further clarify other teachings. The Trinity is a key doctrine in Christianity; it is considered a mystery in that it can't be fully explained or understood. The Trinity had been declared doctrine at an earlier council. It stated that three "persons" exist as one God: the Father, the Son, and the Holy Ghost. Each is fully God, although expressed in one Godhead. The doctrine of the Trinity was further clarified at Ephesus with the statement that God the Father and God the Son (Jesus) were one and the same. Since Mary was the mother of Jesus, she was also declared to be the Mother of God. Her official title became *Theotokos* (Greek: Θεοτοκος, translit. *Theotókos*). Her Greek title is used particularly in the Eastern Orthodox, Oriental Orthodox, and Eastern Catholic churches. Its literal English translations include "God-bearer" and "the one who gives birth to God." Less literal translations include Mother of God.

The power of this declaration has been largely overlooked by Church authorities and members. However, declaring that Mary is the Mother of God reinstates her in her original position as Great Mother or Goddess. Mary went from being the mother of Jesus—no small honor—to being the Mother of God—an undisputable bump up.

The Litany of Loretto, a favorite prayer praising Mary, dates back to the 1500s. It is composed of poetic images reflecting her status in the people's lives. Here are but a few of her titles:

Holy Mother of God, Mother of Christ, Mother of the Church, Mother of our Creator, Throne of Wisdom, Ark of the Covenant, Gate of Heaven Morning Star

Such powerful images speak to the place Mary holds in the hearts of the people, making it difficult for the contemporary Church to override devotion to her. Mary has been both the Church's biggest nightmare and its greatest promotional asset—a one-woman PR department. Church authorities don't know how to quell her power and, at the same time, recognize the attraction she holds for women and men alike.

Today, Mary remains as popular as ever. Her numerous appearances and miracles continue to occur on a regular basis all over the world. For the most part, she is the most accessible heavenly resident and has shown herself to be, ultimately, of and for the people.

God—An Equal Opportunity Employer

For thousands of years, women couldn't own property and there was no place for them other than in their father's house or their husband's. The rise of the monastic/convent movement in the early Middle Ages gave women their first alternative—and they ran with it!

Women developed spiritual communities in convents that gave them a high degree of autonomy, and for the first time, they were under their own direction—sort of. They still had to answer to male authority in the Church, but they were making headway. While life in a convent may not seem a liberating choice today, it was the first career opportunity for women. It gave them a new-found independence, a voice in the Church, and a voice in society as well. The women who founded these religious orders were strong independent spirits with considerable chutzpah.

In addition to prayer and meditation, nuns in these religious orders expressed their spirituality through social action, feeding the poor, and treating the sick. This remained true until the later Middle Ages when papal authority began to usurp the authority of the abbesses in an attempt to bring women's religious autonomy under male control—something that was easier said than done. Convents remained a sanctuary for women, offering independence, education, and employment as teachers and hospital administrators long before these options were available to women in society.

Here are the stories of some of these remarkable women.

Hildegard von Bingen—The Holistic Mystic

Hildegard von Bingen (1098–1179) was one of those remarkable women whose spirit would not be constrained. At a time when the contributions of women largely went unnoticed, Hildegard produced major works of theology, visionary writings, and music. When few women were accorded respect, she was consulted by and advised bishops, popes, and kings.

Hildegard is known for her love of music, which she poetically described as the means of recapturing the original joy and beauty of paradise. According to her, before the fall from Eden, Adam had a pure voice and joined angels in singing praises to God. Hildegard wrote hymns in honor of saints and for the worship of Mary.

Her unique and surprisingly progressive ideas about sex contain the first description of the female orgasm:

> When a woman is making love with a man, a sense of heat in her brain, which brings with it sensual delight, communicates the taste of that delight during the act and summons forth the emission of the man's seed. And when the seed has fallen into its place, that vehement heat descending from her brain draws the seed to itself and holds it, and soon the woman's sexual organs contract, and all the parts that are ready to open up during the time of menstruation now close, in the same way as a strong man can hold something enclosed in his fist.

Hildegard was an herbalist and healer. She wrote about natural history and medicinal uses of plants, animals, trees, and stones. Her holistic and earthy scientific views were based on the ancient Greek cosmology of the four elements: fire, water, air, and earth. She knew sickness was brought on by an imbalance and believed that adding the missing plant or animal element could restore health.

Catherine of Siena—Sage Advice and Tuscan Poetry

Catherine of Siena (1347–1380) was a mystic and a contemplative who devoted herself to prayer. She was a humanitarian and a nurse who sought to alleviate the suffering of the poor and the sick. She was a social activist who didn't hesitate to confront the corruption that characterized the church and society of her time.

Catherine believed that spirituality was based in self-knowledge, and her honesty and straightforwardness earned her a reputation as a person of insight and sound judgment. She didn't learn to write until near the end of her life, but when she retired to Siena, she recorded an account of her visions and other spiritual experiences, along with advice on cultivating a life of prayer. Her legacy includes hundreds of letters in which she shared her practicality and common sense through sage and frank advice.

Catherine wrote in the Tuscan vernacular of the 14th century, and her works are considered among the classics of the Italian language. In them, we can see what has come to be a hallmark of women's spirituality—the mixing of politics and religion. Many of her letters were written to popes, sovereigns, rulers of republics, and leaders of armies; they are of priceless value to history. Others were written to the "regular" folks in her society and today remain as illuminating, wise, and practical in their advice and guidance as they were for those who sought her counsel while she lived.

Teresa of Avila—Christian Mystic with a Yen for Zen

Women in the Middle Ages who had the ability, gumption, and sheer spiritual drive to make it in a man's world were in no way ordinary. They had to be resourceful, independent, sure of themselves, clear of vision, good businesswomen, innovative, and strong-willed. These qualities are not generally characterized as spiritual.

Teresa of Avila (1515–1577) had all of these qualities and more. One of her biographers, Tessa Bielecki, describes Teresa as "a maddeningly beautiful young girl with an irrepressible zest for life" (*Teresa of Avila* [Crossroad Publishing Company, 1994]). Bielecki goes on to say that Teresa operated with equal grace in the kitchen and in the boardroom. She embraced Christ and was likewise a Zen master. She played music, sang, danced, and wrote humorous and insightful poetic notes to friends.

Teresa was born into a wealthy family in Avila, Spain in a time and place where worldliness, militarism, and religion collided dramatically. Her strong spirit was infused with adventure, courage, and religious fervor—a dynamic combination that was challenging and also compelled her to do great things. "God loves courageous spirits," she wrote.

Teresa took her vows when she was twenty-two, and her career as a nun was characterized by ongoing conflict. Her legacy lives on through her writing, which is filled with sensuous poetic understandings of God's loving and nurturing nature. She wrote about God desiring our companionship and needing our friendship.

Teresa was made a saint in 1622 and, in 1970, extended further honor by being elevated to the title of Doctor of the Church by Pope Paul VI—a high position reserved for those whose contributions are considered to be of benefit to the whole Church. Saint Teresa was the first woman to be so honored.

The Inquisition—Hammer of the Witches

Imagine women flying through the air on brooms, mating with animals and the devil, inflicting sickness and death on livestock, crops, and villagers. No, it's not the manuscript for an X-rated Harry Potter book. It's the message preached by the religious and political leaders of Europe during the Middle Ages.

For a long time, the 400-year holocaust known as the Inquisition was directed primarily toward Christians under the guise of quelling various heresies. The net was eventually widened and efforts were directed at Jews and Muslims, calling them "heretics and infidels," and toward women, accusing them of witchcraft. As a result, thousands of women were arrested, questioned, tortured, and put to death—suspected of being "witches."

The Inquisition began as early as the 12th century and became "official" in 1484 under papal orders. Two years later, the *Malleus Maleficarum* (*Hammer of the Witches*), written by Dominican monks Heinrich Kramer and James Sprenger, was published. It became the working handbook for identifying the supposed activities of witches and describing how to convict them—which was essentially through unspeakable torture.

The *Malleus Maleficarum* is rampant with paranoia, blatant misogyny, and the sexual fixation of its authors. It describes women's insatiable lust, infidelity, ambition, and intellectual and moral inferiority. No woman was safe from its reach; however, midwives, herbalists, and healers who were the specialists in women's health were the favored targets of the celibate, all-male clergy. The number of people executed overall is estimated at between 20,000 and 100,000. Among them was Joan of Arc, the seventeen-year-old woman who went to war for her king and country. Known as the Maid of Orleans, Joan was captured by the English. The French, for whom she was fighting, failed to come to her aid. She was imprisoned, charged with heresy, sorcery, and adultery, found guilty, and burned at the stake. Thirty years later, she was declared innocent by Church officials.

Ashore in the New World

The Inquisition of Europe washed ashore in the New World, rearing its head at Salem, Massachusetts in 1692, when 141 people were indicted on charges of witchcraft. Twenty went to the gallows. Fourteen were women; six were men.

After the executions in Salem, most of the clergy in the Bay Colony expressed doubt about the whole affair, and soon authorities admitted they had made grievous mistakes. In 1696, Samuel Parris, who had presided over the Salem nightmare, formally resigned as village minister, bringing an end to the practice in America.

Many women believe the residual impact of these sordid histories is responsible for fueling the anti-female sentiment found in religion and in the larger culture today. Just as African American women carry a residual memory from slavery, women of European descent carry the emotional imprint of terror that prevailed through the 300 to 400 years of the Inquisition.

Wrapping Things Up

Women were active during the ministry of Jesus and following his death, and the early Christian communities were a safe harbor for women and children. As the Church grew in status, women were pushed to the back and men took over the leadership roles. The convent communities of the late Middle Ages provided the first place for women to live in a place where they were not under the control of their fathers or their husbands—almost. They were still under the direction of Rome, but the women had a strong voice and laid their heads down on their own pillows at night. The concerted persecution of the "unfaithful" by the Church, known as the Inquisition, eventually turned against women and many were accused of witchcraft, tortured, and executed. The remnants of the Inquisition washed ashore in the New World in the form of the Salem witch trials. Both the Inquisition and the events at Salem live in the collective memory of women and continue to cause fear at the idea of questioning religion and culture.

Chapter 15

✿❦ ❧✿

CROSSING THE LINE

*C*atholics and Protestants often think of themselves as very different species, but they may have more in common than they realize. This is particularly true of women who are more interested in finding ways to express their spiritual beliefs than they are in religious dogma. These women seem to cross denominational lines quite readily. When today's woman makes the choice to stay in her church, she does so because she is more interested in expressing her spirituality than in maintaining doctrinal principles, particularly those based on theological differences.

Connection, Community, Commitment

Women don't tend to draw clear lines of distinction between faith traditions; they tend to locate common ground and operate within it. They move back and forth between religious "camps" easily, exploring differences and taking what they need to create their own full spiritual expression.

Many of today's Protestant women seek a connection to the Catholic sense of mystery and ritual. This is not to say that they are seeking Catholicism for its theological statement, but rather that they are attracted to many of its practices. In the same way, many Catholic women find that Protestant denominations offer them better access to power through the democracy of their structures and through their willingness to ordain women.

Women go where they feel connected. They seek community where their values are affirmed. And they have a strong commitment to seeing these values reflected in the world. Following are some of their stories, told in their own words.

Olivia—In Search of Mystery

Olivia was raised a Protestant in New England in the predominantly Catholic culture of Boston. In the 1950s, you were either Catholic or non-Catholic. "I was a member of the Congregationalists," Olivia observes, "but referred to myself as non-Catholic." She continues:

> *That began to change when I had a conversion experience while attending the wedding rehearsal dinner for a Catholic friend. The dinner was a big family affair. The priest, a lifelong friend of the groom's family, was there, along with the bride's pastor. As we sat around a large table filled with food and family conversation I had a tremendous feeling of being included in this community from which I had been excluded as a child. There was an interweaving of religion and culture, and I fell in love with it.*

> *What I found among Catholics that I didn't find anywhere else was a wide streak of compassion. The mystery and ritual drew me in. What can I say—I loved the "hocus pocus." It gets places you can't reach any other way. I was able to get past "thinking about God" and tap into the experience of the sacred.*

Eileen—On the Other Hand

Eileen was born into an Irish Catholic family in New Orleans' French Quarter and attended Catholic school for twelve years. Alcoholism made her home a tumultuous place, and she sought the structure the Church gave her. "Church was family," she said. During college, she took a leave of absence from church altogether. "I hadn't separated God from religion yet, so when I dropped out of church, I became an agnostic."

Over the years, Eileen has moved in and out of the Church, each time wrestling with its use of power. Meanwhile, she read the

Bible from cover to cover, and that is where she found her faith. She finally made her peace by leaving the Catholic Church. "I was tired of being angry." Eileen joined the Presbyterian Church two years ago. She belongs to a small congregation, which she describes as friendly and involved in the community. What she likes about her new religious home first and foremost is that women have equal power! Elders run the church, and women can become elders! Eileen says, "I'm finally not angry anymore!"

Ronnie—Bits and Pieces of Faith

Ronnie was born in New York City on the spot where the Schubert Theater now stands, she says proudly. Her mother was a dancer, and her father was a politician. Ronnie has combined the skills she inherited from her parents in her own personality, and the result is a vibrant, composed, outgoing woman of action who loves people. Ronnie was raised in an ecumenical family of German Lutherans, Episcopalians, Greek Episcopalians, Methodists, and Tibetan Buddhists. She chose Catholicism at the age of eleven and was baptized into the Catholic Church.

Despite the problems she encounters in the Catholic Church that cause her to take periodic "breaks" from it, ultimately Ronnie always comes back. This is partially due to the character of her parish, and partially to her own ability to set personality aside and work from principles—in this case her desire to be of greater service.

A few years ago, Ronnie started a writing workshop at Grace House, an assisted-living facility for people with AIDS, an experience she describes as triumphal and joyous. "They are facing the greatest mystery of all—death—and are having the time of their lives. The stories are heroic and painful—a rich mixture of the best and the worst life has to offer. There are also the stories of all the people who come to care for them. I am both filled with gratitude and humbled by this experience." Ronnie is reminding the world that "AIDS has faces."

Although this parish embraces the inclusive worldview that she shares, "big" church, or the organizational church, often falls short of her ideals. When this happens, she takes a break. "Life has taught me how little can be transformed beyond myself," she notes.

> *"Love is the only thing that we can carry with us when we go, and it makes the end so easy."*
>
> —Louisa May Alcott

Annette—Lord, Get Me out of Your Way!

A few years ago, Annette, an African-American woman with a husband and two children, was working as a deacon in the United Methodist Church—a position she describes as being in the eye of the paradox! As a deacon, her job was to connect the church and the world. The paradox is that, as an African-American deacon, she is an enigma in both arenas—church and world.

Annette draws on a rich spiritual inheritance, including a powerful group of elders consisting of two doctors, a nurse, two school principals, and several teachers. They were all summoned together by her "Aunt Henri" to guide and encourage her religious development.

Under Aunt Henri's direction, these family elders made an album of their prophetic hopes and dreams about her. She was less than a year old at the time. In what is an African tradition, Aunt Henri had already recognized the gift within Annette, and had declared that she would become a minister. In their vision of her, her elders saw her as a leader who would work to change the system. They then helped to shape that vision.

Annette's working definition of spirituality is how we connect with God. For her, the connection involves the combined disciplines of prayer, reading scripture, and action. She is a liberationist. "Scripture and prayer always lead me to be an agent of change," she says. For her, political liberation and spiritual liberation are one and the same.

The theme of tolerance keeps Annette on her knees most days. The spiritual challenge of her position in her church is to find tolerance in her heart for Christians who believe that they should be *intolerant* because the world is becoming *too* tolerant. She fights against the temptation to use "being right as a banner," a polarizing position she sees many evangelical Christians take. "The real work is inside of ourselves where we have to get to deeper and deeper levels of faith." Annette believes that "faith lies in knowing God is at work in the world despite the evidence to the contrary; and watching the evidence change before your eyes."

Annette knows that the best way to work with controversy is to find a place where both sides agree, and build from there. Argument doesn't change people's minds as well as finding common ground does.

Annette saw an example of how that works at a conference of religious professionals who represent a diversity of theologies. "Each individual was there because he or she recognized the beauty and joy of life, and was in search of God. The issue on the table was regarding the church's position on ordination of homosexuals." As they broke into groups of ten for discussion, Annette found she was the only person who was in favor of granting full rights to gay and lesbian members. She had signed the Same Sex Union Document, which declared that she would honor marriages between gay people, which pretty much tipped her hand to the group.

I prayed asking God to get me out of the way and began from the position that I didn't know what God's will was on the issue of homosexuality. I admitted that while I had arrived at a different conclusion than they had, I was searching, too.

I told them that I don't pretend to know why people are the way they are, but I do know that they are created by God. I talked about how the church had met 200 years after slavery ended to seek reconciliation and repentance for not treating black people as equals, and that I felt these two issues were somehow related. In both incidences, people were trying to understand God's wishes. I just hoped that we would not be meeting 200 years from now to seek reconciliation and repentance for our treatment of gays. Never give up on finding resolution even to the most complex situations. Time has shown that continued efforts, combined with prayer and meditation, bring both sides of an issue into proper alliance—eventually.

Many people in the group became open to reconsidering their stand. As a group, we decided we had to pray and reflect harder before making a decision. I know that I was able to be useful in that situation because I was honest. I believe our job is to be faithful to what is true for us. It opens the space and creates some wiggle room where dialogue can begin. That's our job. God does the transforming.

Regarding black women's spirituality, Annette believes that today's women are drawing on their grandmothers' and mothers' theology and spirituality—a tradition that asks the question: "How does God call you to act?" She believes much theological writing is done by contemporary authors like Emilie Townes and Maya Angelou. In the black tradition, "theology isn't just an intellectual exercise; it's a direct, affirming, movement. Black women's spirituality is integrated into all aspects of our lives. It shows up in Tina Turner's performances, in Marion Anderson's singing, in Oprah's television ministry, in the Olympic running of Marion Jones, and in the tennis serve of Venus Williams."

Today Annette is facing the biggest challenge of her life—multiple sclerosis. She is dealing with how this disease has changed her and changed the family dynamics. Her relations with her children and husband are strained. She was used to going all the time; now she spends her days in quiet desperation. "God is on the periphery of my life right now," she admits sadly. "I'm angry at the disease; I feel lost, afraid. I don't have a map for this. No, that's not the real problem. The problem is I don't want this. I can't get to the acceptance and I'm blocking whatever blessing is in this and I do believe there is one."

Annette reflects on Maya Angelou's words: "All my work is meant to say, 'You may encounter many defeats, but you must not be defeated.' In fact, the encountering may be the very experience which creates the vitality and the power to endure" (Jeffrey Elliot, ed., *Conversations with Maya Angelou* [University Press of Mississippi, 1989]).

"I haven't gotten there—yet," she admits.

Honora—Preacher Teacher Offers Sage Advice

Honora is a Dominican nun who teaches preaching at a Catholic seminary and a major university, yet is not allowed by her Catholic religion to preach from the pulpit. She is both a progressive and a pragmatist. When I asked how she manages this unfortunate limitation, she offered some very sage advice in a concise two-step process:

- Acknowledge the injustice of it and deal with the emotions it evokes—anger, frustration, pain—whatever.

- Get over it! There are lots of things that need doing that I can do. Make sure the "limits" are theirs, not mine.

Honora further explains, "I'm doing everything I can do, mainly through my teaching, to subvert the mentality that supports the injustice." She defines preaching in the broader context of "bringing the good news of God's all-embracing love." She points out, "There are many places besides the pulpit where this message can be delivered, such as through our individual presence, writing, art, prison ministries, even the Internet." Honora believes that "every creature has a different perception, and all voices are important."

Mary Lou—To Die a Good Death

Mary Lou is a chaplain at a large Catholic hospital. Her job is to minister to patients, family, and staff, assisting them in the face of chronic or life-threatening illness or death. She talks about making peace as the time when everyone involved with the patient comes to terms with or befriends the limits of the illness. She helps patients, family, and sometimes the attending staff find the hope in the situation.

Mary Lou talks about this process as spiritual integration. She approaches her work from an ecumenical position. "If that means bringing in someone of the patient's own religion, that is what I do. I talk with them and find out what needs to happen for them as they approach their death. I assist them in finding out what is important to them and connect them with it."

"The very least you can do in your life is to figure out what you hope for. And the most you can do is live inside that hope. Not admire it from a distance, but live right in it, under its roof."

–Barbara Kingsolver, *Animal Dreams* (Harper Perennial, 1994)

Mary Lou sees spirituality as bigger than religion. "It includes all that gives our life purpose, meaning, and hope. It includes our relationships both here and now and with God. It is the totality of our life experiences and expression—it is dynamic and evolves over time." Her own spirituality was formed by her family and by the fifteen years she spent in the care of the Visitation nuns, the contemplative order that educated her. The nuns taught her about a loving God, and about being still and experiencing God's love.

Lynn Westfield—Hospitality Spirituality

African-American spirituality is one of liberation, born out of survival and resistance to slavery. It is bound together by stories of shared history and connection to the ancestors, which creates a common consciousness. Its roots in African soil connect to a time and a place where the mind-body duality did not exist. This spiritual wholeness is reflected in the embodied style of worship that characterizes their services.

Dr. Lynne N. Westfield, Associate Dean of Religious Education and Graduate Division of Religion at Drew University, published a book called *Dear Sisters: A Womanist Practice of Hospitality* (Pilgrim Press, 2001), in which she identifies a particular kind of African American women's spirituality she calls Hospitality Spirituality. In the book, she talks about the full-bodied Christianity of Africa, the tradition of prayer warriors, and hospitality—African American style.

Westfield isn't sure whether women's spirituality is a product of nature or nurture, but she feels there's an inherently feminine aspect to all spirituality. "Spirituality engages an introspective, quieter, reflective, part of us, aspects that are more cultivated in women than in men" Westfield defines spirituality as: "The awareness that the mind, body, and spirit are one; that we are spiritual beings in a body. Spirituality is God Consciousness. It's the realization that we are connected to God, the ultimate spiritual being." For her, spirituality can't be put into little boxes and marked "For Sunday only." She practices her spirituality every day, in all aspects of her life. She sees her teaching job as a calling to ministry.

Westfield brings spiritual consciousness into her classroom in the way she relates with the students and in preparing the lesson. She teaches the whole student: mind, body, and spirit. While her spirituality also includes a formal practice of meditation and prayer, she feels that true spiritual attunement is practiced in our ongoing interactions in the world, and in our relationship to our jobs, to our neighborhoods, to our families, and to our homes.

Knock, Knock, Knocking on Heaven's Door

There is a historical mystical tradition in African American spirituality that Lynne describes as "ancient, supple, and very much alive."

> *[In] a seamless relationship between heaven and earth, certain members of the community known as Prayer Warriors connect with the ancestors. They have special healing abilities, and they gather and pass along spiritual information. The tradition is transmitted from one generation to the next through personal recognition— a Prayer Warrior recognizes the gift in another. Once the gift is acknowledged, the person spends time alone, learning how it works. As they begin using their gift, word goes out into the community, which then recognizes a new Prayer Warrior.* (Dear Sisters)

Lynne talks about a spiritual hunger that exists in many young people today—a hunger that leads them to many "New Age" practices. She points out, "Nothing is really new about New Age. These practices have existed since the beginning of time. There's a rich source for them within the black church" (Dear Sisters).

Women's Night Out

African American women have a particular kind of spirituality that Westfield calls Hospitality Spirituality, a term derived from biblical tradition and applied to the black women's tradition of coming together in their homes as community, and sharing food and stories. This happens more or less spontaneously when black women gather together around a kitchen table.

Traditional hospitality includes a host and a stranger, meaning someone whose house is opened (host) to people who don't live there (strangers). Westfield, on the other hand, describes African American women's gatherings as stranger-to-stranger hospitality. Because of the degree of disenfranchisement most African American women experience in this culture, they often have no place they can really call home. Few black women own their own houses, and so they often feel like strangers living on the landlord's property, knowing they could be moved out at any moment. Living in this tension is relieved by gathering friends together and celebrating *now*, as it is the only moment.

Safety is a rare commodity for African American women. The racial memory of slavery remains with them. Shared stories that have come down through the ages recalling the separation of families and children sold away while their mothers worked in the field express an alienation so deep that Sojourner Truth described it as a time when "None could hear me but Jesus."

Today, when African American women gather together around the table sharing current stories, there is laughter, warmth, and, of course, food. In these moments, they create a safe place for themselves, a sanctuary. Westfield describes these gatherings as essentially sacramental in nature. Although the women themselves may not consider the suppers spiritual—they gather, they eat, they have fun, and they leave feeling refreshed and renewed in spirit—Westfield calls this a spontaneous kind of spirituality.

Nourishing the Body; Renewing the Spirit

In an embodied spirituality, care of the body equates to care of the soul. Westfield nourishes her spirit by getting massages and taking trips to the spa. However, she finds the best place of renewal to be her mother's kitchen table where her nuclear and extended family gathers to enjoy old family recipes, laughter, and conversation. She says this is where she connects to who I am, whose I am, and what I will become. On the third item, she reports that she gets lots of help in the form of suggestions—many loved ones willing to share their wisdom! Another place of renewal is her work, where she feels she is living out her calling. In her words, "Liturgy means work of the people. Teaching is my liturgy." You can find Westfield's book in the resources listed at the back of this book.

Wrapping Things Up

Women are less bound by denominational differences than men and more focused on where they can find the support they need to do what they see needs doing. Those who find satisfaction working within traditional religions do so by staying active in ministries where they can find expression for their spirituality. Women who stay in the traditional church despite its shortcomings do so with eyes wide open—meaning that they are aware of the injustice and find they can work for change from the inside and still be effective in their service to the world. It is in the nature of systems and structures to become conservative and lose their cutting edge. To avoid this, systems must be challenged by their membership—women are doing just that.

Part IV

❧❧ ❧❧

PEOPLE OF THE EARTH

It isn't necessary to go back to pre-historic times to find examples of matri-archies; Native American societies are organized according to matriarchal principles—it's the spirituality of this land. Practices differ from group to group, but the spirit of cooperation, love for the earth, and concern for its well-being as a living organism are common values among tribes and among other spiritual traditions whose roots go back to the soil. In Part IV, you will read about two remarkable Cherokee women—one who has left her political mark on her people and another who continues a 27-generation spiritual legacy. You'll learn about the School for Witchlets, a woman who runs a sweat lodge, and another who makes flower medicine. You'll also meet two women pioneers in mind-body awareness. Their fascinating work shows how spirituality is encoded in our bodies. These women understand the earth's spiritual intelligence and God's presence in nature.

Chapter 16

❦ ❦

ORGANIC SPIRITUALITY AND NATIVE AMERICAN WOMEN

*T*he spirituality of Native American people is complex and diverse; one cannot talk about native spirituality or religion as a unified set of beliefs. However, there is a common worldview and shared characteristics that can be recognized in the beliefs of most native people. First, we'll look at the Plains Indians to see how the women of this native society lived. We'll also hear about the woman who became the first Principal Chief of the Cherokee Nation. On the way, we will perhaps clear up some misconceptions of what it's like to be an American Indian woman today.

The Ceremonies Are Outlawed

In 1891, the U. S. government made it illegal for Native Americans to practice their religion. For the next eighty-seven years, religious ceremonies and possession of sacred objects were forbidden by law. The ceremonies were taken underground and preserved; however, without direct access to them, the very structure of Native American society was compromised.

Additional destruction to Native American traditions happened through practices that were imposed by both church and government, like the forced removal of children from their parents' homes, forbidding native language, and imposing religious conversion. It was only in 1978, under the Carter administration, that the American Indian Religious Freedom Act was passed and Native Americans were again free to worship through ceremonies and traditional rites.

Each Indian nation is unique and has a particular way to fulfill its spiritual duty. However, there are also certain things they hold in common. Each native nation has ceremonies that relate to the cycles of planting and harvest and the cycles of the moon, ceremonies of purification and renewal, and ways to maintain traditions and cultivate spiritual awareness. The understanding of the living spirit in all things is a unifying belief, although one not honored by our Western culture.

The Iroquois—Origins of Democracy and Women's Rights

The Iroquois are known for their superior political organization. Their political system dominated the first 200 years of colonial history in both Canada and the United States. Proper credit is seldom given, but the Europeans learned about democracy from the Iroquois. The Iroquois tribes had an elaborate system of checks, balances, and law that directly influenced the American Articles of Confederation and Constitution. On Sept 16, 1987, the U. S. Senate passed a resolution officially recognizing that the U. S. Constitution was explicitly modeled upon the Iroquois Confederation.

According to an essay by Sally Roesch Wagner, in her book, *The Untold Story of the Iroquois Influence on Early Feminism* (Sky Carrier Press, 1996), women's rights in Native American tribes were substantial:

1. Children belonged to the mother's tribe.

2. If a marriage proved to be a bad one, the woman could leave and take the children with her. She was free to marry again.

3. When a man brought home the results of a hunt, it was the woman's to use or dispose of as she saw fit. Her decisions were not disputed.

4. A woman kept ownership of her belongings even within the marriage.

5. Women ruled the home front, and all goods were owned commonly.

6. Rape and wife-beating were almost unknown.

7. Women voted on tribal affairs.

8. Treaties had to be ratified by three-quarters of all voters, and three-quarters of all mothers.

9. Women could impeach a chief.

10. Women addressed council meetings.

11. Women could forbid braves from going to war.

Most accounts of Native American life, however, have come through the observations of European men. Women's lives were not usually recorded, or were interpreted by white males. They often painted a picture of the women as downtrodden, mistreated, and subservient, which was not the rule. For the most part, the subtleties of tribal politics were completely lost on early European observers.

The First Women of the Plains

Indian culture among the Plains Indians of North America was matriarchal. UCLA professor and author Paula Gunn Allen, who is a Native American of mixed heritage, laments the price women pay because they don't know about the prevalence of female-based cultures on this continent prior to European occupation.

> I have noticed that as soon as you have soldiers the story is called history. Before their arrival it is called myth, folktale, legend, fairy tale, oral poetry, or ethnography. After the soldiers arrive it is called history. (The Sacred Hoop: Recovering the Feminine in American Indian Traditions [Beacon Press, 1992])

In looking for matriarchal cultures or models of female leadership, Gunn insists, women need to look no further than the first people of our own land.

Tribal Mothers and Grandmothers

Women were indispensable to tribal life, and participated in many communal activities. However, their primary responsibilities were in maintaining the home and family. Women were greatly respected as the life-givers of the tribe. Songs and stories have been passed down through the ages that sing of Mother Earth, and the love and honor the people hold for all females as mothers of the tribe. Likewise, parents had great affection for children, and child-rearing rules were permissive. When discipline was needed, grandparents generally administered it.

The mother-daughter bond was particularly strong, even though (or perhaps because) grandmothers did most of the training, teaching girls to cook, sew, tan hides, and design and make clothing—which was an art form in itself. Bravery was a highly valued virtue in both boys and girls; in some tribes, girls developed their riding and fighting skills. Ordinarily, hunting and warring were left to men, but there were some exceptional cases where women of particular strength became warriors.

Wives were not subject to their husbands. Abuse was rare, and the woman's family had the right to intervene and separate a wife from her husband when there was mistreatment. Indian women maintained their own property, separate from their husbands'. They were free to buy and sell property, as they desired. When a party returned from a hunt, after the animals were skinned, the pelts were given to the women to be used in any way they wanted—they could keep them, sell them, or trade them, and keep the money or goods. Most Native tribes found the treatment of white women disrespectful, and there was concern about what might happen to Indian women when they became citizens and lost their rights.

Marriage was a tribal affair. It was usually arranged, and not always for love. The woman's wishes were considered and she could refuse the mate chosen for her; however, it was not a right often exercised. A suitor brought gifts of horses or other items to the woman's family, and waited patiently for an answer. If rejected, he got his gifts back; if accepted, the family took possession of them. Both families were involved in the wedding arrangements, which included feasting and dancing. The newlyweds generally lived with the bride's parents, as Plains Indians traced descent through the maternal line and children belonged to the clan of the mother.

The end of the childbearing years was an important passage for women of the Plains. Respect and distinction accompanied the older women into their later years. Their opinion was valued for its wisdom and they kept the tribal history. Since the tasks that fell to the younger women took most of their time, grandmothers spent time with the children teaching them the ancient traditions, skills, and crafts of the tribe.

The sacred position of women in Plains Indian tribes is well portrayed in this Lakota song for a womanhood ritual:

> *They are coming to see this!*
> *I am making this place sacred.*
>
> *They are coming to see this!*
> *White Buffalo Calf Woman will come.*
>
> *They are coming to see this!*
> *She will sit in a sacred manner.*
>
> *They are coming to see this!*
> *They are all coming to see this!*
> *(from Patricia Monaghan's* The Goddess Companion)

Women as Shamans and Healers

The Plains Indians knew plants and plant medicine. They gathered and used wild berries and herbs for seasoning food, in ceremonies, and for medicine. Both men and women shared plant knowledge and medicine-making, although it is believed that women excelled at it. Women learned healing from their mothers and grandmothers. Commonly, the road to becoming a medicine woman was a long one. A woman's powers had to be validated by a visitation of a spirit dream, in which she would receive personal instruction and knowledge. This was followed by many years of study and apprenticeship, learning all there was to know about gathering herbs and preparing them. She generally did not qualify to practice on her own until mid-life or later.

Medicine women were considered to have a personal connection to the spirit world that gave them the ability to heal. They approached healing with the belief that emotions influenced health, and supernatural powers were required to rescue the soul and restore the person to health. Healers worked with an ally from the spirit world who guided them, as disease was understood as an imbalance between the physical and emotional world and the world of the spirit. The healer worked to restore balance through the use of herbs and prayer.

The priests of the Plains Indians were called shamans. If a woman wanted to enter this highly respected profession, she did so by seeking training from an established shaman. If she was chosen as successor, she inherited the shaman's position and used her predecessor's songs and formulas, as well those of her own making. Shamans cured illness, predicted the future, and were the spiritual guardians of the tribe. The realm of both medicine woman and shaman were the most powerful roles in the Plains Indian's society, and they were open to women.

Walking Softly on the Earth

Wakan Tonka is the name used by the Lakota people to identify the Great Spirit or Great Mystery, the maker of all who has always been and always will be. Wakan Tonka is in all things—all birds, animals, and fish—and in all people, regardless of color or nationality. The core beliefs of the Lakota people are built on the following maxims:

- ◦ Respect for the Great Spirit
- ◦ Respect for Mother Earth
- ◦ Respect for all men and women
- ◦ Respect for individual freedom

Five principles common to Native American spirituality are:

- ◦ Interrelationship—An understanding of the interrelatedness and interconnectedness of all creation.
- ◦ Sacred world—Respect for all life as sacred and respect for the earth as Mother.
- ◦ Web of experience—Our experience is not time-bound. All actions in this moment affect all others and have lasting effects, both for good and for bad.

- Balance between male and female—An understanding of the differences between male and female, and a mutual respect or valuing of those differences.

- Communal consciousness—Emphasis on our relations and connection, not on the acquisition of goods. If someone is suffering, all are suffering.

White Buffalo Calf Woman—The Sacred Pipe of the Sioux

White Buffalo Calf Woman is a mystical woman who holds a primary place in the cosmology of the Sioux people. She symbolizes purity and renewal; she brought the Sioux the sacred medicine pipe, and seven teachings that form the pattern for all Sioux ceremonies.

> *Remember how sacred the pipe is*
> *And treat it in a sacred manner,*
> *For it will be with you always,*
> *Remember also that in me are four ages.*
>
> *I shall leave you now,*
> *But shall look upon you in every age*
> *And will return in the end.*

> *(Ed McGaa Eagle Man, quoting Buffalo Calf Woman in*
> Mother Earth Spirituality: Native American Paths to
> Healing Ourselves and Our World *[HarperCollins, 1990])*

Rebuilding the Cherokee Nation

In 1838, President Jackson, following a plan conceived by former President Jefferson, ordered federal troops to confiscate Cherokee homes, property, and land. Tribal members were forcibly taken to stockades throughout the Southeast. Thus began the forced march of the Cherokees to Indian Territory in Oklahoma. By the time the last contingent arrived in April of 1839, having marched on foot in the winter with inadequate clothing or blankets, a quarter of them were dead.

The Cherokees' survival as a Nation was in jeopardy; they had to rebuild the tribe. Through their brutal experiences and great loss of life, they bonded as a people. In less than ten years, they made remarkable strides toward re-establishing the Cherokee Nation. They formed a new political system with a new constitution, published a newspaper in English and Cherokee, formed a judicial system, and constructed buildings that still stand today. Most important, they rebuilt their educational system—not only for men, but for women as well—and began the process of healing and rebuilding themselves as a people. The central figure in this renewal was a woman.

Wilma Mankiller—Absolute Faith in Her People

Wilma Mankiller's (1945–2010) concern for Native American issues was awakened in the late 1960s when university students occupied Alcatraz Island to attract attention to the issues affecting their tribes. A close brush with death in a head-on collision began a time of deep spiritual awakening for her, and she embarked on a process of reevaluating her life. A year after the accident, she was diagnosed with myasthenia gravis, a chronic neuro-muscular disease. In a further spiritual awakening, she realized how precious life is and this fired her desire to help her people.

Mankiller had an unshakable faith in the strength of her people. In a talk given at Sweet Briar College in 1993, she talked about the removal of her people to Indian Territory, and of their remarkable recovery as a nation. Significantly, she credited the recovery of her people as a nation to the loss of all their material possessions, and to the establishment of educational opportunities for both men and women.

> [This] was a very radical idea for that particular period of time in that part of the world. Our tribal council had no idea how to run a school for girls, and so they sent a group of emissaries to Mount Holyoke and asked the head of Mount Holyoke to send some teachers back to show us how to put together a school for girls. (from a speech called "Rebuilding the Cherokee Nation," April 2, 1993, Sweet Briar College)

Mankiller earned national recognition as an expert in community development, and eventually was elected as deputy chief of her tribe. Then, yet another life-threatening illness struck. Her love of family and community again became a source of strength when kidney problems forced her to have a transplant. During her convalescence, she had many long talks with her family, and it was decided that she would run for chief of the tribe in order to complete the many community projects she had begun.

From 1985 to 1995, Mankiller served as the first female chief of the Cherokee Nation, the second largest tribe in the United States. Under her leadership, the people prospered. Mankiller tripled tribal enrollment, doubled employment, and established health centers and children's programs.

Her candidacy for chief was opposed by some because she was female—her tires were slashed and she received death threats. She won the respect of the Cherokee Nation, however, and made an impact on the culture as she focused on her mission—to bring self-sufficiency to her people. Mankiller approached her job with "absolute faith and confidence" in her people and their ability to solve their own problems.

Mankiller recalls that the only thing that people wanted to talk about when she was running for election as tribal chief was the fact that she was a woman, not the innovative programs she was presenting. In her frustration at the sexism she was encountering, she consulted an unlikely source—she called a friend on the staff of *Ms* magazine and asked for advice. They had a good laugh, but Wilma says she can't repeat the exact conversation. Nonetheless, she decided to come to grips with the situation as it was and transcend it. And she did, with the help of some words of wisdom she found printed on the back of a tea box: "Don't ever argue with a fool, because someone walking by and observing you can't tell which one is the fool." She took it as good advice and went on to win the election. "Prior to my election," she writes, "young Cherokee girls would never have thought that they might grow up and become chief." Mankiller's leadership earned her an honorary Doctorate of Humane Letters from Dartmouth University in 1991. She has worked tirelessly for the Indian Nations, and for the advancement of females in general. Known for her community leadership, she has also become a spiritual presence for her people and her Nation. Among her many honors is a Presidential Medal of Freedom—the nation's highest civilian award—presented in 1998.

Today, as always, Cherokee women continue to be a powerful presence in their communities. They are active in tribal government, and participate in society as doctors, lawyers, teachers, entertainers, and artists, and in every profession.

Venerable Dhyani Ywahoo— ## In the Voice of Her Ancestors

The Ywahoo lineage reaches back 2860 years, when it was established by the "Keeper of the Mysteries," a mystical teacher known as the Pale One. He instructed the people regarding ceremonies, the building of temples, training for the priest craft, and how to cultivate and maintain peace within each family, clan, nation, and the planet. This body of knowledge was passed down through oral teachings to Dhyani Ywahoo. "Sacred teachings emerge for every era," she observes, "to remind us how to manifest harmony and right relationship" (*Voices of Our Ancestors: Cherokee Teachings from the Wisdom Fire* [Shambala Publications, 1987]).

In 1969, the elders of the Cherokee nation made the decision that certain Cherokee teachings previously kept within the clan could now be given to society at large. Dhyani Ywahoo was chosen to teach this information. She did so by establishing the Sunray Meditation Society.

The Peacekeeper Mission of the Sunray Meditation Society is to encourage and facilitate personal and communal transformation. It is directed toward instilling peace in the hearts of those who are faithful to the practice. Peacekeeper teachings are rooted in the Native American spiritual wisdom of right relationship in the circle of life. Its practices include sitting and moving meditations, chanting, work with sacred sound and shape, and community dream practice. The knowledge and skills have an immediate and practical application to our everyday lives. Techniques develop mindfulness and meditation, bringing clarity that helps us find our life purpose and develop skillful means to accomplish our work in the world. You can find contact information for Venerable Dhyani Ywahoo and the Sunray Meditation Society in the resources listed at the back of this book.

Wrapping Things Up

Native spirituality is the spirituality of this land. It holds the key to creating the transcended relationship to the earth that many people seek today. Women from many races and religions are hungry for a spirituality that expresses partnership, celebrates the living universe, and acknowledges the presence of the sacred here and now. Paula Gunn Allen reminds women that they do not need to go anywhere else to find a connection to a matriarchy; it is right here on our own continent. Native people were denied their religious freedom for almost a century, during which time their survival as a culture was threatened. Today, they are reclaiming their position as teachers and wisdom keepers. Many of these teachings are being shared with non-native cultures today. Many women feel a particular kinship with Native American teaching, as it affirms their sensibility and honors the feminine principle.

Chapter 17

❧ ❧

PAGANS, CELTS, AND
CELTIC CHRISTIANS

*T*he word "pagan" roughly translates to "country bumpkin." It was used by the Romans as a slur against the folks out in the hinterland. It's since come to be used primarily by Christians to identify those who do not believe in Christianity. In the 1960s, the term "Neo-pagan" evolved to describe those involved in the reconstruction of the old polytheistic pre-Christian religions.

Patricia Monaghan, contemporary poet, writer, and pioneer in the women's spirituality movement, describes this transition in the context of Celtic spirituality:

> *A large percentage of Americans describe themselves as Irish-Americans, but it's not only Irish-Americans who are attracted to Irish spirituality. For those looking for a European tradition that has the kind of metaphoric power that we find in Native American religions, Irish or Celtic mythology and folklore has a great deal of appeal. There are those wonderful female characters, human and divine: Maeve, Brigit, Macha, and so many more. And there is the sense of connection to a living tradition, which is unlike, say, the divinities and rituals of classical Greece. So it is no surprise that interest in "Celtic traditions" is high. This usually means Irish traditions, as Ireland has maintained an indigenous spirituality into*

the present and is more often written about than the related tradi-
tions of Wales, Cornwall, Scotland, Brittany and the Isle of Man,
which together constitute the traditional Celtic lands. (The God-
dess Companion [Llewellyn Worldwide, 1999])

Pagans—Exchanging Original Sin for Original Grace

Neo-pagans believe in original *grace* rather than original sin. Sin to a Neo-pagan would most likely be social sin—the failure of a society to address the needs of its people adequately. They believe that life is good, and that to be alive is rich with spiritual potential. They basically believe that men and women are spiritual equals and honor both a female and male deity—the Goddess and God. Sometimes, this Godhead is expressed in the singular, but more often the two aspects of this spirituality appear together, as a *pantheon*. Values generally associated with masculine and feminine archetypes are respected equally in these communities, with a slight emphasis on feminine values as a means of balancing today's patriarchal culture.

Practice, but Don't Preach

Pagans fall short of their own ideals and make mistakes like anyone else, but the emphasis in this tradition is on restitution and reaffirming a commitment to ideals, rather than on sin or punishment. Neo-pagans strike a balance between the need for personal autonomy and awareness that all actions impact the whole of society. For them, society includes all life forms, including the earth—which they hold as a living organism. They understand this relationship between individual and community and earth to be a dynamic one that is always in need of renegotiation. Negotiation calls for introspection and self-honesty. Thus, many Neo-pagans become vegetarians, animal-rights activists, pacifists, and environmental activists. However, individual choice prevails. Depending upon their individual beliefs, you may find Neo-pagans eating a Big Mac, grabbing organic salads at health-food stores, or steaming their own veggies at home.

Sex and Sexuality

Because Paganism is not patriarchal, it is almost free of bias regarding sex and partnering. Neo-pagans consider sex to be one of the good things in life, to be enjoyed without guilt and without abuse. They are tolerant of sexual preferences and alternative relationship lifestyles. In this community, you will find heterosexuals, homosexuals, bisexuals, trans-genders, and some who are undecided. These folks may be in monogamous relationships, be in one or more polyamorous relationships, or have no romantic relationships at all. This tolerance can be viewed suspiciously by those of stricter religious traditions. However, Neo-pagans do not tolerate deviant practices—meaning sexual abuse of any kind. If someone is guilty of that kind of behavior, it is dealt with in the same way that the culture at large deals with it.

Ritual and Ceremony

Neo-pagans follow the Wheel of the Year as laid out in chapter 11. They observe the solstices, equinoxes, and phases of the moon. They honor rites of passage like birth, puberty, personal dedication to a given deity or group, marriage, ordination, and death. You will no doubt find a strong connection between these beliefs and ceremonies and those identified as women's spirituality—both are earth-based and, like Native American beliefs, have much in common with each other.

Neo-pagans respect and love nature; they believe that people are part of it and not the "rulers over it," or walking around "on it." In fact, what has come to be known as "the Gaia hypothesis" is commonly attributed to a Neo-pagan named Tim Zell. The Gaia hypothesis states that our planet is a living organism that exists as a cooperative, interactive system. This hypothesis sits in contrast to Darwin's competition model, expressed in the principle of survival of the fittest. It focuses on all the ways in which nature is in symphony with its various aspects.

Paganism is more a way of life than a formal practice; it has virtually no concept of heresy. You will find Neo-pagans who belong to various faith communities, and they place a high value on respecting one another's beliefs. Many Neo-pagans enjoy participating in activities with members of other faiths who share similar values. The Unitarian Universalists are one of the first established religious traditions in the United States to recognize the Pagan community officially, and the Covenant of Unitarian Universalist Pagans (CUUPS) has become one of the largest and most active subgroups of the Unitarian Church.

For the record, don't confuse the worship of Satan with Paganism. The devil is not present in Pagan philosophy or religion. Pan, a nature spirit, appears throughout Greek mythology as the Horned God. He's an archetype of male virility and sexuality, which is how he may have come to be confused with Satan among Christians. He is understood among Neo-pagans as a fertility figure. Cults that worship Satan are not part of the Neo-pagan tradition.

Celtic Christianity

Christianity influenced the Celts and the Celts, in turn, put their mark on Christianity. Many of the stories of Celtic gods and goddesses became entwined with Christian saints. Sacred springs and wells and other Pagan temple sites became the locations of cathedrals. Today's Celtic Christianity connects its followers to their roots in the ancient cultures of Europe.

They've Got That Magic Touch

The current revival of Celtic culture through music, dance, art, and spirituality speaks to a need within many people to link to their past. They do so to feed their ecological imagination, and to ground their spirituality back into the soil from which it sprang. Nothing so captures the imagination as Irish folklore and Celtic stories. Indeed, it is sometimes difficult to separate fact from fiction regarding these seemingly magical and mysterious people. Perhaps that is precisely the appeal this tradition holds today for those who are searching for the magic that is missing in our overly technological world. For whatever reason, many people are exploring the Celtic world through Celtic Christianity and Celtic spirituality.

God and Landscape as One

The Celts were intimately involved with the sacred through the constant interplay of ritual and life, acknowledging the divine presence in the natural world. Like other indigenous people, they transmitted their teaching by oral tradition rather than by written word, using poetry, song, and mythological stories both as poetic expression and to facilitate memory. The Celtic people were tribal, and they bonded through their connection to local gods and goddesses, who inhabited the forests, lakes, and streams, making religion and landscape one.

Thou King of deeds and power above, Thy fishing blessing pour down on us. I will cast down my hook, the first fish which I bring up, in the name of Christ, King of the elements, the poor shall have it at his wish.

–A Celtic fisherman's prayer

Celtic Women—From Battlefield to Bedroom

Because women's position in the culture is often ignored or misinterpreted, no one seems to know or agree on the precise status women held in Celtic society. Some sources say that Celtic women occupied a place in the culture equal to men, owning property, choosing their marriage partners, and retaining their independent status and property in marriage. Other sources say that their place was almost, but not quite, equal to men. Still another source reports that it varied from region to region, and over time. All seem to agree that women appear to have had some rights and liberties in Celtic culture. The details will never be known, but the relationship between men and women was apparently good.

In *Sacred Texts by and about Women* (Crossroad, 1994), editor Serenity Young points out that Celtic women seemed to have more status in practice than by law. For example, some codes show limits on women's ownership and sale of property, yet deeds, wills, and the oral literary traditions indicate they frequently inherited, bought, and sold property. In Moyra Caldecott's *Women in Celtic Mythology* (Destiny Books, 1988), she tells us that women enjoyed a high place in Celtic society and that it is revealed through their mythology. Oliver Davies and Fiona Bowie, in *Celtic Christian Spirituality* (Continuum, 1995), however, caution the reader not to think that Celtic women enjoyed too great a privilege in the culture. Despite powerful stories like those told about Bridget, the ancient goddess who became a Christian saint, they say the culture was only marginally less patriarchal than other societies of its time.

Celtic heroism certainly was not the exclusive realm of males. Women were known to be fierce fighters, battling side-by-side with their men. Celtic heroes were often named for their mothers. Women took part in politics, but to a lesser degree than men. A woman's primary role was as wife and mother. However, a Celtic woman could get a separation from her husband and remarry, thus her status was not that of property.

All sources agree that the status of some Celtic women was high and that women in northern Celtic lands enjoyed a higher place in society than they did under Christianity. Celtic women were respected in their culture, even becoming priests—a practice that, at this time, was not common in the neighboring cultures. Celtic women were known to be "seers" and soothsayers, and were consulted as intermediaries between the natural and supernatural worlds. According to some stories, Saint Bridget became the bishop of Kildare. As the Celts met the Catholics, it was over the status of women that they had their greatest disagreements. Women were ordained in the Celtic church, but not in the Catholic Church.

Bridget, a favorite goddess of the Celtic people, was later adopted into Christian stories, where her legend continued as Saint Bridget. Her feast is celebrated on February 2. Bridget's praises have been sung and prayers like the following have been offered to her for thousands of years.

> *Every day, every night that I pray to the goddess, I know I shall be safe: I shall not be chased, I shall not be caught, I shall not be harmed. Fire, sun, and moon cannot burn me. Not lake nor stream nor sea can drown me. Fairy arrow cannot pierce me. I am safe, safe, safe, singing her praises. (The Shield of Brigid [sic], Irish Prayer from* The Goddess Companion *by Patricia Monaghan)*

Spiritual Inheritance

Druid priests were magicians and poets, counselors and healers, shamans and philosophers. Their ancient teachings add an important dimension to the Western spiritual and mystical tradition—most notable in the Catholic mystical spiritual practices. Incubated in the Druid/Celtic culture, Catholicism remains what is called a mystery religion today—meaning that many of its core beliefs rely on faith and cannot be supported by fact or science. Most Christian denominations share a belief in the Trinity, virgin birth, God made man, resurrection, and ascendance into heaven. Catholicism goes a bit further, with its belief in transubstantiation or the absolute presence of the living Christ in the bread and wine when consecrated by the priest.

These deeply held and greatly cherished beliefs cannot be proven in the way we think of proof—thus maintaining the sense of mystery and magic infused by the Celts. The Celtic reverence for the natural world, as seen in their invocation of the elements—earth, air, fire, and water—also connect earth spirituality with the sacraments of the Catholic Church. Notice how the elements reappear as road, wind, sun, and rain in this traditional Celtic blessing:

> *May the road rise up and welcome thee,*
> *May the wind always be upon thy back,*
> *May the sun always warm thy face,*
> *And may the rain fall softly on thy fields.*

Today Celtic Christianity remains close to the earth, keeping its link with the natural world and its poetic understanding of God's mystical presence. Where once gods and goddesses spoke to the Celtic people, the voice of the risen Christ who dwells in nature now speaks to them. The presence of the Holy Spirit as a creative force in the Celtic imagination is as apparent today as it was in the past. The Celts continue this living relationship through poetry, music, dance, the arts, and, most profoundly, in their continued connection to nature. Celtic Christianity is calling Christians back to their roots in the soil.

Regardless of whether women achieved positions of power in Celtic society and religion, the structure of the culture itself was more affirming of feminine values than what many women experience in today's institutions. The characteristics of Celtic spirituality that have been passed down through history to Christians today are the same qualities with which many women strongly identify and are seeking today:

- Intuition
- Imagination
- Lyricism and poetry
- Interconnectedness
- Earth-based values
- A sense of the world as community

By pursuing and embracing these characteristics, women today keep the magic of Celtic spirituality alive in our modern world.

Wrapping Things Up

There is no agreed-upon definition of pagan or Paganism. A common thread connects the religions of the ancient world to the modern one—a thread based in a love and respect of the earth and all creation. Neo-pagan is a term being re-appropriated by today's spiritual seekers who feel a connection to the values of an earlier world. The primary focuses of today's Neo-pagans, in addition to respect for the earth, include love of community, freedom to express their religion, and freedom for others to express theirs. The Celtic culture of Old Europe provides a vital link to today's Christianity. It grounds people in an earth-centered spirituality and connects them to their historic roots. Women look to Celtic spirituality because of its values. They find a home there. Since Paganism has more to do with our relationship to the earth than to a specific deity or theology, we can be pagans and still belong to another faith community.

Chapter 18

❦ ❦

WHEN YOUR OTHER CAR IS A BROOM

*I*f your head is filled with images of black hats, black cats, and broomsticks, you may be in for a surprise—the woman standing next to you in line at the supermarket may be a witch! The practice of witchcraft, or Wicca as it is often called, is on the rise—exchanging its position in the underground subculture for a living room in your neighborhood.

Wicca is an ancient religion or spirituality with roots going back in time and deep into the earth; it has always been primarily a women's spirituality. Wicca is gaining popularity among women, men, and many young people for the values it expresses—honoring the Goddess and God, and making a strong ecological statement. The word "wicca" stems from the Saxon word *witega*, meaning "a seer or diviner." Wicca, sometimes called witchcraft, is a revitalization of an old folk religion; it is constantly changing form. A witch in tribal societies is one who practices healing, divining, or other magical crafts; today's craft is based in those qualities.

Witches—Would You Want Your Brother (or Sister) to Marry One?

Wicca falls under the general heading of Pagan religion or spirituality, leaning more toward spirituality. It's practiced in small groups called covens and professes no doctrine, but instead works from an ethical base. The craft has no written codes and is taught according to oral tradition. However, there is an increasing amount of material written on the subject, and workshops and seminars abound.

There is no witchcraft central office or board of directors. The rule of the craft is simple: *Do what you will and harm no one*. This succinct ethic is backed up with the understanding that, whatever you send "out there," comes back to you threefold. Similar to the Golden Rule we all grew up with, this ethic is simple and direct—but it also bites back.

The resurgence of the craft in this country can be traced back about fifty years to a retired British civil servant of Scottish descent named Gerald B. Gardner. Many consider him the "grandfather" of the Neo-Wiccan movement. The story goes that Gardner was initiated into a coven of witches in the New Forest region of England in 1939 by a high priestess, Old Dorothy Clutterbuck. At the time, witchcraft was still on the books in England as a capital crime. Laws forbidding its practice weren't repealed until 1951. At that time, it became clear that the craft had not been eliminated, but was alive and well. Gardner released his book *Witchcraft Today* in 1954.

Witches, Wiccans, and Good Ole' Girls

Today, people who follow this tradition may call themselves witches or Wiccans, but just as many don't identify with either of those terms. The craft has an element of privacy or secrecy around it, which adds to its power in the cultural imagination in both negative and positive ways. Its mystique no doubt feeds the old fears that have surrounded the practice; but it also draws people to it. Anyone seeking membership in a coven must wait a year and a day after formally presenting her or his request. This gives the group an opportunity to find out if they want the new member, and also is used as a time of study and preparation for entrance.

The Devil Does Not Make Them Do It!

As mentioned earlier, the confusion regarding witchcraft and devil worship goes back to medieval and early modern Europe. For many years, mainstream Western religions—Judaism, Christianity, and

Islam—have held witchcraft in fear and contempt, perhaps falling victim to some of their own press in the process. They have lumped together many practices—cards, runes (characters from an ancient German alphabet used for insight), magic, sorcery, New Age philosophy, crystals, yoga, and sometimes meditation—describing them all as occult and attributing them to devil worship. Witchcraft has no association with the devil.

Imagine That!

Magic is core to the practice of Wicca. The word "magic" comes from "imagination." Magic follows the same law as any other creative act; it originates in the imagination and brings something into being. Magic begins by imagining a situation or a condition *the way you would like it to be.* For example, a powerful way to work for world peace is to imagine the world already living in peace and harmony, rather than thinking about the destruction of war. Peace is energized in ceremony and prayer, and, as it takes form in the lives of those who are creating it, it becomes a reality. This means, of course, that you have to walk the talk or your intention remains wishful thinking. Working magic is sometimes referred to as casting spells. Contrary to common understanding about wishing warts on your neighbor, spells can be compared to prayers.

Witchcraft has been the subject of controversy and misconception for a long time. However, when you examine the craft and what it means to be a witch or a Wiccan with an open mind, you can see that it believes in pretty much the same things as traditional religion: identifying the God or Goddess of your understanding and creating ways of expressing that in a group of like-minded folks.

The traditional characteristics of witchcraft—its four pillars—are:

- Faith
- Will
- Imagination
- Freedom

These core elements of Wicca relate directly to issues in women's spirituality. Here are the stories of three women who made that connection.

Starhawk—Bewitched and Bothered, but Not Bewildered

Starhawk is the hands-down living goddess of the Wiccan arm of the women's spirituality movement. She leads rituals, teaches earth spirituality, and counsels women. Born Miriam Simos in 1951 in St. Paul, Minnesota, she was raised Jewish and given a Hebrew education. She went on to the University of California and later received a Master's degree in Feminist Therapy at Antioch University.

Starhawk taught at the Institute for Creation-Centered Spirituality under the direction of Matthew Fox, theologian and former Dominican priest. His institute was housed at Holy Names College in Oakland for many years. It was Starhawk's presence on the faculty in the mid 1980s that caused the pope to censure Fox, silencing him for one year. Fox was forbidden to speak in public or publish during the allotted time. Such a papal order is seldom invoked in modern times. To some, it seemed like a profound affirmation of the power of Starhawk's work.

Spiral Dancing with Starhawk

Starhawk is the founder of Reclaiming: A Center for Feminist Spirituality and Counseling. The Reclaiming community offers classes, workshops, and public rituals. She is a feminist who includes men in her ceremonies and as members of the community. Her theaology is based on the sacredness of the earth and she integrates social and ecological activism into her spirituality and rituals. The Reclaiming community was one of the first Pagan groups to engage the political structures directly and has participated in demonstrations against nuclear power plants and military bases.

Starhawk has written extensively on the connection between politics and spirituality; her book *Spiral Dance: A Rebirth of the Ancient Religion of the Great Goddess* (Harper & Row, 1979) remains a classic. She teaches and lectures around the country at colleges and universities, including Union Theological Seminary in New York, the University of California at San Francisco, and California State University at San Jose and Chico.

The Charge of the Goddess

The Charge of the Goddess appears in many places, but no one knows its exact origins. Starhawk's version, in which she has updated the language, appears in *The Spiral Dance*. Here is part of the piece:

> *I, who am the beauty of the green earth and the white moon among the stars and the mysteries of the waters, I call upon your soul to arise and come unto me. For I am the soul of nature that gives life to the universe. From Me all things proceed and unto Me they must return. Let My worship be in the heart that rejoices, for behold—all acts of love and pleasure are My rituals. Let there be beauty and strength, power and compassion, honor and humility, mirth and reverence within you. And you who seek to know Me, know that your seeking and yearning will avail you not, unless you know the Mystery; for if that which you seek, you find not within yourself, you will never find it without. For behold, I have been with you from the beginning, and I am that which is attained at the end of desire.*

Margot Draws Down the Moon

Margot Adler is the New York Bureau Chief for National Public Radio and author of *Drawing Down the Moon: Witches, Druids, Goddess-Worshippers, and Other Pagans in America Today* (Penguin, 1997), a comprehensive study of Neo-paganism that is still considered one of the definitive books on the subject. Margot is a witch who travels throughout the United States, leading rituals and workshops and speaking about Wicca and other Neo-pagan traditions.

Ritual Born of Desire

Adler's longing for ritual ignited when she saw her Catholic friend's First Communion dress and veil. She was raised in a Jewish/Marxist/Atheist home; her father told her she belonged to "the brotherhood of man," a neighborhood she found spiritually boring. Now Adler talks about ritual as a way human beings can connect to each other. She talks about ending the feelings of alienation that are so much a part of the human condition—at least in modern technological society. Making connection to one another and to the earth in ritual ceremony creates earth community, she says. "Ritual returns us to our sense of attunement with the universe, to reconnect us with who we really are."

Adler knows it's difficult to squeeze one more thing into our busy lives. She suggests "spiritual multi-tasking" and talks about calling on the elements as you take a shower or in blessing your food. Adler demystifies ritual by reminding people that they don't have to have all the bells and whistles. She describes an integrated approach to spirituality, describing how, sometimes, a ritual can be performed by a quick glance at an altar on top of a filing cabinet at the office.

Encounters with Artemis and Athena

Adler knows the importance of having young girls grow up with powerful images of women. She remembers encounters she had with Artemis and Athena during a year she spent studying in Greece when she was only twelve. The basic philosophy of women's spirituality is that *we* are sacred. Both the women's movement and earth spirituality give women permission to celebrate their bodies and minds—making everything we do sacred. Adler sees women's spirituality as supporting and enriching feminism by empowering women, removing any limits to what they can accomplish in their own lives and in their communities, and giving them the power to remake the world:

> I believe the women's spirituality movement has gained such tre- mendous momentum so quickly because it helps women see them- selves as part of divine reality. Traditional religions don't have a place for women—we were disinherited from the ministry centuries ago. Let's face it—women were left out of the deity game. (Draw- ing Down the Moon)

A challenge Adler sees as the movement grows is how to avoid the temptation to institutionalize it as it shifts from a private spiri- tuality to a more public one. She wonders if the movement will sacrifice autonomy and diversity, and considers how it will handle issues of power and dogma if it goes main-stream. Adler believes women's spirituality does well as a minority religion because it provides a critique of the larger society. Regardless of the chal- lenges, however, she is in it for the long haul. She agrees with the philosophy of women's spirituality and finds the practice satisfying.

Straight Up with Zsuzsanna Budapest

Uncontrollable, outspoken, charismatic, troublemaker, and vision-ary are words used to describe the legendary Zsuzsanna Budapest, founder of the feminist religion called Dianic Witchcraft. Her Hun-garian lineage is a direct link to the practices of Old Europe, and she learned the craft at her mother's knee. Dianic covens are for women only, but are open to women of all sexual, cultural, and religious orientations. They draw their name from Diana, the Roman version of Artemis, the virgin Goddess of the Moon. They generally honor the Goddess exclusively.

Budapest, or "Z" as she is known, was born in Hungary in the middle of a Siberian blizzard in 1940; she calls herself a genetic witch. Her early Goddess consciousness was formed at her mother's knee, watching her sculpt statues of the female divinity. She learned herbal remedies from her grandmother and was raised with the sto-ries of the gods and goddesses. Budapest traces her family tree back to 1270. She is an author, ritual leader, and teacher.

Like other forms of Wicca, Dianic Witchcraft is a nature-based religion that pays respect to both the God and Goddess; however, only the Goddess is worshipped. In tipping her hat to the male principle of the universe, Budapest assures students that he is a "good boy," but "we just don't pray to male gods." In her teaching, she also points out that women are daughters of the moon; the female's reproductive cycles and psyche are ruled by the moon.

Living Room Witches Need Not Apply

In the early 1970s, the feminist movement made little mention of religion or spirituality. Many feminists dismissed spirituality as navel-gazing that took time and energy away from activism. Buda-pest saw it differently. She believed the movement needed spiritual underpinnings, and she offered what she describes as "a new kind of trust—we are learning to trust our souls." She brought the spiri-tual and political camps together and created a new religion that affirmed feminist values. Budapest takes credit for originating the term "feminist spirituality."

Pushing the Hexing Envelope

Of all the concerns raised regarding the craft, the one guaranteed to raise the hair on the collective necks of all detractors is hexing! Hexing smacks of lawlessness, black pointed hats, and dolls with pins in their backs—the very things most witches are accused of and staunchly deny. It is no wonder that, when Budapest advocates for hexing, she pushes the envelope.

Budapest is talking about women taking back their power, however—specifically and only in cases of rape. She encourages them to plead their case to the Goddess and to seek retribution through her, but to make no requests as to how that retribution should happen. Rather than collapsing into a victim mentality, the hex or spell becomes a proactive demand for justice. How that is effected is left up to the Goddess; the woman performing the hex simply asks that justice be done. According to Budapest, the fear people have about hexing translates as a fear of women gaining power. But giving women a sense of empowerment is necessary to healing. Budapest reminds us that what we're really talking about is balancing the patriarchal scales and the absolute imperative of the craft that whatever you wish upon another will be returned to you threefold!

Wrapping Things Up

Wicca belongs to the Pagan movement that is currently resurfacing, primarily among women, in the United States and in many other parts of the world. It is a religion that has roots in pre-Christian Europe, but is not to be confused with false accusations that were made about it during the Inquisition of the Middle Ages, some of which continue today. The practice of Wicca in no way invokes the devil or engages in negative behavior like wishing bad things on people or their animals. Wicca promotes positive images for women, equality between the genders, and ecologically sound living. The four pillars that support the craft are: faith, will, imagination, and freedom. Wiccans believe that everything we do comes back to us threefold—a belief that really puts teeth in the Golden Rule.

Chapter 19

❦ ❦

MOTHER'S MEDICINE CHEST

Many holistic practitioners consider their healing work a spiritual practice. It calls on them to walk the talk—to live a balanced life. This often involves meditation and prayer, as well as other health-conscious practices. Holistic healing involves all aspects of a person—body, mind, and spirit. It is best described as a process. Its relational meaning is about creating a different relationship to yourself, and to your life and the choices you make in that new relationship. Building a relationship takes time.

Traditional healing or allopathic medicine is faster. It gets in there and gets the job done—and that is important, too. However, it often fails to get at the underlying factors that spawn the disease state. It is focused on a procedure or medicine that will be applied or ingested rather than on the practitioner and the patient.

Holistic therapies approach healing in a more maternal way— the comfy quilt on the sofa, chicken soup, mom's hand on your forehead, or your feet in her lap. *It is also based in sound principles of healing.* In this chapter, you'll hear from three holistic practitioners in their own words—practitioners who have studied their art well and applied it successfully for many years. Holistic healing works at the soul level—slower and deeper—and its effects are life-changing for the one who practices it, as well as for those who receive it.

Catherine Abby Rich—Singing Their Praises

Catherine Abby Rich has been an herbalist for more than forty years and has studied the wild medicinal herbs of Europe, India, and the United States. She lives in Marin County, California, and earns her living gathering herbs, making medicine, and teaching others how to listen to the secrets of the wild plants. Her earliest encounter with the plant spirits came at age nine, when she read the biography of George Washington Carver and learned about his spiritual understanding of growing things. "In the book he said that he learned everything by watching and loving them [the plants]," Catherine adds. "They gave him direct transmissions on how to use them. His book filled me with inspiration."

"All flowers talk to me as do hundreds of little living things in the woods. I learn what I know by watching and loving everything."

–PETER TOMPKINS and CHRISTOPHER BIRD, *The Secret Life of Plants* (Harper & Row, 1972)

FIGURE 18. Catherine Abby Rich taking time out from an herb walk to love the plants, Marin County, CA.

Catherine refers to herself as a "culinary Jew" rather than a religious one, meaning she knows how to make matzo-ball soup, but she doesn't attend services in the temple. She was raised in a Jewish home without traditional religious training, but very much in accord with Jewish ethics. Her parents were liberals who walked in picket lines. They believed in education, kindness, non-sectarianism, service, and peace. Catherine says that these values are her "truth." Her spirituality is expressed through her love of nature and the healing herbs, and, she says, "The creation brought me to the creator."

Plants + Prayer = Power

Almost four decades ago, Catherine left Queens, New York where she was an elementary school teacher, "to have an adventure of a totally new kind." Her adventure took her to Bavaria, where the local midwife introduced her to the world of plants and plant medicine. "They opened up my intelligence—ignited my spirit. My passion to learn about herbs and making medicine was voracious." For the next five years, she worked with local teachers, beginning with plants that were used to support pregnancy, childbirth, and childrearing. She later expanded her interests to a wider variety of conditions. She learned German and Dutch so she could read as many local herb books as possible and collaborated with friends to write her own book, which became a best-seller in Germany.

Catherine left Bavaria for India, where she met and worked with Dr. Lad, an *Ayurvedic* doctor in Poona. They shared their love of plants and exchanged information—Catherine taught him what she knew of Western herbs, and he instructed her in the precepts of Eastern medicine.

> He taught by singing the plants. As we ground the roots he honored the plant by singing its story. He sang of the plant's history on earth and how it was used for more than 6000 years to heal people. He would sing the specific qualities of the plant, praising it and thanking it. He chanted and I OMMMMMMMMMMMed! From him, I learned the formula of making medicine: plants + prayer = healing power.

Today, Catherine makes her medicine the way Dr. Lad taught her, and every batch contains praise and gratitude for the plants and prayers for the health of those who will receive it. She was given another important instruction in the form of three yarrow sticks brought to her by an elderly woman herbalist. "She told me I would go on to make powerful medicine, but reminded me that God put the power in the plants, I did not," Catherine recalls. "She cautioned me never to call myself a healer. I can pick the herbs and prepare them; I can know how to extract the properties; and I can add my prayers. But it is not by my power that the healing happens. That is done by the creator."

Catherine moved to California in 1984. Over the years, she has introduced thousands of people to flowers, herbs, and medicine-making at her booth in the San Rafael farmer's market and on walks along the coastline of Marin and Sonoma counties.

School for Witchlets

Catherine has a degree in Elementary Education; she finds that children are especially drawn to the herbs and love knowing the uses of the plants. "Children are naturals," she says. "They haven't been taught that the spirits of the plants don't exist, so all I have to do is introduce them to the plants and they begin talking with each other."

The recent Harry Potter craze brought potion-making out of obscurity, and gave Catherine a new approach to herbal education: the School for Witchlets. "Now kids are seeking me out," she says. "They want to know if I can show them how to make a spell—in the first class! I tell them we call it prayer, and yes we can do that." Even though Catherine has never had children of her own, she feels she was born to be a mother. Working with children has helped her express that side of herself, and she has numerous "fairy god-children."

In the School for Witchlets, children have an opportunity to develop their natural sensitivity to the environment through intuition training. They are taught to be careful with plants and to respect nature. Catherine says, "Even children with short attention spans become enthralled when looking for plants. Because they're closer to the ground, they see things that adults miss. They find caterpillars, ants, and every little thing completely interesting. They learn to identify many plants and to give thanks to the creator for this glorious creation."

FIGURE 19. *Young students stirring up a pot of Boo-Boo Balm at Catherine's School for Witchlets, Marin County, CA.*

Coyote Kid Camp

Ocean Song is a non-profit learning center in the hills of Western Sonoma where environmental awareness and skills for healthy living are taught. They sponsor Coyote Camp for children, and I accompanied Catherine to a class she was teaching there.

Working with five different age groups, Catherine was able to captivate her young audience, engaging them in making her specialty, Boo-Boo Balm. The children picked the herbs and flowers that would go into the mix, and infused them with intention. "Please help my brother's knee heal. He is learning how to ride his bike and he falls down a lot," said one. "Please help my dog's ears, he scratches them too much," said another, until everyone had spoken. They left that day with a small jar of cream and an imprint of nature as healer that they won't forget.

Beyond Chicken Soup

Catherine teaches that food is medicine:

> *If possible, eat locally grown organic produce and seasonal food— the fresher the better. Shopping at farmers' markets can give you*

the opportunity to look into the eyes of the person who grew your food! You can find the nutritional or medical information you need in a book and then eat the things that you need. For example, blueberries are good for gout, nettles are good for arthritis, and corn silk is good for the kidneys. There are common foods and seasonings that are powerful medicine when prepared properly. Garlic, parsley, cilantro, shiitake mushrooms, ginger, all the seasonal vegetables, oregano, basil, thyme, chili flakes, and cayenne all have medicinal qualities. You can boost your mood and your immune system at the same time by adding the right seasonings to your soup.

Here, she shares a recipe for a delicious and nutritious soup. Many of the ingredients can be found in Asian markets or health-food stores.

MOTHER'S MEDICINE SOUP

1 handful dried nettles (or fresh if you know where to find them)
About 2 inches of seaweed (Kombu or nori)
1 burdock root, sliced
4 to 5 garlic cloves, crushed
Several shiitake mushrooms, chopped
2 red onions, chopped
1 carrot, sliced
2 celery stalks, chopped
2 handfuls spinach or kale leaves
Chili flakes to taste
1 handful cilantro, chopped
1 handful fresh parsley, chopped
1/4 cup Bragg's All Natural Liquid Aminos
3 quarts water
Optional seasonings: basil, dill
Boil ingredients in large pot for 15 minutes or so. Freeze leftovers!

Genie Marie Guthrie—Dreaming Laughing Winds

Genie Marie Guthrie lives in rural Tennessee, where she cares for a piece of land and the things that grow there—including the men and women who have come together to create a community. She has a Master's degree in Health. About twenty years ago, she began a formal study of herbs and herbal medicine, apprenticing with Susan Weed, an herbalist who specializes in women's health and specifically how to use herbs to support women through menopause.

Genie has always loved the earth and dreamed of starting a community where she could live close to the land with others who loved nature. She thought her work would be with women; she was surprised, when she began to create her dream, that men also came to help. In fact, men were among the first residents of Laughing Winds.

Caring Versus Caretaking

Genie understands her work as balancing the male and female energies in herself and those who come to the community to partake of the sweat lodges, drumming circles, fire walks, and other gatherings and teaching events. Genie doesn't have any children of her own and sees herself as helping people energize the mother within them so they can love and nurture themselves. She talks about the difference between *caring* and *caretaking*—modeling her work on caring. It takes a strong sense of boundaries, she says.

Genie has observed that, all too often, for people who have had no mothering or have suffered from "smothering mothering," their feminine side is confused—shut down or overdone. As she talked to me, cultural images of "mother" flashed through my mind—from June Cleaver to Rosanne, mothers take a bad rap in our society. "Many of us don't know how to love ourselves," Genie says. "We try to get loved through sexual relationships—mistaking sexual love for the unconditional love we all seek. No wonder so many partnerships fail.... We're looking for someone else to do what only we can do for ourselves—give ourselves unconditional love. The kind of love that only Great Mother can provide."

Great Mother's Womb

Genie offers sweat-lodge ceremonies throughout the year and sees the lodge as the place where it all comes together. The lodge itself is a female form—it replicates the womb of Great Mother. Going into the lodge is like going back into the womb. It is dark and warm. People enter with many different expectations; during the ceremony, they have all kinds of experiences. Most come out having experienced some kind of transformation or spiritual rebirth. "Both men and women become vulnerable in the lodge—it's a practice of opening and receiving. It doesn't matter who you are on the outside; in the lodge, we let our defenses down and spirit can work with us," Genie says, smiling.

Genie prefers using local herbs in the ceremonies. Mugwort grows abundantly in Tennessee and she burns it for smudging the lodge and those who enter it. Mugwort—a variety of artemisia, which is considered a female herb—is also called the dreaming plant. Genie likes it because Laughing Winds is a dream in process. She mixes mugwort with Cherokee mint, which opens the sinuses and the psyche to the experience of the lodge. She puts the herb osha on the rocks for its antibiotic and anti-histamine qualities, along with lavender, which supports balance and smells good.

Genie makes a spring salad fit for a 5-star restaurant. The ingredients grow wild in the yard—violet blooms and violet leaves, chickweed, dandelion greens, and plantain mixed with some fresh leaf lettuce from the garden. "A few local herbs like these added to food can provide most of the support we need," she says. Genie isn't an organic food "freak," although she does grow most of her vegetables. But she likes to shock her students by eating a hamburger just to let them know that healthy eating doesn't have to be an all-or-nothing deal—again, it's always about balance with her.

Although Genie's dream at Laughing Winds is very much about Earth Mother energy. It's also about creating a co-operative model. In that regard, it is like a matriarchal culture—not women ruling men, but men and women working together. She knows that balance won't happen if women simply change roles with men or expect them to "get their girl on." Both are going to have to learn how to love and nurture themselves and respect each other—a process she refers to as good mothering.

Allie O'Conner—Making Flower Medicine

Allie O'Conner has tended a flower garden since she was five years old—that's sixty-six years ago. She lives in Paducah, Kentucky on the banks of the Ohio River. She loves flowers and digging in the ground. "It makes me feel right," she says. She has a Master's degree in Education and has studied several alternative therapies, including clinical hypnotherapy and insight meditation. She learned to make flower essences about twenty-five years ago under the direction of Catherine Abby Rich, whose story you read earlier in this chapter. Allie describes her role as healer:

> When presenting yourself as an alternative healing practitioner, it's customary to identify people whom you studied with since the practices are not taught in traditional schools, but through apprenticing with an experienced teacher. It's also necessary to know the boundaries of the medicine you're working with. For example, I wouldn't 'treat' someone's illness. I would send that person to a health-care provider. However, I might work with that person to identify the emotions he or she is struggling with and offer support.

Flower essences became popular in the 1930s when an English physician and homeopath, Edward Bach, intuited that flowers contain healing energy transmitted by vibration. He tested different plants using kinesiology and began to create a system for transferring the vibration to water so it could be ingested or applied topically in the prevention and treatment of many conditions and illnesses.

Bach believed that illness is the result of an inner conflict between our soul purpose and the personality or ego's point of view. This inner battle creates disharmony, which results in physical disease. He treated disease by addressing the emotional and spiritual conditions that underlie it—an understanding that is common to alternative healing modalities. Bach sometimes treated disease states directly, as well. His famous Rescue Remedy brought him fame and continues to be widely used to help manage stress. Despite the failure of flower essences to prove themselves in clinical tests, Rescue Remedy and other essences are used by thousands of people, perhaps bringing relief through a belief in their ability to heal.

The Inner Healer

Allie is well aware of the lack of evidence to support the healing properties of flowers, yet she knows from experience that making them provides healing to the practitioner! She loves making the medicine. "It is a meditative process of focusing on healing and specifically what you are asking the plant to give you. Whether the plant is transmitting healing or is the vehicle for connecting a person to his or her own inner healer doesn't really matter." Making those kinds of distinctions, she believes, isn't as important to alternative therapies as it is to traditional medicine.

> We understand that healing occurs at many different levels and treatment modalities are a process—they address all aspects of a person as well as lifestyle. In this regard, the flower essence is the focus of a much larger piece of work. To isolate an essence and test it without the rest of the process won't necessarily yield the same results. Holistic healing is based in a different paradigm than what we call traditional medicine.

Allie points out that traditional healing isn't all that traditional and certainly not universal. "Cultures all over the world rely on herbs to maintain health and treat illness. Allopathic medicine is a recent development—and an important one. However, it exists in relationship with many other approaches to healing."

Teaching the Process

Allie thinks of herself more as a teacher than as a practitioner. She teaches others how to make essences, and her classroom is the garden or a field of wild flowers. Students spend the day in meditation, focusing on their potential healed state. "We walk in beautiful places, sit on a blanket on the ground in the sun, laugh, pray, meditate, and make medicine—sometimes we bring a picnic lunch. Every time they take the medicine they remember the experience of making it and reinforce the power of nature. What's not healing about that? I guess it's a matter of semantics."

Like most holistic herbalists, Allie believes in gathering your medicine as close to home as possible. She makes flower essences with local flowers and will also travel to work with a flower that doesn't grow in her area of the country. She begins by noticing what is blooming at any given time of the year, looking for healthy plants and flowers that are at the fullness of their growth cycle. Before using a flower, students meditate with it, connecting with its essence—its spirit. The plant will often "self-select" flowers to be used. It's not unusual for one blossom to start vibrating or for a bee to land on it, signaling ripeness or readiness.

Allie uses several flower essence books, as well as intuition, kinesethic testing, and the signature of nature to help determine the right flower for the right condition. Kinesiology is the principle employed in dowsing—using a device to telegraph physiological energy that resonates with substances being tested. This is the same principle used in lie detectors. It's possible to know when your body is giving you a positive reaction—you feel uplifted. A negative reaction feels like a disappointment. Each person may have his or her own inner system. Recognizing what your body is telling you is a big part of healing in the mind/ body system. It is based in the belief that the body has intelligence and that nature does, too—God present.

The signature of nature is the understanding that a plant has certain characteristics that help communicate its uses. For example, yellow flowers often pertain to the liver, red ones to the blood. Blackberry helps with grieving and depression; its purpose is reflected in its color and the thorns on its stems. "None of this is exact," Allie observes:

> It's intuitive but that doesn't rule out its effectiveness. Yes, it works on the placebo effect, but many medical studies show that the results from placebos are often as good as those obtained with allopathic medicine. The time spent in nature—mediating, being listened to, imagining your healed state—have all been clinically proven as effective in the healing process, equal to and in some cases superior to the use of drugs. I'm not ruling out the flower's ability to heal by vibration. I'm sure they do. I am only saying they work on many levels—but they do work.

Recipes for Recovery

Allie works in the addiction-recovery field and has made special formulas to treat the conditions that often accompany addiction. She preserves her medicine in vegetable glycerin rather than brandy, which is the basis of Bach's medicine. Some of her formulas include:

Morning glory for healing addiction

Blackberry for relieving grief, depression, fear of dying

Forget-me-not for calming anxiety

Zinnia for laughter as a healing medicine

Sunflower for opening the heart for giving and receiving

Bells of Ireland, cedar, and chamomile for relieving stress (as well as lifestyle changes)

Comfrey for security

Jasmine for spiritual attunement

Allie spends time with her students, listening to their stories and helping them gain insight into their underlying issues. She works with them to identify what is going on below the surface and what they would like to develop within themselves. She sometimes combines as many as three essences to create a formula specifically for that person. Part of the process includes naming the medicine—it sets the direction of their healing, as her teacher taught her. For example, someone who is struggling with anxiety may name his or her medicine "Calm, Cool, and Collected." Allie says that identifying what you want and energizing it is good medicine.

Allie orders bottles for her medicine from France. "They are a very particularly lovely shade of cobalt blue," she says. "You know flowers are very vain. They know they're beautiful and they want you to pay attention to them. You have to put them in beautiful bottles to honor them for their good looks as well as their healing power. In that regard, they work on the twelve-step concept of attraction not promotion!"

Wrapping Things Up

The plant world feeds us and heals us. You can connect to the natural healing properties of plants by finding a beginner's book and identifying a few that grow close to your house. Your intuition will lead you to where you need to go next. Children have a natural connection to their environment and learn plant identification and medicine-making quickly. For thousands of years, people have gone to nature for their healing and for their medicine. As a culture, we are just beginning to remember the importance of natural healing. The women you just read about led the way in developing healing arts rooted in ancient history –they have studied their medicine well.

Chapter 20

❧❦

BODY AND SOUL

Women's spirituality is based in relationship and connection. It understands that spirit and body are one and that our spiritual journey and our human journey are one and the same. It shares many beliefs and practices with the practices of holistic healing. Both are based in the belief that instinct and intuition provide guidance for our mental, emotional, physical, and spiritual development. Holistic practices are about getting us back in touch with our instinct and intuition—the map that was pre-installed on our hard drive, the body's spiritual intelligence.

What Is Holistic Healing?

In both women's spirituality and holistic healing, balance is considered a spiritual principle. Holistic healing believes that, when body, mind, emotions, and spirit are balanced and supported, we generate healing energy—or life force. This life force carries directives for living, or human instincts. Holistic healers apply natural healing techniques and remedies to assist in balancing and supporting the whole person. Balance and support include personal desire, intent, and lifestyle choices that support health. Spiritual seekers, as well as those seeking healing, are encouraged to lead balanced lives, including eating a healthful diet, getting regular exercise, rest, creative expression, working toward a positive self-image, cultivating friendships, and participating in a spiritual practice. Like many things in nature, this philosophy has a high degree of common sense behind it.

Holistic healing is based on anatomy and physiology, and on the energetic system that flows through the body—the life force, or *chi*, as it is called in Eastern culture. Chi (sometimes written as *CH'I* or *qi*) is the energy or life force of the universe, believed to flow around and through the body and to be present in all living things. Spiritually, this equates to sacred presence—the Goddess or God within.

When this energy is open and flowing, the body enjoys its naturally healthy state. When this energy is weakened—which can happen for a variety of reasons, like poor diet, toxins, worry, or any other stress—the flow of chi is blocked and health is compromised. Holistic healing supports keeping the energy flowing, which strengthens the life force. When the life force is strong, the body's natural defense systems protect it from disease. In women's spirituality and in holistic healing, maintaining one's health is a spiritual practice.

Soulbody—Healing and Wholeness

The term *soulbody* describes this unified physical, emotional, mental, and spiritual presence. Healing engages all aspects of self or soulbody. Western culture, specifically in the U. S., stands alone in its suspicion of these ancient beliefs and practices—but that is changing. For example, the medicinal use of herbs is standard in Europe, India, Asia, Africa, and South and Central America, and is gaining ground in this country. Acupuncture is widely practiced all over Asia, as well as in many other countries around the world; it is increasingly being accepted by Western practitioners. Many traditional medical centers now offer classes in yoga, meditation, and guided imagery; hypnosis, and massage are part of the treatment process. These practices were uncommon only a few years ago.

Common Holistic Practices

The following are descriptions of several common holistic practices currently being used in traditional Western medical settings, as well as in holistic clinics throughout the country. They're based on ancient practices that are resurfacing as part of the "new" paradigm. They've been tested by science and proven to be effective in assisting the body to heal disease and alleviate stress by supporting the soulbody. They are often used in combination with traditional treatments.

- Acupuncture: originated in China and is used to treat a variety of disorders by inserting needles into the skin at points where the flow of energy is blocked.

- Acupressure: based on the same principles as acupuncture, but uses finger pressure rather than needles on specific points along the body.

- Herbology: applies knowledge of the healing property of plants both internally and externally to prevent illness and to rejuvenate the soulbody's systems.

- Hypnotherapy: engages the subconscious mind in the healing process and can assist in healing trauma that can cause illness.

- Imagery: an ancient technique that heals through the imagination, directly engaging a person in his or her healing process.

- Reflexology: applies direct pressure to points on the feet or hands that correspond to organs and systems in the body, relieving tension and resulting in positive changes .

- Reiki: a healing technique in which practitioners sense the client's energy field and, through a series of movements, assist the flow of energy.

An increasing number of medical doctors are seeing that patients are healing faster and more effectively when they are treated with both Western and holistic medicine and they are bridging the gap between the two worlds; women have led the way in this bridge building.

"Medicines do not cure; nature alone cures."

—FLORENCE NIGHTINGALE (1820–1910)

Holistic Healers

Holistic healers are having an increasing impact on Western medicine. Here are the stories of six women educated in both Western, or allopathic, medicine and Eastern, or holistic, medicine who are combining techniques and offering patients the best of both worlds.

Carolyn Ross—Treating the Whole Person

Carolyn Ross comes from a long line of physicians and healers. Her grandfather was a well-known doctor who opened his own hospital and nursing school. Her grandmother was a Cherokee medicine woman. She wanted to be a doctor ever since she was nine years old and worked summers and vacations in her grandfather's office, accompanying him on house calls, helping him deliver babies, and learning how to dispense medications in his office pharmacy.

Ross followed her dream and completed her undergraduate degree while working as a full-time mother before returning to school to complete her pre-med requirements and going on to medical school. She had already made the connection between medical problems, lifestyle, habits, and the stresses of modern living, and began exploring complementary and alternative therapies and the use of herbs and supplements. She completed a residency in Preventive Medicine at Loma Linda University and set up practice in San Diego, California, where she opened three women's centers for primary care and gynecology. She integrated the best of Western medicine with complementary and alternative therapies like yoga, acupuncture, chiropractic, and nutrition counseling. Her holistic practice and nutritional awareness combined in her visionary and comprehensive treatment of eating disorders.

Ross continued her studies at the University of Arizona's Center for Integrative Medicine, where she completed a two-year fellowship in Integrative Medicine, studying with Dr. Andrew Weil. Ross treats the whole person. She looks at the context in which patients live—their work and home life, the stresses they live with, and how they handle them. She believes in good nutrition, which often can mean adding vitamins, herbs, and minerals to their diet.

Ross' approach to medicine is whole-person centered. She considers the mental, physical, emotional, and spiritual aspects of health and recognizes the body's natural ability to heal with the right balance and support. Her approach is about healing the person rather than treating the illness. She heralds the transformation that is possible, and celebrates its arrival in Western medicine. Contact information for Dr. Ross, along with information on her books, can be found in the resources listed at the back of this book.

Caroline Myss—A Medically Intuitive Theologian

Caroline Myss has an undergraduate degree in Journalism, a Master's degree in Theology, and a Ph.D. in Energy Medicine. She is a *medical intuitive* who draws on theology as well as biology. She is able to diagnose illness intuitively, using her medical training to accurately interpret and understand what her intuition is telling her. She has discovered that the great spiritual teachings of four world religions—Hinduism, Buddhism, Judaism, and Christianity—are all saying the same thing: spirituality is encoded in the body.

The sacraments of the Catholic Church (baptism, Eucharist or communion, confirmation, marriage, reconciliation or confession, holy orders, and the sacrament of the sick) are physical acknowledgments of God's grace supporting us through life passages. They have a prescribed form, which includes the use of elements like water and oil to anoint the body, along with holy candles, bread, and saying certain words.

Myss' observations show how the chakra system of Hinduism and Buddhism, along with the mystical teaching of the Jewish Kabbalah and the Christian sacraments, form an integrated spiritual instruction book for health and well-being. The ideas, although expressed differently in these religions, all deepen our understanding of life as a soul journey. "The universal jewel within the four major religions," she tells us, "is that the Divine is locked into our biological system in seven stages of power that lead us to become more refined and transcendent in our personal power."

Chakras—The Soulbody's Energy Centers

There are seven major energy centers in the body called *chakras*, a Sanskrit word meaning "whirling light." Each governs the functions of particular organs and emotions, and also contains the "instruction book" for our spiritual development. The chakra system shows how the body and spirit are one, and how our spiritual journey is energized by our connection to source, unfolding from within us. Each chakra relates to a Hindu god or goddess present in the embodied spirituality of the system. Each energizes particular physical, emotional, and spiritual systems that correspond to the major nerve or endocrine centers in the human body.

Knowledge of the chakras comes to us from the *Vedas*, the oldest written tradition in India (2000 BCE–600 CE) and the foundational scriptures of Hinduism. Like all sacred material, however, the teachings of the *Vedas* belong to the whole world. These scriptures are particularly important to our discussion for several reasons. They consider the body and soul as an integrated whole, and they create a link between today's religious and scientific understanding and the wisdom of the ancient world, when an integrated understanding was common.

Figure 20 shows the seven major chakras, or biological energy centers, and the spiritual power each one contains, based on Myss' observations and drawing on a variety of other sources as well.

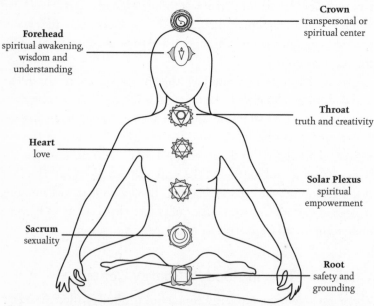

FIGURE 20. The seven major chakras, or energy centers, from bottom to top.

Root Chakra—Oneness

The first chakra is called the root chakra. It's located at the base of the spine—the sacrum—and is foundational to health and well-being. In women, the root chakra is located at the opening of the vagina; in men, it relates to the gonads. This chakra governs reproduction and contains our instinctual need for security such as food, shelter, and family. It corresponds to the Kabbalah's teaching called Shekhinah, God's feminine name, which honors nurturing and the unity of the family or tribe. It also relates to the Christian sacrament of baptism, an initiation into the community symbolic of "tribe." It instructs us instinctually on the need for bonding and belonging.

Parts of the body energized by the first chakra are: legs, feet, bones, large intestine, spine, nervous system, red blood cells, womb, menstrual cycle, and fertility. Imbalances in this chakra can result in insecurity, inability to bond, feeling like an outsider, as well as opposite conditions such as being overly dependent and failing to individuate and move ahead in our lives. It can contribute to problems of infertility.

Positive emotions affected by the first chakra include enthusiasm, belonging, and joy. Negative emotions include fear of survival, insecurity, disconnectedness, longing, and distrust.

The first chakra contains our inborn instructions on how to establish trust, seek safety, live a healthy life, and create a home and family. It teaches us that right relationship comes from safety, belonging, trust, and bonding with our people. It is foundational to building a successful life. If it is compromised, the entire system suffers.

Sacral Chakra—The "Other"

The second, or sacral, chakra is located halfway between the pubis and the navel. It relates to the ovaries in women and the spleen in men. Its functions overlap somewhat with the root chakra in women, because it governs some aspects of fertility and menstruation. Issues of sexuality are located there. It contains intuition and emotional memory. It's where we become aware of relations—and likewise the beginning of individuation, seeing ourselves as existing separate from others in the family, yet still belonging to the family. This chakra connects with the Kabbalah's teaching regarding the procreative force of God. It relates to the Christian sacrament of Eucharist or holy communion—the essence of nurturing and being nurtured—being fed by Mother/Father God.

Parts of the body energized by the second chakra are: skin, reproduction organs, kidneys, bladder, circulatory system, lymphatic system, adrenals, orgasm, and the flow of fluids in the body. Imbalances in the second chakra can result in asthma, allergies, epilepsy, coughs, kidney disease, and arthritis.

Positive emotions affected by this chakra include the ability to care for self, comfort with self and others, ability to give and receive pleasure, our desire, and passion. Negative emotions include fear, anxiety, lust, inability to nurture self and hanging onto painful emotions.

The second chakra contains our instinctual instructions for friendship and partnership. Human relationship begins with our ability to accept sensual pleasure (cuddling the baby), thus creating the capacity for emotional intimacy. It teaches that good relations begin with family. If this does not happen, early relationships must be healed, or all subsequent relationships—personal or professional—as well as emotional and physical health will be challenged. Creativity originates in this chakra.

Solar Plexus Chakra—Personal Power

The third chakra is located in the solar plexus, just above the navel. It's the center of personal power, which is necessary for effectiveness in all aspects of life. It connects to the Kabbalah's teachings of endurance and strength and relates to the Christian sacrament of confirmation, which also imparts endurance and strength in the practice of personal faith and ideals.

Parts of the body energized by the third chakra are: intake and absorption of food, digestion, glands, diaphragm, stomach, duodenum, gall bladder, liver, and endocrine functions of the pancreas. Imbalances in the third chakra can result in diabetes hypoglycemia, eating disorders, digestive upsets, ulcers, urinary infections, and skin problems.

Positive emotions affected by this chakra include willpower, self-empowerment, the ability to get needs met, the ability to be effective in the world, self-confidence, and taking things to completion. Negative emotions include mood swings, depression, powerlessness, feelings of victimization, excessive introversion, and loss of the will to live. It can also result in bullying, controlling or overpowering others, and insisting on having our own way.

The third chakra contains the instinct for personal power and right use of will, the development of a code of ethics, and the strength of character to be true to our ideals. It teaches that compromising our integrity affects physical strength; corresponding organs are likewise negatively affected.

Heart Chakra—All Is Love

The fourth chakra is located near the heart, under the breastbone between the breasts. It connects to the Kabbalah's teaching on compassion, harmony, and beauty. It relates to the Christian sacrament of marriage, opening the heart, and blessing love.

Parts of the body energized by the fourth chakra are: heart, thymus/immune system, circulation, infections, lungs, respiratory system, arms, and hands. Imbalances can result in heart disease and a weakened immune system, causing infections and guilt.

Positive emotions affected by the fourth chakra include the ability to give and receive love, self-love, healthy self-image, trust, openness, compassion, charity, altruism, beauty, sensitivity, belonging, and joy. Negative emotions include loneliness, isolation, longing, self-hate, bitterness, resentment, fear, and guilt.

The fourth chakra contains our instinctual understanding of the power of love—our innate need to love and be loved to survive. It carries the energy for imagination, the magical child within, and playfulness. Its lesson is that love and forgiveness are necessary for our physical and emotional strength and it teaches us how to develop those essential qualities.

Throat Chakra—Creativity and Truth

The fifth, sixth, and seventh chakras are associated, not with emotions, but rather with abilities. The fifth chakra is located in the throat. It is the creative center, especially after menopause, when the creative energy of a woman's reproductive center in the second chakra is transmitted to the fifth.

The fifth chakra relates to the Kabbalah's teachings on how speaking with love and mercy make our communications truly powerful. It relates to the Christian sacrament of confession, in which forgiveness is granted through the spoken word.

Parts of the body energized by the fifth chakra are: nervous system, female reproductive organs, vocal cords, ears, thyroid, and parathyroid. Imbalances can result in headaches, migraines, sore throats, creative blocks, anger, asthma, anemia, laryngitis, and skin or respiratory problems.

The fifth chakra strengthens our ability to communicate— to find our voice and speak our truth. It helps us hear the deeper meanings in communication and energizes singing, music, and deep insight. It contains our instinctual instructions for speech and the need for clear, honest communication. It energizes all creative projects, sending them out into the world. It teaches that we must speak our truth to be strong and healthy. Living a lie creates negative consequences in the body, mind, and emotions.

Forehead Chakra—Awakening Wisdom

The sixth chakra is the called the "third eye" and is located in the center of the forehead between the two eyebrows. It energizes intuitive perception and governs wisdom. Through it we see the big picture, the paradoxical nature of truth. It connects with Kabbalah's wisdom teachings. It corresponds to the Christian sacrament of ordination, and because of our expanded awareness and wisdom, all occupations take on the dimension of a priestly vocation.

Parts of the body energized by the sixth chakra are: eyes, nose, ears, brain, pituitary gland (main hormone balancer), women's intuition and knowing, and white blood cells. Imbalance can result in multiple sclerosis, degenerative disease, headaches and migraines, mental and nervous disorders, colds, flu, pneumonia, sinus, rigid thoughts, irritability, confusion, stress, and neuritis.

Abilities supported by the sixth chakra include psychic development, clairvoyance, telepathy, wisdom, finding our right work, integration on many levels, including merging of our male and female selves and living by one's own rules. It holds the energy for spiritual awakening, for coming into our own being and living our truth.

Crown Chakra—Union with Goddess or God

The seventh chakra is located outside the body, just above the head. It is our energetic connection to the divine source connecting our personal energy field with the big energy field, the source of all spiritual energy. It corresponds with the Kabbalah's teaching on "the supreme crown of God." It also relates to the Christian sacrament of extreme unction, assisting at the time of death.

Parts of the body energized by the seventh chakra are: endocrine or pineal glands, white blood cells. Imbalances can result in vision problems, stress disorders, insomnia, anxiety, mental and nervous issues, tumors, and strokes.

The seventh chakra carries our instinct for fulfilling our spiritual journey—enlightenment—and the realization that there is no death—or life after death. Self and other are no longer experienced as separate. It is the fulfillment of spirit become human—through it we experience unification.

Joan Borysenko —Spiritual Wiring

Joan Borysenko holds a Ph.D. in Biology and is a licensed psychologist and a leader in mind/body medicine. She brings a further understanding of our spiritual instinct grounded in the body and activated through natural biological functions. She has identified the spiritual map that's found inside women's bodies that guides us on our journey of life. It shows that spirituality is not separate from physiology.

Ceremonies and spiritual practices assist in awakening these energy centers in the body, empowering our physical, emotional, and spiritual passages. "Spirituality," she tells us, "is our deepest sense of connection to self, to nature, and to God or Spirit, characterized by feelings of love, harmony and being the moment—accompanied by awe and belonging" (*A Woman's Book of Life: The Biology, Psychology, and Spirituality of the Feminine Life Cycle* [Riverhead Books, 1996]).

Borysenko divides our life into seven-year segments. She describes the intuitive, holistic thinking of little girls from birth to age seven as one of life's greatest gifts. Young girls' moral compass is guided by their intuitive understanding that the world is alive. Brain scans on children show more activity in the right hemisphere in girls than in boys—the location of relational skills, imagination, and mystical experiences. This organic edge, combined with socialization, creates a women's spirituality that is centered in relationships.

Family and friends relate to little girls with more emotion, Borysenko points out, smiling more when speaking to them and holding and cuddling them more than boys. This encourages relational skills like emotional development, intuition, and empathy in girls. From then on, they use these qualities in making decisions in all areas of life, including how they understand moral truth. Borysenko describes this natural wisdom as "heart" logic.

As a young girl approaches the onset of her menstrual cycle, according to Borysenko, the chemicals produced in her brain deepen her emotions, sharpen her intuition, and increase her sensitivity to cultural messages. If she is receiving positive messages about herself, she grows strong and confident and has a clear sense of herself. If not, she begins to question herself at the deepest level.

FIGURE 21. Two little girls marvel at the magic of a starfish during an afternoon at the beach.

As a young woman enters the later stage of adolescence, ages fourteen to twenty-one, she faces her essential spiritual task or challenge, as Borysenko sees it. She must resolve what she perceives as a dilemma of choosing either herself or "other." When a young woman resolves this conflict, she can create a centering point within herself from which she can safely reach out and help others. Her natural empathy and relational skills can be used without losing herself in the process. She will be firmly grounded in her own healthy self-esteem.

The window for a woman to individuate closes in her mid twenties. If she is unable to solve that dilemma, she will struggle against issues of self-worth for many years and will be left with deep feelings of inadequacy that play out in a variety of ways—poor body image, lower school grades, eating disorders, addictions, unhealthy dependency on others' opinions, people-pleasing, and other coping mechanisms that often lead to depression. In her struggle to be free, she may turn to anti-social behavior—*fighting against*, rather than being effective in, the world. She will spend much of her productive years dealing with her damaged ego.

Borysenko notes that women are given a second chance at individuation in mid-life. Their biology creates another powerful mixture of chemicals as menstrual cycles decline, presenting them with the opportunity to complete their process. Mentoring by a woman who has passed through this gate, or belonging to a women's group focused on self-discovery rather than doing for others, is an important part of successfully making this transition.

Borysenko added to our understanding of aging by giving us the biological basis of the freedom and wisdom available to us at this stage of life. Chemicals produced by menopause open "conduits of higher wisdom," as she describes them. The years from sixty-three to eighty-four and beyond are a time of great perspective and personal power that produces freedom and authenticity. This is when women speak their truth, regardless of the consequences.

Carol Gilligan—Whole-Brain Logic

Carol Gilligan, psychologist and professor of Gender Studies at Harvard University, is the author of *In a Different Voice: Psychological*

Theory and Women's Development (Harvard University Press, 1993). Here, she identifies similar differences in how males and females approach moral decisions. She found that males come from an understanding that individuals have basic rights that must be protected. For them, morality is a system of limitations, like the Ten Commandments, stated as "thou shalt nots." Females naturally perceive morality as a responsibility to others. Morality calls them to care for others, as expressed in the biblical injunction to "love one another." Females factor circumstances into moral decisions. They mitigate justice rather than follow the letter of the law.

As girls grow, they add left-hemisphere skills to their natural intuitive skills and become whole-brained. This additional connective tissue between the right and left hemispheres of the brain gives females a balanced and holistic way of thinking and making decisions. In making choices, including moral choices, girls perceive the complexities of a situation, seeing a big picture that includes the motives and circumstances of everyone involved. They engage morality in an interactive dynamic that is informed by law and guided by the spirit.

Gilligan observes that traditional religion, which excludes women's experiences, can seriously hamper young women's spiritual development. Relational skills like awareness of others have to be developed in males, but the opposite is true for females. Females need encouragement and support in realizing that their own hopes and dreams are important, and that it's right to take care of their personal needs before giving to others. Religious instruction that continually directs a woman to focus on the needs of others without spending adequate time developing her sense of self-worth increases pressure and adds guilt. Girls are left with the feeling that, no matter how much they give, it isn't enough. Gilligan notes that, while religion remains primarily in the hands of males, this is the message it gives to women.

Growing Old and Wearing Purple!

Sandra Haldeman-Martz's *When I Am an Old Woman I Shall Wear Purple* goes a long way toward reframing how many people feel about aging. The book gives poetic insight into the freedom of growing older and the innate wisdom that accompanies the process. At this point in her life, the spiritually vibrant woman has broken through her conditioning; she has met her true self and likes what she sees! The confrontation with death that accompanies the aging process only raises the bar as far as truth and integrity are concerned, and there is a re-dedication to the principles we hold dearest. Here is a story of a woman who has entered this phase of her life, told in her own words.

Dorothy Robinson—Listening to the Soul

At age sixty-five, Dorothy Robinson had spent fifty-five years as a professional actor, director, producer, and writer, and had begun exploring the world of digital movie-making. She describes the shift that began for her a couple of years ago as "becoming aware of life's rhythms"

> I have become a "seer." I "see" why things have happened in my life and understand the innate wisdom of the experiences. I can "see" the evolution of my consciousness, my soul. I also "see" through the propaganda of the culture!

"I think most organized religion completely misses the boat," she says. "All those rules as if you can control spirituality, or need to!" Dorothy defines spirituality as "knowing you fit into the universe," a place she describes as both "simple and vast." She nourishes her spirit by spending time with friends, sharing meals, playing cards, and benefiting from the restorative power of sleep. Her early mornings are spent looking out her window at the river. "I am lazy in the morning. I don't want words or thoughts infringing. It's my time for just being."

However, "just being" for Dorothy, at age seventy-five, may exceed the cultural standard. For her, it included writing a book in which she shares her years of experience on both sides of the footlights. The book, *What Makes an Actor: A Director's View of Acting* (Blue Ball Publishing, 2010), illustrates the connection between spirituality, psychology, acting, and life. See the resources listed at the back of the book for contact information and how to find her films and books.

Wrapping Things Up

Soulbody describes our unified nature. Holistic health operates from *soulbody* philosophy, supporting the whole person and engaging the body's natural healing ability. Energy centers in the body called chakras maintain physical and emotional health and contain our spiritual instructions as well, guiding us on our transformational journey. This highly integrative system is identified by four world religions: Hinduism, Buddhism, Judaism, and Christianity. Throughout our lives, chemicals in the body open levels of consciousness according to a divine plan—grace or the indwelling of the Holy Spirit. The soulbody has long been recognized by indigenous healers and many other natural healers, who understand the system intuitively and energetically.

Chapter 24

❦❧ ❦❧

EMBODYING PRAYER

Women's spirituality acknowledges divine presence here and now, and women's prayer life reflects this integrated spirituality. Many rely on traditional forms of prayer and many prefer non-traditional practices you may not have thought of as spiritual disciplines. Rather than specific prayers, we'll explore some time-honored prayer practices that are somewhat unconventional to the Western mind, and also some newer approaches to renewing the spirit.

The Labyrinth—Ancient Mind Body Meditation

Labyrinths are circular geometric forms that define sacred space. Their patterns are considered archetypal, having been found carved or scratched into stone as grave markers, etched on pottery, woven into baskets, and stamped on coins all over the world. Labyrinths have been discovered in Greece, Egypt, India, France, England, Ireland, Algeria, Scandinavia, and Iceland, as well as in Native American and Mayan cultures. Probably the most famous remaining labyrinth is in Chartres Cathedral, build about 1200 BCE near Paris. It provides a direct link between ceremonies of the ancient world and contemporary religion.

Labyrinths are closely associated with women because of their circular pattern and also because some of the earliest were found in Crete—the last great Goddess culture dating back 4,000 to 5,000 years ago. It is believed that women presided over the labyrinth there and conducted the ceremonies surrounding its use.

Labyrinths are an example of how external space intersects with inner space, connecting us to a very natural and physical sense of spirituality that affects brain waves and can be felt in the body. It is said that you "experience" the labyrinth. Other geometric forms, such as Stonehenge, pyramids found around the world, and, more recently, temples, cathedrals, and mosques are further examples of sacred geometry. Like the labyrinth, they use space to help us reach higher states of consciousness, assisting us in connecting with our inner goddess or god self.

Seven Circuits—Seven Chakras

Labyrinths exist in three basic designs: seven-circuit, eleven-circuit and twelve-circuit. The most common design found today is the seven-circuit design pictured below. It's the pattern found in Knossos on the Greek island of Crete. The seven paths take you to the center and correspond to the seven-chakra system energizing the body and renewing the spirit.

FIGURE 22. A seven-circuit labyrinth design. The seven paths resemble the configuration of the brain.

As you look at a labyrinth's pattern, it may remind you of a simplified sketch of the brain. As you follow its seven-circuit path, you are taken on a series of 180-degree switchbacks, "waking up" consciousness by stimulating and balancing the right and left hemispheres of the brain. Balancing generally means quieting the left hemisphere (the cognitive side) in an effort to be in a more internal and meditative state. It reduces stress and has an immediate effect on health.

The labyrinth belongs to everyone. It has been in continuous use for thousands of years, and even today, people from all spiritual or religious backgrounds enjoy walking its pathways. Somewhere along the way, the journey of the labyrinth has been described as the threefold path of enlightenment: release, illumination, and integration. This is a soft description, however—continuing to take us beyond our ability to define it, the labyrinth remains a mystery.

1. *Release:* The path to the center is the path of letting go. *Release* There is a release and an emptying of worries and concerns as you make your way through the winding path.

2. *Illumination:* Standing in the center can bring clarity; it *Receive* invites illumination or insight. The center generates a receptive, meditative state.

3. *Integration:* The path out of the labyrinth is one of inte- *Return* gration. Insight gained in the process is woven into your thoughts, ready to be manifested in the world. Integration continues indefinitely.

Walking the Labyrinth

The experience of the labyrinth is unique to each person who walks it, and one's experience can change with each walk. For some, it symbolizes the womb. For others, it might evoke the soul's journey into the center of creation, or to one's own center of being, and back out again to the external world feeling rebalanced or realigned— even reborn. The Hopi people consider the labyrinth a symbol for Earth Mother; it functions similar to a ceremonial Kiva.

Mazes are similar to labyrinths. However, a maze's purpose and the experience it offers are very different. For example, a maze is designed to confuse the participant; it has a series of dead ends and the way out is hidden. Walking a labyrinth, on the other hand, is about the journey, not the destination—its winding path will guide you to the center and lead you back out again. Labyrinths allow you to let go and trust the process, rather than trying to figure it out.

It's recommended that you pause to collect yourself before beginning your journey into the labyrinth. Let go of expectation, empty your mind, and bring your awareness into the moment. That may mean simply looking at your feet and watching them as they navigate the twists and turns of the path. Take a few deep breaths and walk slowly to the center. Spend as long as you like there. Again, just let the experience continue, rather than trying to interpret it or analyze it. When it feels right, begin your journey out again, walking slowly, paying attention only to your feet as they follow the path. Spend a few moments in quiet meditation following your walk. It isn't necessary to have a big flash of insight—the changes can be very subtle and may continue for the next few days or even weeks.

The power of the labyrinth's circular configuration is ancient, and walking one can be a time for prayer, meditation, reflection, personal healing, creativity enhancement, relaxation, and sometimes just an interesting experience. Labyrinths can assist you in resolving an inner conflict: if you begin your walk with a particular concern or question, you might emerge with a solution; but most likely, the answer will emerge in time. Those who walk a particular labyrinth regularly talk about the interactive property of the space: the labyrinth transmits something to the participants, and it is also energized by those walking it.

Insight Meditation

While both women and men meditate, the form itself is considered feminine. It develops female qualities, specifically the quality of receptivity and quieting our active mind. It's about being rather than doing (an attribute generally considered masculine). An ongoing meditation practice will balance the right and left hemispheres of the brain—thus balancing our female and male aspects of self. The balanced mind leads us toward "right action," meaning action that is consistent with our deep values.

Meditation provides insight into our thoughts, emotions, and physical feelings. Our body often makes healthy adjustments naturally through the practice of meditation and we don't have to know all the details to receive the well being it offers. Medical science is now adding to our societal understanding of the interconnection of spirit and matter. The physical and emotional benefits of a regular meditation practice are being validated through brain imaging as well as evaluating the healing process among those who have a practice and those who don't.

Getting Started

Oftentimes people approach meditation believing they are supposed to have a peaceful experience and feel they are doing it wrong if they don't. However, insight meditation is about noticing what is going on in your mind and not doing anything about it—observing without judging. You step out of the argument and just observe yourself as you are in the conflict. The mind eventually quiets because your attention or resistance to the chaos is not energizing it. Meditation develops your ability to be in the non-judgmental observer mind, sometimes called "wise mind." The ultimate goal of a regular practice is to be able to meditate anywhere at any time, maintaining a calm state no matter what is going on around you. This doesn't necessarily result in a passive state, but rather an appropriate one. Actions or responses to your environment will be formed in a calm or peaceful state of mind rather than a confused or fearful reaction. Here are some basic steps to meditation:

1. *Make time to meditate.* Set aside time in your daily routine for meditating, beginning with a few minutes and gradually increasing to thirty or more. Consistency is more important than length of time, which will increase naturally as you develop. Avoid meditating immediately after meals or if you are already hungry. The same is true of being too tired. Many people find the morning is the best time to meditate, before the day grabs all your attention. But that is up to you.

2. *Find or create a quiet, relaxing environment.* Turn off anything that beeps, buzzes, binds, or vibrates. Turn off the

television. If you play music it should be calming, repetitive, and gentle so it won't intrude on your concentration—and no favorite tunes, which tend to engage your memory and get you singing along rather than quieting the mind.

3. *Sit up straight, but don't be rigid.* Stack up the vertebrae in your spine so that they are balanced one on top of the other, supporting your body, neck, and head. When you do this correctly, you will feel as if no effort is required. Uncross and relax your arms and legs. If you tend to fall asleep when you close your eyes, leave them open and soften your gaze. Looking at a candle helps.

4. *Focus your attention on your breath.* Feel it coming in and going out. Listen to it. Feel the temperature of the breath as it comes into your nose. Feel it as it goes down your throat. Feel your body expand as you inhale. Feel your muscles soften as you exhale. Make no judgments, just observe. Gradually increase the depth of your breathing, but don't exaggerate it. The breath becomes the focus for emptying the mind of all the chatter. Beginners might find it helpful to count as they breathe to help hold the focus. Count from one to six on the inhalation. Hold for a few counts, then release while counting from one to six again. You might also simply count the breaths one to seven and then begin again.

5. *Visualize a place that calms you.* It can be real or imaginary. Imagine you are in a comfortable place in nature, and notice exactly how that place looks, smells, sounds, and feels. Continue this until you find yourself relaxing. Some people picture a staircase and relax as they imagine descending the stairs. Others prefer to imagine rising above their thoughts. If you find these techniques distracting, you may try simply letting go and relaxing.

There are many ways to meditate, and you can try out different styles. They are basically about accomplishing the same thing. It is helpful to have a teacher to remind you to breathe and help you avoid the pitfalls of judgment—beating yourself up for not getting it right, for instance. It seems that everyone's mind wanders. Observe this human phenomenon and practice letting it go. You will find that over time your mind slows down when you approach your time to meditate. You are retraining it.

Meditating in a group is helpful. However, avoid turning your practice into an Olympic event—it's not meant to be a competitive sport, it's a way of life. After meditating, most people experience a general feeling of satisfaction as well as relief from conditions such as anxiety and depression. Meditating releases serotonin, dopamine, and other mood-enhancing chemicals, and it improves mental clarity, creativity, and promotes general peace of mind. It's been shown to be an effective pain treatment and even has an effect on sleep patterns and maintaining a healthy weight.

Yoga—5,000 Years of Holistic Health

"Yoga" is a Sanskrit word meaning "to merge, join, or unite." It promotes integration between the practitioner's spiritual and physical nature and seeks to unify the whole person with the Divine. Yoga involves a group of disciplines that promote awareness of body and soul, health, and well-being through breathing exercises, postures, and rituals. It works on principles of God present, and spiritual and physical health through balance. "The supreme Godhead resides in the heart of every being," a traditional yoga saying tells us. Yoga helps the practitioner become more aware of that presence. Yoga was traditionally used to prepare students for mediation by releasing stress and making room in the body for the spirit to expand. The earliest evidence of its use can be traced back to about 3000 BCE, making it about 5,000 years old. Today, yoga is used for a variety of reasons: to relax, to build flexibility and strength, and as a spiritual practice.

Both men and women practice yoga, and like other spiritual disciplines mentioned here, it works to balance the inner male and female aspects of self. Many stress management programs in businesses and medical facilities use principles based on yoga, such as breathing exercises and gentle postures designed to aid in the recovery of a variety of stress-related illnesses. The following story tells how one young therapist uses this ancient healing modality in her work and in her own life as well.

Corey Emerick: Yoga as Therapy

Corey L. Emerick holds a Masters degree in Professional Counseling and is currently pursuing a doctorate in that field. She specializes in the treatment of eating disorders, assisting clients in self-exploration using a variety of approaches including insight therapy, DBT (Dialectical Behavior Therapy), RTR (Rapid Trauma Resolution), and yoga. Here, she talks about herself as a lifetime student as well as a teacher of yoga—how it changed her life and how she uses it therapeutically to help others make changes in their lives.

> Yoga is often translated as "union," meaning the union of body, mind, and spirit. When I first began to practice yoga, that definition was lost to me; yoga was a way to exercise, get in shape, and not get bored. How my definition of yoga would change! Back then, I used yoga to show off, improve my self-esteem by engaging in advanced asanas (poses), and to gain admiration or approval. When I talked about my yoga "practice," I viewed yoga as an external experience. Today, I view yoga as an internal experience and that can include prayer, healing, grounding, release, inspiration, forgiveness, energy or awareness raising, or a combination of many of the above.

> Over the years, yoga has become a way for me to let go of shame, make peace with my body, learn to love myself, and find freedom. My best friend—a wonderful yogini, passed on to me a lesson from her teacher: to treat the yoga mat as my "universe" so that what others did on their "universes" did not matter to me. That teaching has helped me come back to myself, to the moment, and to the union of my body, mind, and spirit many times. Yoga has allowed me to slowly quiet the "hamster wheel" that speeds around in my mind and allow the outside world to slowly melt away while I practice.

Corey points out that this is a transferable skill—we ultimately learn to live from our center rather than in reaction to the external world—thus we find the peace of mind most of us seek.

> Yoga is a gift that revealed itself to me, gradually and slowly. Today, I experience yoga as conscious movement and not exercise. It gives my body the motion, stretching, and relaxing that it seeks. It calms me and brings balance—both relaxing and energizing my mind, which then balances my emotions. It ultimately allows me to feel the

love and nurturing my soul deserves. Yoga has transformed my life and carried me through suffering toward joy and through self-hatred toward self-love many times. So, it is an honor for me to be able to offer it back to those who are searching for healing and freedom.

Yoga allows people to shift away from "right and wrong" or "black and white" thinking. It is all about prana (breath); you cannot do yoga "wrong," as long as you are allowing your breath to flow through your body. It teaches that each body is different; therefore, flexibility and the ability to get into advanced poses does not make a person a better yogi/yogini than another. I often see yoga help people reduce anxiety and/or depression, since it can quiet the mind and activate the parasympathetic nervous system. Humor is an essential function of yoga as well, encouraging those who practice it to laugh at themselves and not take themselves so seriously.

Yoga is a great healing tool in the treatment of eating disorders and addiction. As an eating disorder therapist and a person who has healed from one as well, I see yoga as a way to teach my clients how to connect to their bodies, since such a large part of eating disorders is about being able to disconnect from our own bodies as often as possible. When teaching my clients yoga, I aim to help them identify and set their intentions for each practice, recognize thoughts and feelings that surface—then, name, feel, and allow the feelings to flow through their bodies. Sometimes the feelings are released and other times people need to sit with them. Yoga can help build self-esteem and confidence, and help people find themselves.

Is yoga the "cure" for eating disorders, addictions, anxiety, depression, or plain old misery? No. Yoga is what you make of it and what you allow it to make of you. It is also a phenomenal foundation in our journey toward healing and/or recovery. To me, yoga is a doorway to freedom. I am still guided by a quotation that I used in my senior yearbook: "One body—respect it; one mind—feed it; one life—enjoy it."

Corey is on staff at Integrative Life Center in Nashville, TN, a wellness-based intensive outpatient program focused on treating the whole person in recovery from addiction and the accompanying disorders. You can find contact information for her in the resources listed at the back of this book.

Retreats—Feeding the Body and Nourishing the Soul

Retreats offer an embodied kind of spirituality, and they don't require an overtly spiritual focus to be a prayer. Retreats are based on the premise that caring for the creation, nurturing and caring for ourselves while relaxing and enjoying the company of others, is intrinsically spiritual. A retreat can provide opportunities for one to open doors to deeper healing. Like other spiritual practices, retreats can work on many levels, often benefitting the organizers as well as the attendees.

Following are stories of women who have opened doors (literally and figuratively) for themselves and other women. These stories show a broad range of approaches to hosting retreats—a simple yet elegant county-style hospitality; a fun-filled weekend at a mountain retreat; or a homegrown, bring-your-own-sleeping-bag affair. All offer a chance to experience peace and partnership, and they share the spirit of community, rest, regeneration, and tending to body and soul.

Spirituality and Chocolate-Chip Date Cake

Mary has a cottage on a small lake near Star Prairie, Wisconsin. It is the gathering place for family and friends from the Twin Cities, an hour and a half away. She says she can feel a sense of relief and connection when she crosses the St. Croix River and heads for the lake. "It feels like the rules change. I can breathe deeper." For her, spirituality is natural, not supernatural. The closer she is to nature, the easier it is to connect spiritually. Mary describes spirituality as sensuousness. "The senses connect us to life, nature, people—everything."

Mary talks about communion as the ritual of cooking "sacred recipes" passed down through her family. She recalls her mother's chocolate-chip date cake, and how there was always enough to share, regardless of who showed up at her table. "When people eat alone, they don't absorb the nutrients as well as when they eat with other people," Mary notes. She uses the word "conviviality" to describe getting together and sharing food. Her spirituality is bound up with the senses, food, and good conversation. "It's the coming alive of the spirit in the body."

As Mary and I spoke, Sadie, the neighbor's brown-and-white springer spaniel, appeared in the kitchen window, her nose pushed hard against the glass. There was a look of fierce determination as Sadie locked eyes with Mary, insisting on help. Just then, we heard thunder growling in the distance, across the lake to the north. Sadie intensified her efforts. Mary opened the door and the dog made a beeline for the narrow space between the couch and the wall, where she took shelter from the storm. Outside, the rain began to pelt against the front window, wiping out our view of the water below. The scene with Sadie captured the essence of what Mary's retreat center is all about.

Mary sees spirituality as understanding ourselves as an extension of God. She loves setting people free in their minds and bodies. "Here, in our country, we aren't oppressed in the same way people in other places in the world are; for us, the struggle goes on inside of ourselves. We are oppressed by greed—sometimes our own and sometimes the greed of others. In the materialism of this culture, people lose touch with reverence and respect for life." Every day Mary spends at her home by the lake brings her an opportunity to participate in the observance of a holy day.

An overdose of organized religion had left Mary feeling despair. She is "pastor-shy," as she describes it. "Religious leaders have the definite tendency to take over the show," she believes. "It quickly becomes about them and the church, not about the people and God. Today, I have a growing satisfaction with my life," she says. "I journal every morning, spend time in nature, and am nourished by my Artist's Way group—they have become my tribe. Sometimes, I visit the Quaker Meeting House and enjoy quiet respectful meditation there. And my music is coming back to me. I have always been able to sing my way out of anything! I want to get back to my guitar and my singing. When I play, I feel myself yielding to the creative spirit, and time and space are suspended."

The storm that brought Sadie to Mary's window moved through and the sun glinted off wet branches that dripped on our heads as we walked down the hill to the lake and boarded Mary's boat. With her at the wheel and Sadie riding shotgun, I pushed off and jumped onboard. We putted slowly around the lake, savoring each view as if we were turning the pages of an old photograph album. The air smelled as if someone had just opened a fresh bottle of ozone, and the colors were surreal. Long purple stripes stretched across a persimmon sky.

After dinner, Mary turned down the quilts on an old iron bed on the sleeping porch, and I crawled in between flannel sheets— which felt good on this midsummer night. Sadie was sleeping on the back porch, and our hostess was down the hall in her room. The storm thundered back through, and I slept what my mother used to refer to as the sleep of the just. I awakened to the morning chatter of a bird outside my window and the smell of coffee, which I drank as I enjoyed a serving of Mary's mother's chocolate-chip date cake, guaranteed to renew the spirit

Diane Conway—Sparks Fly at a Women's Retreat

Today's busy women often find weekend retreats are a helpful way to rebalance their lives. Here's the story of how one woman finds respite by assisting other women in finding theirs.

Diane is a woman who wears many hats. She's been a whale watcher in Maui, an instructor at bad-drivers' school, a model, a one-woman comedy show, an author, a national speaker, a fairy god-mother, and a creativity coach. Once a year, she takes women into their imagination for a complete get-away weekend where spirit has a chance to work the miracle.

Diane has been facilitating women's retreats for many years. Her specialty is a yearly gathering that has turned out to be the most rewarding activity of her life—she gets as much as she gives, she assured me. "Seeing women open up their spirits, play and laugh [a retreat activity Diane calls practicing playfulness], and support each other unconditionally has been life-affirming to the women who attend and for me personally," she told me.

When you choose a favorite spot, it says something about you, as well as something about that spot. Marin County, California holds up the north end of the Golden Gate Bridge. It is known through-out the world for its natural beauty. Rocky seacoast, sandy beaches, golden hills, old redwood forests, and Mount Tamalpais looking down through the clouds all combine to make it a paradise on earth. Diane describes her favorite retreat location, and the effect it has on the women and on her.

> *I hold most of the retreats at a magical mansion on Mt. Tamalpais in Northern California. It was built in 1914 by an early founder of Mill Valley for his wife, and it even has a huge heart-shaped lawn in front. Sometime during the weekend, I'll look up from below and see women on the first-floor porch, or the second- and third-floor balconies and I see playful, spiritual beings. They're in touch with their playful side and their spirit is soaring; they have relaxed into being-ness instead of doing-ness. They've maxed the course!*

When people ask Diane what she does at her women's retreats, she tells them:

> *We laugh, eat, nap, dance in the woods, make crowns and totem dolls, and indulge our inner little girl. Then we laugh, eat, and play some more. We pray by writing our fears on scraps of paper, attaching them to a stick, lighting them on fire, and circling around the fire. We watch the sparks floating up to the stars—and laugh some more!*

> *I always thought it would be utterly divine to have an all-woman church. I didn't want a weekly responsibility, so I do the retreats a couple of times a year. As you know by now, there's a lot of laugher, spontaneous joy, and boundless Ah-has throughout the weekend— and for me spirituality, joy, and play are all wrapped up together. Some smart person whose name I don't recall said, "Joy is the infallible sign of the presence of God."*

Diane explains:

> *I come from the twelve-step traditions where we are encouraged to have a God—as we understand God. One of my best friends, Jan, says her personal deity looks a lot like Mae West. Mae was one of the richest and most powerful people in show business at a time when men dominated it. She explored spirituality, but never a male-centered theology.*

Women feel free to practice our own kind of spirituality when men are not around. The centerpiece of the retreat is the Sunday morning circle. I lead a guided meditation, then ask the women, What would you do if you had no fear? As each woman declares her dream (because that's what naturally bubbles to the surface when we release fear) we all visualize her having or being what she wants.

It's common for women to be totally surprised by what comes out of their mouths, as if they're hearing it for the first time—because by this time in the retreat, the intuitive has taken root. Women have declared the most beautiful, startling, brave, fanciful things. A common one is, "I'd quit my job and do as my heart calls." We all gasped when a woman spoke for us all as she said, "I'd make more noise, and I'd be more me."

Diane recalls dreams revealed by women a recent retreat: I'd paint my front door purple; I'd skydive; I'd open a second-hand store in a small artsy town; I'd paint in Provence; I'd leave my relationship and find real love! "After an eerie moment of silence," she remembers, "we applauded, shouted, stomped our feet and whistled!"

Diane accounts for this reaction like this:

In some mysterious and profound ways, asking that very simple question—What would you do if you had no fear?—produces a jolt of energy, a divine flash that brings assistance into the circle like a bolt out of the blue. Women have reported that amazing coincidences begin popping up after the retreat, sometimes as quickly as on the way home. One woman declared she wanted to travel to Thailand, but had no one to go with. She gave a woman from the retreat a ride home and that women said, "I'll go." I have a picture of them on an elephant in Thailand.

After witnessing the power of that question, I declared at the next retreat that I wanted to write a book with the title, What Would You Do If You Had No Fear? I set about interviewing everyone from clerks to CEOs, cops to former robbers. The experience was spiritual and it changed me in life-affirming ways, just as it did the people I interviewed. In true serendipitous fashion, one of the women from the retreat took the manuscript to a friend in publishing and that's how I got a book contract. I still get fan mail from men and women who say the book produced life-affirming changes for them.

There's just no telling what can happen when you get a bunch of women off by themselves dancing around the fire at night and laughing in the face of fear. It's pure magic!

You can find contact information for Diane Conway and her retreats and books in the resources listed at the back of this book.

Donna Rabuck—Center for the Sacred

Donna Fontanarose Rabuck received her Ph.D. in 1990 with women's studies and writing as her focus. She administers a writing program at the University of Arizona and directs the Center for the Sacred Feminine—a teaching circle and retreat center she created in Tucson, where she nurtures a women's community. The circle has become international, as women come to celebrate sisterhood and experience a paradigm of peace and partnership.

Donna has written extensively in the field of women's studies. Using her academic background in archeology, history, psychology, Western literature, Eastern studies, yoga, and Native studies, she uses the Greek goddesses as archetypes in assisting women in their process of self-inquiry. Donna weaves archetypal images of maiden, mother, wise woman, and crone, along with the cycles of the moon and seasons of the year, creating rituals of celebration and healing.

The Center of the Sacred Feminine offers a spring and fall retreat on the banks of the San Pedro River, where the goddesses of the season are celebrated in nature and within each participant as they practice relaxation, meditation, singing, dancing, and enjoying community with other women.

You can find contact information for Donna and her retreats in the resources listed at the back of this book.

Goddess Gathering, Homegrown Style

Several years ago, I was living in California in a small community house at Muir Beach. We had friends up and down the coast. We began a tradition of Goddess Gatherings, getting together at each of our houses for a weekend of girl time. There were usually about seven of us. Everyone brought food, bedroll, CDs, videos, drums, and rattles. We hiked, watched movies, ate popcorn for dinner, slept late, sat on the beach, took naps, kayaked, and spent nights around the fire talking. The gatherings were affordable, easy (we took turns cooking), and fun. They weren't "spiritual retreats" in the traditional sense—we didn't pray, meditate, or wrestle with deep meaningful questions. We just had fun—Goddess style. We met about four times a year for several years.

These Goddess Gatherings prove that, although going on a formal retreat is good, you should never rule out a homegrown one. They're cheaper and can be just as renewing.

Twelve-step Programs—Walking the Talk

Twelve-step recovery is a grass-roots movement that has an important place in contemporary spirituality. Its primary focus is on embodying our beliefs—as indicated by the chapter in the Big Book of Alcoholics Anonymous entitled *Into Action*. It provides a proven example of how a spiritual program can function according to what can be described as "feminine principles." It has a holistic understanding of addiction and recovery—seeing it as an illness of body, mind, and spirit—and recognizes that healing comes through the spiritual component of the program.

Twelve-step programs are built on the idea of a higher power, as defined by each individual. There are no commandments (only suggestions), no hierarchy, and no authority outside of self and each person's commitment to honesty. Men and women are on equal footing and share leadership. Wisdom is passed through a tradition of sharing personal stories of hope and strength; listeners draw whatever lesson is meaningful to them. There is no preaching, and no one interprets anything for anyone else. And it's ultimately about action—being available to a person who may be in need. But that outreach is by attraction only—never by promotion.

While many places of worship espouse this way of life, few accomplish it in the simple straightforward way that twelve-step communities do. Churches and temples often get caught up in defining God for their members and the necessity of maintaining buildings and parking lots. Twelve-step communities do not own property, but rather meet in a variety of locations, renting space in church basements and clubhouses around the country, therefore avoiding the additional problems of maintaining physical structures.

Twelve-step communities have regularly scheduled meetings that are spontaneous in nature. There are stories of meetings being called in airports or bus stations by travelers in need of support by paging: "Will the friends of Bill W. please come to gate___." Sometimes a crowd of up to thirty people show up for a stranger. This spirituality embodies Matthew 18:19–20: "Wherever two or more are gathered together in my name there I am in the midst of them."

Wrapping Things Up

Space and movement are ancient prayer forms. They assist in the transformational process in a holistic and integrated way—working with the body and renewing the spirit. Women find nourishment in traditional prayer forms and also non-traditional forms that are "new" to the Western world. Getting together as a community of women nourishes the feminine spirit. As women design retreats for each other, they strengthen their spirits, nourish their bodies, and have a good time as the stress of the world falls away. The twelve-step recovery movement is essentially a grass-roots and spontaneous community with no structures; it exists through its embodiment in the lives of its members. It provides a model of spiritual community functioning on feminine principles—non-hierarchal with shared leadership.

Chapter 22

CREATIVITY AND SPIRITUALITY

We are co-creators in an unfinished universe. Our souls long to participate in this process. In the past, as well as now, women's creative spirit has contributed to the development of culture through art, music, dance, literature, philosophy, and healing. Creativity itself is a prayer and a meditation. When you create—whether you take your art form to the professional level, or simply create because when you do so it restores your soul or expresses your spirit—you participate in a spiritual process. Spirituality is creative and creativity is spiritual. Here are the stories of three women who built creativity into their personal, professional, and spiritual lives, told in their own words.

The Friendship Beading Company

Elizabeth recently celebrated her fiftieth birthday. She lives in Alaska with her husband, her two children, and her dog, Neva. She and her husband feel the early years of child-rearing are important and, despite the fact that they cut their income in half, they were willing to make the financial sacrifice for her to be a stay-at-home mom while her children were small. They're now seventeen and twelve; Elizabeth has gone back to work and Bob has become the house-husband for the family. Elizabeth, a nurse, manages two departments at a local hospital—Home Health and Infusion. During her stay-at-home years, she began exploring her creativity and that exploration continues today.

Elizabeth tells how her own personal creativity opened new doors for her:

> *Friendship Beading Company began when one of my friends at church needed a birthday gift, and I offered to make her a piece of jewelry. I got the catalog out and began looking for beads and realized that, if I ordered enough for ten pieces, I could save a lot of money. Even though I had no idea what I would do with the extra nine, I ordered the larger amount. With two kids at home, I needed "grown-up" time, so I got the idea of having a bead party. I used to make quilts, and I know how great it is to sit around and work on a quilt together. I wondered if this feeling would translate into beading. It did, and Friendship Beading Company was born.*

> *I began having parties—kind of a cross between* How to Make an American Quilt *and* Tupperware! *It was fun, and everyone left really happy and proud of the creation they took home. I charged them for the beads and a slight fee for instruction, but my goal wasn't necessarily to make a lot of money. I attend Unity Church and believe in tithing, and I did it right from the start. My beading parties increased, and people wanted to buy my finished products, too. I began to take special orders, and a local shop started carrying my stuff and it was selling very well.*

Letting Go and Letting Goddess

When the time came for Elizabeth to go back to work on a full-time basis, her company was about ready to take off, but she wasn't sure that's what she wanted.

> *I'm happy when I'm in the act of creating, but I don't want all that goes with a larger business. So far, it's all been an almost 100 percent organic and intuitive process. I've followed what makes me happy. I have always loved handwork in any form—beading, quilting, knitting, you name it—and I like people. I discovered a way to bring those two parts of my life together*

My advice is to stay true to what you "feel" like you want to do, and let go of trying to figure it all out. If it's supposed to develop, it will. This is a spiritual principle that I have been attempting to integrate into my life since I first heard it in the twelve-step world as "Let go and let God." I don't think I was able to really get what that meant. Friendship Beading Company is teaching me.

Elizabeth talks about her unique design, which came out of her varied experiences:

I was raised Catholic, and I guess beads get into your genes or something. I have also developed my spirituality through a twelve-step program. As I said, I belong to Unity, and I also follow an earth-based spirituality. Again, by pure synchronicity, all this has converged into one of my best designs—affirmation beads.

Affirmation beads represent mind/body/spirit. The four sections represent the four directions and the four elements. Individual beads set the intention for that decade. There are ten beads in each section, because the number ten symbolizes completion.

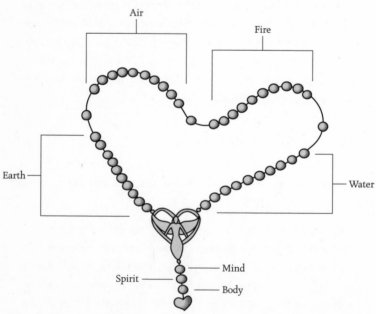

FIGURE 23. *Affirmation beads.*

Elizabeth's advice regarding getting your creativity started is simply: "Do it! Carve out the time and space and be willing to guard it like a bull dog." She feels lucky because her family understands how important her art is to her. It feeds her creative juices and makes her life work. She has a room in the house dedicated to whatever art form she is currently pursuing. "That makes a big difference in my life," she says. "Whether your thing is art, cooking, walking, or whatever, make sure you make room for it in your life. Women have trouble letting themselves have what they need. But it's important. You may have to let some other things go—like folding everyone's clothes, or keeping the house like a magazine cover—but choose your battles and move on!" See the resources listed at the back of this book for Friendship Beading Company contact information.

Following the Impulse

Sydney is a sculptor who nestled into a slice of land between two steep Tennessee hills thirty years ago and built a house and studio. She designed the space and created almost everything in it, from the bathroom sink to its eleven handcrafted doors. Much of who she is grew out of her relationship to the land.

Pushing the Edges

Sydney pushes her art to the limits. Her life as an artist began as a result of what she was "not"—in this case, a good student. "When I couldn't make a nice, smooth handle for a clay pot, I made them into tree trunks or other irregular forms," she says.

> Later, I mastered the techniques, but my personal style had been created out of those earlier shapes. When I couldn't keep my pots perfectly centered on the wheel, my art pushed deeper into the boundaries of that irregularity. My difficulties at school left me searching for the thing that would give me a place on the planet. Art became the vehicle for that search. Clay provided a strong physical connection—I loved its earthy sensuousness and what I discovered evolved naturally out of me.

Sydney is an artist of many mediums; she sees them all as extensions of the same impulse. Here, she describes her relationship with her land and her art—spinning poetry out of words.

> I live in a valley of water and light moving the seasons. Between soft round mounds of moss and frosted stars. Long limbs of naked winter hardwood dance ever-changing from whatever moon, wind, mist, storm breathes a new view. I eat and drink these images, and they have become the seeds of dreams. Chant of the angel toads and vibration of a woodpecker's African drumming on the edge of a spring-lit forest. This texture is the soil of soul and calls me home gut-driven and working across an alchemist playground. Hammering a vision. Welding the puzzle. Pounding the subtext. Carving the rhythm. It's the beat of the earth I work. A journey longing for form from chaos and madness to some kind of peace. Built out of land, the hand, and a large dose of magic.

Hornet Spit and Ginger Ale

A large copper sculpture mounted on a wooden platform floated across the pond in front of us as Sydney and I talked, and water trickled over rocks and down a waterfall she had built. She points to the sourwood trees growing along the bank and talks of the particularly sweet honey that comes from them. A newly formed hornets' nest hangs on a low branch just outside the screen porch. "Did you know that whole thing is made of fly wings and hornet spit?" she asked. I didn't, but was totally captured by the image.

Sydney doesn't separate spirituality from nature and from her artistic expression. She talks about the balance between masculine and feminine—the natural order. When that balance is compromised, as it is among humans right now, there are problems. She referred to the out-of-control building going on all over her county as "the male psyche run amok," adding that women participate in this craziness, too. "When nature is balanced, there is an amazing dance of creation," She observed. We tossed around our ideas on this topic and came to the conclusion that "nature" will survive, even if our little corner of creation as human beings does not!

Just then, a small troop of hornets came out of their nest and began repairing the paper-thin layers that make their home—spitting and patting the fly wings. We lifted our ginger ales and toasted them. "We're every age we've ever been," Sydney told me. "Our history is imprinted in us. Our visual image changes as we grow; the old form breaks open and new forms emerge. My job as an artist is to open the form and give the new one freedom to fly."

Work = Love = Beauty!

Jackie sees spirituality as the business of soul work. It's getting to the essence of self and why we are here—and pursuing it. According to Jackie, we can't always get there without a bit of trial and error! "Assignments," she calls them.

"Spirituality makes you a bigger container for God's love—it builds on what you have and prepares you for the next encounter here or in the next life," Jackie says. She feels that Spirit guides the process—if we are willing to follow where it leads. The way that works the best for her is to find what you resonate with and pursue it—enlarge your sensitivity to it. She recently practiced that principle in regard to her music and her growth as a person, and produced her own CD aptly named *Insoulful*. In her music and in her life, she attends to her soul work.

Jackie is a professional musician, singer, songwriter, and counselor. She draws no distinction between her creativity and her spirituality. She grew up with music. Her father was a jazz musician and a professor of Musicology at a local university. He played the viola in the symphony and jazz on an upright bass. Her mother's gift to her was teaching her to be true to herself. The combination has made Jackie an artist in her music and very much her own person. Her ancestry is rooted in African, Caribbean, Native American, and Caucasian cultures, which feed into her music, making it a unique fusion of jazz, blues, classical, and black Southern gospel. One of her favorite songs on her CD is "Solomon's Love Song," which she composed drawing on images from the scriptural Song of Solomon.

Jackie asked me to play the CD while we were talking, because she wasn't sure of the lyrics. "The words came out as I was singing; I didn't write them down or memorize them," she told me. "That particular piece has a different composition than most songs—it's not made up of verses and a chorus—rather it is a story." For her, the story tells of "a wise and balanced kind of love. Sensuous rather than sexy—it portrays love and sexuality, not in an enslaved way, but as a gift from God. It is saying to a couple. 'Love this human like you love God.' Not to be confused with making the other person or the relationship your God, but to infuse it with the love of God."

Jackie describes two kinds of love she learned about in studying the *Course in Miracles*—special love and enchanted love. Special love grows when partners draw from each other. They come into it needing or wanting, and take what they need from each other. This, of course, runs its course and ultimately fails. Enchanted love grows when each partner is spiritually connected to source and the relationship becomes the container into which they pour God's love. This kind of love is boundless.

Making her album was a spiritual process, according to Jackie. There were times when her ultra-critical side took over and she hated to hear her voice played back.

> It was a raw part of myself I didn't want people to know about or to hear. It made me feel too vulnerable. Now when I hear it, I am struck by how good it sounds—I forget it's me and want to say, "Come over here and listen to this! This sister is good."

In the process of making the CD, Jackie had to open up and trust her fellow musicians. It was a case of art mirroring life—trust and being open are her spiritual challenges. I asked her what changed for her in making her album. She said, "I changed from being a performer to being a singer," a relationship she described as "more about myself and my music than about entertaining someone else."

Jackie carries on her family traditions as teacher, mentor, and liberator—helping women in their journey to becoming themselves. She counsels women in a local addiction-recovery center in Nashville. She works with them individually and in groups, and also has developed a therapeutic process using music as a healing modality. Jackie describes how it works:

> Music is a universal language. It can alter your mood and your mind just as well as any drug. For patients, music breaks down

defenses, creates a bridge, increases a sense of well-being, and decreases stress. It is a common denominator, leveling out differences internally and externally. For caregivers, it can be an energizer. I tell my colleagues, we are so steeped in trauma every day, go home and take a music bath!

Jackie has a daughter who has her own relationship with her source and as a parent. This is the accomplishment of which she is most proud—that she encouraged her daughter to question, to seek, and to practice spiritual principles in all areas of her life. Her seven-year-old granddaughter, named Grace, lives up to her name—not to mention that she looks like an angel. See the resources listed at the back of this book for *Insoulful* contact information.

Wrapping Things Up

Spirituality celebrates our ongoing involvement in creation. The women in this chapter create because they feel the spirit. Making money or turning their art form into a business is not off the screen for them—some are financially successful artists. But creativity as spiritual expression is the driving force behind their work, rather than money or fame. Our creativity doesn't always receive the attention it deserves, but it is a soul expression that simply won't be stopped. Through our creative outpouring, we learn more about ourselves, more about the human story, and more about God's action in the world. Artists offer encouragement for women to find the time to do what they love to do, and to be willing to guard it. Find what makes you happy and do it. That's how spirit leads us!

Part V

TRANSFORMING CULTURE

This section looks at the innovative work of women who are impacting society through healing, teaching, and creating social systems. You'll see the progression of ideas as these holistic concepts that began outside traditional systems are eventually woven into nursing-school curriculum and practice. We'll look at multi-level projects that began healing racial relations between black and white women in the South, and two social programs that integrate services, cross boundaries, and address needs in visionary and practical ways. It concludes with a project about women and power that has gained national recognition.

Throughout history, as we are doing today, women express their generous and caring spirituality by stepping forward and doing what needs to be done—not for fame or fortune, but because it needs to be done. This reflects our sense of justice and concern for others. As you read this section, notice the particular character of the work and the projects; they carry the unique imprint of women.

Chapter 23

❧❀❧

HEALING BODY AND SOUL

Women's spirituality identifies the separation of body and soul as the wound of Western culture. In this chapter, you'll hear about women whose pioneering efforts have developed healing modalities that address that wound. This a story of women who stepped outside the system, developed their healing arts, eventually seeing them become part of the educational system. Their pioneering work has improved traditional health care, both in theory and practice.

Sarah Stewart—Integrated Healing Arts

Sarah Stewart puts a whole new spin on the term "born again"! A health-care provider for more than forty years, she is a visionary and pioneer using both allopathic and holistic modalities. She draws on her experiences as a nurse, massage therapist, yoga teacher, herbalist, hypnotherapist, mother, and grandmother. Stewart is a member of the Pre- and Peri-Natal Association, the American Council of Hypnosis Examiners, the Holistic Nurses Association, and the International Massage Association. Her school, The Institute of Integrated Healing Arts, was founded in 1982. In 1987, it expanded to include instruction on clinical hypnotherapy and yoga. A sister school was opened in Nashville in 1992. Stewart maintains a private practice in Sonoma, California. Here is her remarkable story—in her own words.

God's in the Rooster

Stewart grew up in a small house on the family farm.

> My grandfather was Cherokee, and my grandmother was pure country. She didn't believe in the God you find at church, but her faith was very strong. She used to say, "See that rooster over there? God is in that rooster, and he will feed you. We're going to kill that old bird and have it for dinner!" She would grab it by the feet and chop off its head. The feathers would fly, and the rooster would be in the pan before they hit the ground.

Stewart talks about life on the farm as holistic in the truest sense of the word.

> We plowed the field, planted the seed, harvested the crops, fed the animals, watched the eggs hatch, and saw the horses and cows mating and knew it would result in baby animals in the spring. There wasn't any part of the life cycle we weren't directly involved with—including death.

Stewart describes holistic practices as engaging *chi*, the body energy that is the basis of most non-Western medical models. As we learned in a previous chapter, chi is the living force that runs through the body along meridian lines. If the meridians become blocked (think of kinks in a hose), the energy can't get nourishment to all parts of the body. Systems and organs begin to break down. Massage, hands-on energy work, herbs, acupuncture, acupressure, meditation, or even a walk in the woods can reduce the stress and open the channels again, allowing the life-giving energy to flow. We can pass this healing energy to others (think battery cables and jump-starting a car) and stimulate their innate healing abilities. Stewart talks about her introduction to being a healer:

> My mother died in childbirth when I was thirteen years old, and my new-born brother died with her. She had three other children born healthy and easily at home under the caring supervision of my grandmother—in the same room in which she was born. What

went wrong this time? Well, the doctor was going on vacation, and three pregnant women were due at the same time. He put all three in the hospital at once and induced labor. My mother was one of these women. She hemorrhaged to death as a result of being induced and of not being properly attended during her labor, and my brother strangled with the cord around his neck.

When she died, her image came to me in a vision. There was peace in her eyes as she looked directly at me and smiled, "Take good care of the kids for me. I have to go now." Then she disappeared, and I was left holding my eleven-month-old brother and looking at my eleven-year-old sister in the corner of the room. A few hours later, they came to tell me she had died, but I already knew it. That experience left its imprint on my life in ways that are still being discovered.

"Baby" Consciousness

Stewart wanted to be a doctor, but with her mother's death, there would be no chance. So she did what many women do: she went to nursing school.

In addition to her traditional education as a nurse, Stewart's professional training included many years of practicing yoga. She knows that this spiritual discipline strengthened her and opened up many levels of awareness that she uses in her healing work today. In her thirties, she traveled to the Philippines to work with the psychic surgeons she had heard about. Her healing abilities were recognized, and she was allowed to assist them and ultimately to work side-by-side with them. Although she does not use psychic surgery in her practice, she knows that the experience opened more levels of healing within her.

Stewart continued to pursue her studies in the blossoming field of holistic health, this time with Dr. David Cheek, a pioneering obstetrician/gynecologist practicing in San Francisco. Cheek was a friend and associate of Dr. Milton Erickson, who is considered to be the father of hypnosis in Western medicine. Cheek believed that babies had consciousness in the womb, having both sensory and cognitive awareness. He treated many of his clients with hypnosis to relieve stress during pregnancy and to facilitate pain-free and drug-free deliveries. He encouraged starting the parent-child relationship at the beginning of pregnancy.

Before Rebirth—Reconception

Building on Cheek's work, Stewart began to design a process she calls Reconception, in which she uses regression to take a person back through their experiences of conception, their gestation in the womb, and birth.

> The mother's emotional state, her spiritual awareness, as well as her physical health all create the climate in which the baby spends almost the first year of life. Re-birthing is popular, and it's a good way of clearing birth traumas; however, many additional things have already happened to the mother and child at the time of conception and throughout pregnancy that leave lasting imprints on the soulbody.
>
> I have worked with pregnant women and their families for many years as a spiritual midwife to the whole family. I prepare them for birthing at home or in the hospital using yoga, breath, hypnosis, massage, and just being there during the pregnancy and delivery. My goal is to help parents and siblings realize that the child within has consciousness. I also emphasize that the family can help this spirit feel loved and wanted. This takes many forms, including stories by the big sister, conversations with the baby, and the traditional preparations of gathering the baby's things. When arrangements are made lovingly with the intention of welcoming the baby, the child is much more likely to be a secure, loving person. This establishes a lifetime pattern that affects every aspect of being a full person, and these positive feelings will be transmitted to everyone he or she meets.

Stewart is currently writing a book about her innovative process entitled *Reconception*.

An Integrated Vision

Stewart was on retreat at an ashram in India when a vision of her school came to her, showing her the combination of healing arts that she would offer. She describes her work this way:

The body contains our emotional memory. If the memories are good, they contribute to good health. If they are painful, the opposite is true. By combining the hands-on healing of massage with deep relaxation and hypnosis regression along with yoga breathing exercises, emotional trauma from the body can be released.

Stewart has worked with hundreds of students, teaching them her integrated approach to healing. She approaches her teaching in a very personal way.

Everyone brings individual strengths and offers a little different approach to their healing work. This is important to recognize. The philosophy of Integrated Healing Arts is to use this diversity to create powerful healing modalities that work with the same set of principles, yet honor the individual healer. The "integration" factor of Integrated Healing Arts works at many levels. It integrates right and left hemispheres of the brain by teaching cognitive skills and developing intuitive healing abilities; it integrates new techniques with the body of knowledge each student brings with them; and it integrates past with present, allowing the future to be a transformed one.

Stewart reminds her students and clients: "There is no need to carry the pain from the past into the future." Her school is licensed and leads to a certification in clinical hypnotherapy, massage therapy, or yoga instruction.

When Stewart looks back over her life—her childhood, the loss of her mother, letting go of her dream to go to medical school, and the subsequent events that have taken her all over the world to study with the healers of many different cultures—she feels a powerful affirmation of being on her true spiritual path. "I am doing the work I feel I was born to do, and I love doing it. I have followed my visions, my intuition, and my inner guidance, and it has served me well. I guess I will continue to follow it."

See the resources listed at the back of this book for contact information for Sarah Stewart and training events at Integrated Healing Arts.

Betty Stadler—Curiosity Leads Her

Betty Stadler is certified as a family nurse-practitioner, healing-touch practitioner, healing-touch instructor, clinical hypnotherapist, and

Reiki master. She is a medical consultant, helping bridge the gap between traditional Western medicine and alternative healing arts. She has had a private practice in mind/body health since 1993, and has been teaching holistic nursing seminars and healing touch since 1991. Stadler sees herself as supporting holistic health as a lifestyle. Her vision is to see conventional health care bridged with complementary health-care practices to facilitate a philosophy of treating the whole person. She had an opportunity to see her vision into reality. She was instrumental in developing the Holistic Nursing program at Tennessee State University in Nashville—one of the only programs like it in the country.

Regarding her transition from Western to holistic medicine, Stadler believes "It's always a mystery how we get where we are. I guess the bottom line is that curiosity leads me."

Following the Urge

Besides her natural curiosity, Stadler credits yoga with facilitating some of the changes in her life. She began practicing yoga at a self-awareness center, which led to a workshop where she learned intuitive decision-making. Through the process, she found herself making decisions she would probably not have made using straight-up left-brain logic. From there, her intuition "opened up a whole chain of events," one of which was the study of Reiki, an energetic healing process from Japan. Her advice to those in the healing professions is simple: "Every now and then you should ask yourself why you're doing this work. It helps keep your ego out of the way."

Stadler's interest in Reiki was just the beginning:

Curiosity led me to the American Holistic Nurses Association, where I found healing touch. I felt the urge to investigate, and it turned out to be a major component in my life. I had gone back to graduate school to recapture some of the excitement I had once felt about nursing. As my career developed, I was getting farther away from the people and more involved in administration. I wanted more hands-on nursing. Healing touch brought it to me. I knew almost instantly that I would learn it and teach it!

Healing touch is a healing technique that works with the energy field, affecting body, mind, emotions, and spirit. Its philosophy believes all healing is self-healing. The practitioner aligns the energy flow, reactivating the mind/body/spirit connection to eliminate blocks to self-healing.

University of Miami's Medical School documented studies showing that the use of hands-on techniques like healing touch facilitates a person's recovery from surgery and burns. Premature infants have a higher growth rate when healing touch is part of their care. More than 30,000 hospitals in the United States now use these modalities and consider them legitimate medical techniques. In most major cities, it is becoming increasingly common for teams of medical doctors and nurses to combine allopathic medical skills with hands-on and energy techniques.

Reawakening Spirituality

Stadler's work with healing touch led her to spirituality. "I consider healing as a ritual—through my work I have come to a deeper understanding of my religion," she says. Healing touch reawakened her earlier sense of spirituality. She was raised Catholic and talks about how religion and spirituality were all wrapped up together in the church experiences of her childhood. As meditation became a regular part of her yoga practice, she realized that she had actually learned how to meditate as a child, in time spent silently sitting in church. She talked about the smell of incense, Gregorian chants, ceremonies, and rituals of her childhood—particularly the May crowning:

> Girls wore white dresses and carried baskets of rose petals. We had a procession all around the church, singing as we walked. As we passed in front of the statue of Mary, we took handfuls of rose petals, kissed them, and dropped them on the floor at her feet.

The physical body was very much a part of these rituals—walking, singing, wearing special clothes, carrying rose petals, smelling the incense—"wiring" the brain spiritually and holistically. Stadler discovered that food plays a part as well:

> I have recently discovered how great a part food plays in our spiritual development as well as our health and well-being. When we eat fresh fruit and vegetables, and eat slowly with intention, our energy field expands, getting much bigger and energized. When

we eat denser food, and eat on the run, our energy field compresses. Even during the preparation of fresh food, your energy and the energy of the food begin to interact. It is actually transmitting its life force to you.

Food is very spiritual, and preparing food is a spiritual act. I nourish my spirit continually and in many ways: daily meditation, checking with my inner connection with the divine throughout the day, prayer, and nature. One of my favorite ways to feed my spirit is by a walking meditation in the woods. I sleep with my windows open so I can listen to the birds at sunrise.

Stadler goes on to say: "It is like coming full circle. I draw on those early experiences in the spiritual aspect of my work—I know from *experience* that the body and spirit are one."

Stadler considers healing touch and her medical practice as ministry. The course work she teaches incorporates a spiritual history of healing in the Judeo-Christian tradition, grounding it in scripture. For her, it was personal experiences both as practitioner and patient that made the body/mind/spirit connection a physical reality she experienced, not just a philosophy.

Healing Images

Stadler studied hypnotherapy and found it increased her understanding of how she enters an altered state of consciousness along with her client, giving her insight into the client's process. She calls this a spiritual realm. Insight may come through images, words, or thoughts. This requires therapists to develop the ability to distinguish personal thoughts and feelings from those coming from the client. Therapists therefore become actively engaged in their own process. Stadler adds that, when there is any doubt, she checks things out with her clients, letting them know what she is seeing or intuiting and asking them what it means to them. In this way, she can be the means by which a client gains insight. "It isn't about me getting it right, but about being an instrument in the healing process," says Stadler.

This is the predominant character of holistic healers. In recognizing the innate healing abilities of each person, the practitioner's ego stays out of the way.

It's obvious to me when it creeps back in. I feel a charge inside of myself, a need to be right, and I immediately step back. I don't know if we ever completely eliminate ego, but we can recognize its presence. There are three things I learned early in my career in healing touch that create the environment in which healing can occur: intention, presence, and acceptance.

Before working with someone, I set my intention, turning the healing process over to God. Presence happens by my staying focused on the client, paying good attention to what I am sensing and feeling. Acceptance is where I as the practitioner completely let go my agenda; that is, I let go of the need for anything to happen and get completely out of the way. Then I can open up to the process. In those moments, something bigger comes through.

The Truth about Aging!

Stadler finds that spirituality differs among individuals, regardless of whether they are men or women.

It comes in many shapes and forms and is often not recognized for what it is. We have so intertwined religion and spirituality that people often don't recognize their own spirituality. I help people find their passion and realize how their passion connects them with the divine. Men are generally farther away from recognizing their spirituality than women because, in our current society, they are taught to be less connected to their feelings—to "suck it up," be strong, and don't show emotions.

Stadler believes that her therapeutic skills get better with age because of developmental shifts that happen as we get older, and also because of her own spiritual progress. "At this point in life, I realize it's all spiritual. I've become aware of the interconnectedness of everything and everyone." She talks about finding the intrinsic beauty in even the smallest things throughout each day. "When I was younger, I was busy doing and discovering the world outside myself; now it is about the inner space," she notes. It's through this deepening that she is able to provide the freedom for her clients to make the connections for themselves. She smiled a knowing smile and said, "Aging is the opposite of what society tells you it is."

Betty Stadler passed away during the writing of this book. She leaves behind her many contributions to the healing profession. She is missed by her many students and friends.

Deanna Naddy—Ironweed and Other Wild Things

The first time I met Deanna Naddy, I found her crouched behind the back porch of her old Victorian farmhouse planting flowers. She put down her garden tools and asked me if I'd like to see the farm. She disappeared around the corner for a few minutes and reappeared at the wheel of an old 1984 Nissan pickup, which, coughing and gasping, transported us across fields where ironweed and other wild things towered over our heads. We lurched over hill and dale, finally coming to rest near a beautiful stream. From there, we set out on foot, climbing a series of good-size hills, where we checked on the wild ginseng.

On the way back to the house, we crossed a grazing pasture, made our way through a herd of cows, passed two barns, and stopped to throw a load of wood into the huge furnace beside the garage. Then we came through the side door into her kitchen. Without pausing to rest, she pulled a couple of pieces of salmon and two small steaks out of the refrigerator and began to toss a salad. "How about lunch?" she asked.

This was obviously a woman of considerable strength and more than a few facets. We ate and retreated to the front porch swing, where we talked for hours, interrupted periodically by a grandchild or two (twelve in all) coming through on their way to Grandma's kitchen.

Getting to the Roots

Naddy is the former head of the Nursing program at Columbia State Community College in Tennessee. She grew up in Kansas and began her career at the University of Kansas, where she completely accepted the Western medical model of working with disease. She remembers being horrified to find out her mother went to a chiropractor. She went on to get her Master's and doctorate, specializing in mental health. Her career has included working in public health, a medical surgery unit in a small hospital, operating-room nursing, managing a clinic in Jordan for the U. S. Embassy, and thirty years in nursing education.

Naddy describes her transition from allopathic to holistic medicine as following her natural curiosity and recognizing that traditional Western medicine does not get down to the issues that underlie disease. She recalled her mother's trips to the chiropractor and realized that medical doctors could treat back pain only with surgery or drugs; they didn't get to the root causes. She observed her own patterns of stress and how high levels of it often resulted in getting sick. At the same time, people began to come into her life and introduce her to different holistic practices. She was open to explore and receive this new information.

In 1995, 41 percent of the population of the United States used one or more alternative healing methods, either to complement or substitute for traditional medical techniques. It is now estimated that 60 cents out of every health-care dollar is spent on alternative therapies.

One of the first holistic healers Naddy met was Betty Stadler, the woman in the preceding story. Naddy invited Stadler to teach a class to her Nursing faculty (mainly so she could learn the fascinating healing-touch technique, she confessed), and then observe the results on the faculty as well as herself. "Despite the fact that many in the class didn't believe in the process, they began to get better anyway—their energy levels rose and they laughed more."

The Joy of Learning

Naddy signed up for subsequent courses in many holistic healing techniques. Her philosophy expanded, particularly regarding the belief that healing begins when people take charge of their own health. She was introduced to the important use of herbs and natural products as alternatives to prescription drugs. She began to explore other modalities, like the use of guided imagery, meditation, yoga, tai chi, Reiki, Earth philosophy, and hypnotherapy. The most transformational experience for her came after a class in Bowen Therapy, a gentle hands-on body technique from Australia.

Naddy traveled to Peru and Israel, where she learned to be silent and go inside herself, and to listen to the voice of creation. "You know, you can be still and learn things," she said to me with amazement in her voice.

Today, she assists people in their healing by listening to their stories and using her extensive background and training to recommend appropriate therapies. She knows her experience in both the allopathic and holistic worlds gives her expertise and also credibility. Sometimes, she uses her own story as a way of connecting with her clients, knowing that her transformation from a straight medical practitioner to holistic healer helps them trust the process.

Naddy believes that spirit is the energetic basis of all life. She nourishes hers in nature and by connecting with God. This year, she and her partner planted several hundred blueberry plants—she may have overshot her goal, she adds. Rather than an "Aha!" kind of spiritual awakening, she describes hers as a process—a series of smaller steps rather than one big leap (with the possible exception of the blueberry project). "I know I get guidance; I know I miss some along the way because I don't always listen; but I know it's there when I need it." As to what motivates her to continue to learn and grow, she says simply "It brings me joy."

Debra Wilson—Buddhism, Tibetan Medicine, and Nursing Theory

Debra Rose Wilson has a doctorate in Health Psychology with an emphasis in psycho-neuro-immunology (PSI). This field of study has provided a scientific basis for holism and proved to be absolutely necessary for holistic philosophy to be taken seriously by established medicine. It's based in the understanding that beliefs, emotions, attitudes, habits, and cultural and family dynamics impact health in both positive or negative ways. Wilson's doctoral thesis illustrated the connection between early abuse, particularly sexual abuse, and a multitude of health problems.

Wilson is an assistant professor in the graduate Nursing program at Middle Tennessee State University (MTSU) and also teaches for Walden University's online program in Psychology. Before she took her current position, she was an instructor at Tennessee State University, where she shaped the innovative advanced-degree program in Holistic Nursing mentioned in Stadler's story. Her current position has taken her to Botswana in Africa, where she has helped strengthen the educational process for nurses and promoted nursing as a career choice.

Pieces of the Mirror

Wilson's understanding of holism comes from Buddhism and Tibetan medicine, as well as from the nursing theory of Rosemarie Parse, who developed the Human Becoming Theory. Wilson identifies holistic nursing as meeting the needs identified by the patient in that moment, as perceived by that person. Her experience working with children on the street taught her the wisdom of that philosophy. She gives this example:

> When talking with a pregnant teenager on the street, regardless of the circumstances—such as homelessness, an active addiction, cocaine, cigarette smoking, or anything else—if she thinks she needs to drink more milk and everything will be okay, that's where you begin. If you try to tell her what you think the real problem is, you've lost her. If you go with what she presents as her greatest concern, you've got a way in to the whole person.

Wilson sees spirituality as a developmental process of recognizing wholeness. "Religion can be one of the ways we develop our spirituality, but there are many ways to do it," she declares. She uses the analogy of God's reflection in a mirror:

> The mirror breaks, scattering the pieces—but each contains part of the image. If a religion picks up one of the shards and believes it has the whole picture rather than just a piece, it's problematic. Spirituality is about finding wholeness, and that is a two-fold process of self-discovery and connection with others who are on a similar path. You must find your truth, stop along the way and sort through your old beliefs, and find out what is true and not true for you. It's like the snake shedding its skin—as it grows bigger each year, it gets too tight.

Paradox and Creative Tension

For Wilson, truth is found in paradox. "The tension between two opposing beliefs can be creative," she says. "When you can identify the conflict and sit with it, a solution arises. It is our nature." An example can be seen in her relationship to her grandmother, whom Wilson describes as "a Hungarian healer and extraordinary herbalist."

At the same time, she had a mean streak. She sought power from her healing. She could sense vulnerability and go right for it. I could see it even as a child. Should I negate all her abilities because she was so mean? Do I pretend she wasn't mean so it doesn't conflict with my idea of a healer? Both observations were true. My thinking had to expand and accept the paradox. My grandmother was both those things—a healer and a mean woman!

Wilson believes this is life's essential dilemma. When we identify the opposing parts in a situation and hold them in tension, creative solutions result.

Wilson follows the theory of creative paradox in healing, believing as Buddhists believe that disease and other challenges come as both the problem and also the transformer. "When a person can locate the meaning the disease has for them," she believes, "they can transcend the illness or the challenge they are facing and get on with life."

Wilson's holism is both imaginative and pragmatic—she refers to it as existential and transformational at a practical level. She encourages patients to recognize their traumatic injury and draw power from it—asking how it can become a positive influence in their lives *today*. Getting on with life doesn't always mean curing the disease. It can mean changing your relationship to the disease—how you experience it.

"Disease prevention is an important ingredient in holism, too. Good nutrition and other health practices are part of the process," Wilson says. Her bottom-line philosophy is that those seeking healing hold the key to their own recovery. They know what they need. The job of the practitioner is to pay attention. She believes she needs to walk the talk in her own personal life as well.

Nursing is a demanding profession, as is teaching. Wilson knows you have to make conscious choices to maintain balance and good health. For example, she walks her dog, Barkley, when she is stressed. "I may not feel like walking him, but I know it's the right thing to do." She gardens, and recently spent a month at her lake home in Canada, near where she was born. She talks about setting boundaries and eliminating negative people from her life. She describes her relationship with her husband as based on respect and love, and as one of the places where she is nourished. She also meditates and finds it a source of renewal.

Wrapping Things Up

The four women's stories in this chapter show how changes happen in the system. Sarah Stewart began her career as a nurse. She stepped outside the box and began developing non-traditional healing arts, opening a school in which she has taught many, including Betty Stadler, who was instrumental in developing a university program in Holistic Nursing. Stadler influenced Deanna Naddy, who further integrated alternative healing with nursing. A generation later, Debra Rose Wilson earned a doctorate in Health Psychology with an emphasis in psycho-neuro-immunology (PSI), which provided a scientific basis for holism. It's important to note how relatively quickly (in one generation) these huge changes have been made—with women leading the way.

Chapter 24

❦❧ ❦❧

BUILDING BRIDGES AND
CREATING CULTURE

Women's spirituality isn't just a female thing. It encompasses the repository for social values that both men and women share. In this chapter, you'll read about three projects that are transforming culture. The first is the work of a woman from the Dominican Republic whose insight and expertise developed a multi-level project dealing with race relations. The second was developed by a woman from Tennessee to provide a safe place for African American women and their children to heal from addiction. The third story tells how three people from very diverse backgrounds came together to show that women's spirituality isn't just a "girl thing." In this story, men and women work together on a creative project that will to help make a better society. Here are their stories—in their own words.

Noris Binet—Black and White
Women Building a Bridge

In 1990, Noris Binet, a native of the Dominican Republic, moved to Tennessee. Soon after, she had a vision for a project that could begin the healing process between black and white women in her community. She spearheaded a multi-level project called Black and

White Women Building a Bridge in the Land of the Native American. It began on the 500th anniversary of the European occupation of the Americas.

Binet's project unfolded over a four-year period and involved rituals, small group discussions, public forums, and an art show—all focused on issues of race. Binet's qualifications for such a project are unique. Born and raised in the Dominican Republic. she lived for thirteen years in Mexico, where she studied with the Huichol Indians. For the past twenty-one years, she has made her home in the United States. Her Caribbean ancestry includes African, Native American, and Caucasian influences.

Tapping into Huichol Wisdom

Binet's work has brought her to a realization of the importance of creating environments where women can be truly themselves—places where their visions and identities are acknowledged and validated. When this safe space is created, they naturally explore and embrace who they are—they find their creative and spiritual identities.

Binet believes women are innate healers and naturally see connections. She had a vision of how women artists could come together and begin to build a bridge between the races that would create new experiences of each other and provide a new way of seeing themselves. She set out to help design and build that bridge.

Binet brought many years of experience to the project—gained through immersion in and study of native and international culture, as well as her study as a sociologist and therapist. She had participated in many large celebrations in Mexico, where art, theater, dance, ceremony, and politics all freely mixed on a regular basis. She knew the power of these celebrations:

Every time you look out the window you see the priest, altar boys, men, and women carrying candles and holy pictures processing down the middle of the street. Many are wearing costumes or carrying big masks representing whatever local politics are going on. It's the natural way for Latin people.

In addition to her training and experience, Binet brings her particular gifts of creative thinking, tireless energy, and a vision of how even a few can make a big difference.

> This project explores the multifaceted aspects of bridges. It is not only the physical bridge created by the very existence of the artwork of this group of women, but that this group of women worked together in several workshops, building emotional and spiritual bridges and exploring one of the most important bridges—the one that each individual started to build within herself, with her body, with her inner self, with her creative process and her healing energy.
>
> (Women on the Inner Journey [James C. Winston, 1994])

The model Binet used to create her far-reaching project of social healing is an ancient Huichol Indian ceremonial form. She felt that was particularly significant, because the project would begin on the 500th anniversary of European occupation of America, and because she knew firsthand what a powerful transformational process it offered.

> I had to begin by getting a clear picture of who I was in this project and what my intention was. I saw myself as a bridge. I am not black or white; I am both. I'm also an outsider; I had been codified differently. My culture is more inclusive; everyone is racially mixed. There is a statue outside of the Museum of Modern Art in the Dominican Republic acknowledging the mixing of race. Here in the United States, at least in Nashville in 1990, it wasn't talked about. Yet most blacks have white and Indian blood, and most whites have black and Indian blood. I could look at the women and see how they were alike, rather than different. The issue isn't skin color; it's conditioning—it is how you are taught to see.

Breaking Old Boundaries

Binet talks about the project:

> The prejudices I had to deal with were my light skin color, which made the black women uneasy; my "not white, either," skin, which made the white women uneasy; and my status as a foreigner from a third-world country that made everyone uneasy. Because of the level of distrust that existed between the two groups of women, I designed this project as a process rather than an event. I knew it

would have to be deeper than just a showing of art; we would have to deal with the past. I also knew we should not begin with words, as words would lead to accusations, guilt, and run the risk of further separation. Words express thoughts, and thoughts are always in the past. They are reflections on our experience. If things were going to change, we needed new experiences of one another. That would give us something new to reflect on.

Perhaps the most essential part of this project is that it is created and developed by common people who believe that something can be done to create change. Using their personal resources, they are taking responsibility for creating a better place to live. It is time for people from small places to be heard. It is not only people in cosmopolitan urban areas who have options to offer.

Binet remembers:

The white women were filled with fear, guilt, and denial. The black women were filled with fear, anger, and denial. I also recognized that sheer panic existed just below the surface and the volatility of what we were attempting. I knew we needed to build a common spiritual ground on which healing could happen. We needed an altar, a ceremony, and a new way of being together.

We began with a series of workshops in which the women could get to know each other. We built our altars, danced, and even created music together. We were breaking through the isolation and individuality of this culture; the women were thirsty for the experience and for the expression of community. We were breaking boundaries— women who had been afraid to touch each other's skin were dancing together. They were looking at each other's faces and seeing into each other's eyes. We were breathing the same air, laughing, and crying together. Soon we had footings for our bridge. By the time the show opened, we could actually stand there together, holding hands, moving together, singing the music we had composed, looking at our art hanging on the walls. Now we had something to celebrate!

Signs, Symbols, and Synchronicity

Shortly after Binet conceived Black and White Women, the impressive statue of Athena Parthenos was unveiled inside Nashville's

Parthenon, a full-scale replica of the ancient Greek temple. Artist Alan LeQuire's rendering of the Goddess of Wisdom fills the building, standing over three stories tall. Binet talked about the synchronistic meaning of the event for her. "Athena represented a new archetype to the people of Greece. She symbolized a new partnership, birthing a new order of divine and human relationship."

> On the opposite side of synchronicity, the Rodney King riots coincided with the workshop. People were in the streets in thirteen cities all across America, and the media was totally focused on it. Suddenly it was clear: We have a racial problem in this country, and we can't hide it. We didn't know what would happen. We even wondered if the Ku Klux Klan might be outside. But we felt that we could make a difference that day, and we did. On a very personal and intimate level and as a society, healing happened. In light of the King riots, I think everyone in the community was pulling for us and praying for us.

Binet feels the project was successful. "We went through a process together, and our lives were changed. We saw how it wasn't always necessary to work on a big scale, that a few coming together could change our perceptions and perhaps provoke a change in the larger culture."

Binet is presently involved in community-building among Anglo, Latino, and African-American women in the Sonoma Valley of California. One of the projects is creating a multi-cultural altar for the celebration of the Day of the Dead. The purpose of the project is to create a safe place for women's spiritual expression and to build bicultural community.

SISTERS—Building a New World

Women's spirituality is often directed toward transforming culture and bettering society. Since the very earliest days of this country, women have been on the forefront of social change, advocating for justice, instituting social services, and fighting for equality. This tradition continues today among the women who create and continue to develop healing places for women and children recovering from the trauma of addiction.

One such program is the SISTERS program, a unique and successful alcohol-and-drug treatment program that is now in its eleventh year of helping African American women get clean and sober. SISTER stands for Supported Intensive System of Treatment Empowerment and Recovery. The program began out of the realization that black women face the same problems that white women face while battling addiction, yet very few of them were seeking treatment.

In 1990, Darlene Fowler-Stephen, with twenty-one years of experience in the alcohol and drug unit of Meharry Hospital in Nashville, Tennessee, set out with a team of others to remove the barriers between African American women and recovery. The program she began, which maintains very high visibility by its famous bright-pink jackets and pink flyers, provides an ongoing outreach directly into the communities, housing projects, jails, and prisons where women are often trapped in their addictions. The most important ingredient in their success is their heartfelt dedication to their mission.

Over the years, the SISTER program has been featured on NPR and *ABC World News Tonight* and in *The Los Angeles Times, Parade Magazine,* and *Family Circle* magazine, as well as in local newspapers. The model has been exported to several other towns in Tennessee, as well as to California, Louisiana, Wisconsin, Florida, Alabama, and Indiana. They also train staff for other programs.

The Pink Badge of Honor

Fowler-Stephen recounts:

> *That first trip out into the projects was a little intimidating. We didn't know what to expect. We made our way through drug dealers and teenagers to deliver flyers and talk with the women about addiction.*

Soon, however, their bright pink satin jackets with the name SISTER proudly displayed on the back became a badge of honor around town and in the projects. On one hot summer day, Fowler-Stephen remembers heading into the housing project without her jacket and being hassled by some young boys who kicked rocks at her and her companion as they approached. They went back to the car and put the jackets on, and the boys' attitude sharply changed. A voice announced their approach to the others, saying: "Leave them alone! Those are the SISTERS—they're here to help!"

FIGURE 24. *Two delighted little girls whose mother is in SISTER care. (Photograph courtesy of Dr. Carlene Hunt.)*

"Once a Sister always a Sister!" the project's literature proclaims:

When a woman joins the SISTER program, she is a member for life—regardless of her ability to stay clean and sober. Many have relapsed; however, they know they can return without judgment and be met with love and compassion. Some women who are still using refer others to the program, saying, "I'm not ready yet, but this person needs help. I told her you can help."

The bottom line of the SISTER program is: "If you want to get clean and sober, we'll help you no matter what." The program's philosophy is empowerment, and they use every opportunity to encourage, praise, and love women into making a choice for a better life. "It takes a certain type of person to work here," says Dominique, one of the counselors. "Not everyone can do this work. It is very demanding. We stay available to the women at all times."

The program takes every woman who wants to come as soon as the space is available. "Some of them arrive in pretty bad shape straight off the street; some have just been beaten by their boyfriend or husband; some are angry and abusive to the staff at first. You have to be able to hang in there with them, and not everyone can do that." Regina, a professional singer and staff member, told about standing at the foot of the bed and literally singing a woman to sleep. "She just wouldn't settle down any other way," she said.

It Takes a Village

"It takes a village to raise a child," an African proverb tells us. And that is how the SISTERs fulfill their mission. The greatest barriers to women getting into treatment are their children. That's a catch-22. Women won't and can't leave their children because the Department of Children and Family Services will take them, and many women are afraid they won't get them back. They're also afraid they'll lose their jobs, which is often the case, or that they'll get thrown out of their apartments, which is also likely to happen. When a woman is admitted as an inpatient, the SISTER program finds safe places for her children.

"We have surrogate families, aunties, and grandmothers all over town, or we'll pay for child care," says Fowler-Stephen. If a woman is an outpatient, the SISTER program often ends up taking care of the children—making the old African proverb a reality! Dominique told about how she was waiting to be interviewed for a staff position while three children belonging to a client were climbing all over her. She played with them, not showing any signs of distress. The secretary got up and went into Fowler-Stephen's office and apparently told her: "You better hire this one—she can handle the kids!" Dominique got the job!

The SISTER program offers a home environment and a chance to make the choice to trade misery for a new way of life. Over the years, over 1000 women have made that choice and learned the living truth of the SISTER program's motto: "There is hope."

The Ark—What Happens When...?

What happens when a veteran social worker, a visionary priest, and a legendary singer-songwriter walk into a bar together? If it's Jennie Adams, Charles Strobel, and Emmylou Harris, the answer will most likely be: A new project! And that project will be innovative, multi-dimensional, pull a network of people together, and improve the community. And if the bar is in Nashville, chances are it will involve a song at some point. And let's not forget our four-legged friends. The project you'll read about here, aptly named The Ark, has brought together an unlikely alliance of people and canine critters, and placed them all in a beautiful setting.

This project really began in 2002, not in a bar, but in a local restaurant when the three principals met for lunch. Father Charles Strobel, local legend and former Nashvillian of the Year, had started a project known as Room in the Inn over twenty years before. It began on a cold December night in 1986 when he was pastor of Holy Names Catholic Church. Strobel's concern for the people sleeping on the front porch of the rectory where he lived reached a peak one night, and he invited them into the church, where he served them peanut-butter-and-jelly sandwiches.

Since that night, the Room in the Inn project has grown into an inter-faith community of over 200 congregations, with thousands of volunteers providing shelter for several hundred guests every night. It's now called the Campus for Human Development and provides a full range of services to residents—from food and shelter to medical care, job training, and permanent housing. Ten similar communities have sprung up around the country. Now here is the next chapter in this ongoing story of service to the poor and underserved.

The music of legendary songwriter and musician Emmylou Harris transcends categories—she is aptly described as an American artist. Harris has long been an activist dedicated to both human and animal rights. She promotes feminism in her music and has performed at Lilith Fair—a traveling music festival promoting women in music that raises money and consciousness for women's charities throughout North America. Harris has also organized a tour called Concerts for a Landmine-Free World. All proceeds go to supporting the Vietnam Veterans of America Foundation (VVAF). More recently, she has been a major force for the National Resources Defense Council (NRDC) in a campaign to stop the destruction of Appalachian mountaintops through coal mining.

A few years ago, Harris founded an animal shelter in Nashville known as Bonaparte's Retreat, where she assists in her "spare time." The shelter rescues death-row dogs and rehabilitates them for adoption. The dogs (and a few cats) are treated by a veterinarian, have their shots updated, and receive basic obedience training. Beyond these services, and of equal importance to their rehab, they are loved by Emmylou and the staff until they virtually shine.

Jennie Adams is a social worker and master web-weaver. She has stirred more kettles of soup than Mr. and Mrs. Heinz and the Campbells put together. Jennie knows everyone! She has worked for several organizations, including the YWCA, where she developed a summer program for ninety children by tapping into her network of generous citizens, who provided the funds. She was one of three who founded the Bayview Center in Clearwater, Florida, a retreat and healing center for exhausted clerics. The Center combines counseling and spirituality in a unique partnership between religion and mental health.

The Over the Hill Gang, another of her creative projects, provided a place for aspiring entrepreneurs to present their vision to a room full of seasoned professionals who could offer guidance and provide connections in the business community—on a volunteer basis. They met for fifteen years and helped launch numerous projects and businesses. In 1985, Adams co-founded Nashville Psychotherapy Institute (NPI), an organization for mental-health workers. Here, she developed an arena for communication among professionals that remains a unique and vital resource in the community.

Adams is a key link in the chain of events that led to the building of The Ark. She knew both Strobel and Harris, and saw the natural connection between their two dreams. She played the role of a visionary and of godmother to the project. She is a master at putting the right people together for the right purposes and watching things grow. In fact, watching things grow and blossom is Jennie's life work—she does it with organizations, with people she guides in her private counseling practice, and in her bounteous garden.

Harris, Adams, and Stroebel met and talked for several years. Jennie saw that the dream was in danger of stalling out and got a friend to put together a "Come to Jesus" retreat that helped them make the leap from dream to reality. Committees were formed and progress began at a concrete level. They are currently looking for a location for The Ark at the Crossroads Community Campus.

The Ark Dream

The Ark at the Crossroads Community Campus is a non-profit career-advancement center where young adults and other men and women seeking stability and career opportunities can learn all aspects of pet care, including training, grooming, and business skills. The vision of The Ark has identified a weak place in the social services system, specifically young people coming out of foster care with no place to go and little means. It hopes to address this need. The Ark will become self-sufficient and provide paid positions for students and graduates. The facility will include:

- Animal care in a no-kill facility and adoption center
- Residential quarters for students
- Onsite food preparation and service
- Large-scale community gardening where food will be raised for the facility and where neighbors are invited to participate in the growing and consuming of organic produce.
- Community dog park and neighborhood park with walking trails
- Tree and nursery and arboretum
- Education and business incubation center
- Administrative offices
- Construction and land use practices that will be "green" and environmentally sustainable—e.g. solar and geothermal

Emmylou Harris and Bonaparte's Retreat staff will guide the development of pet services, which will be extended to the larger community. Services will include grooming, boarding, adoption, basic obedience training, a dog park, and lots of love. Harris has been instrumental in raising funds for the project.

Jennie Adams talks about her vision of developing a program to work with the many volunteers who generously give their time to this project. Adams believes volunteering gives a face to what is the spirit of this country in a way that is sacred. It fosters a sense of compassion and community and belonging that people are hungry for. She wants to involve the local residents and the public at large in The Ark to help create an open and involved community.

When Father Strobel is asked why he thinks the poor need all the services he provides, he answers "Because you need them." This simple philosophy defines the mission.

Strobel and Adams are creating a new language in which to talk about the people they will be serving on campus. They believe the term "homeless" lacks dignity and offers no hope. They consider their guests as people in transition and their services as assisting in that transition. The goal is to offer support to men and women in making the journey home—to their own homes as fully functioning people. Contact information on The Ark Crossroads Community Campus can be found in the resources listed at the back of this book.

Wrapping Things Up

Successful social programs are the result of vision and hard work. They are powered by love and guided by good management. Women's projects are multi-dimensional, creative, and transformational—to those who participate and ultimately for the culture at large. No dream is too big to become a reality—we are invited to expand ourselves and to work together to make dreams come true. Those who do find fulfillment and satisfaction on a day-to-day basis. They hold the vision of fruition and work in the now.

Chapter 25

❦ ❦

WOMEN, POWER, AND SPIRITUALITY

*T*iffany Ludwig and Renee Piechocki may have the best handle on how women, power, and spirituality all fit together. Since they began working together in 2001, they have interviewed over 600 women from South Carolina to Alaska, asking the seemingly innocent question: "What do you wear that makes you feel powerful?" They collected these first-hand testimonies under the title *Trappings: Stories of Women, Power and Clothing.* In 2010, their complete work was archived at the Schlesinger Library of the Radcliffe Institute at Harvard University. The library exists to document women's lives and endeavors. Because of the success of *Trappings*, I wanted to know more about the artists. Here's the result of our conversation, along with two women's stories of power, spirituality, and clothing told in their own words.

> Mary: *I'm curious, how did you decide to focus on women's power and how did you connect it with clothing?*
>
> Renee: *When we started collaborating as artists, we spent about a year talking about our work and figuring out what we had in common. We discovered we both wanted to do a project that involved women; we wanted to create a work of art that was very different from our personal studio practices; and we wanted to create a work of art outside of the studio environment. We were both in our*

mid to late twenties. We saw that women were rejecting the label of feminist, which confused us, since they seemed to be benefiting from all feminism created. So, we considered asking women about feminism. We quickly realized that this would be a very polarizing discussion—one that would not allow us to dig any deeper into women's feelings about their own sense of power.

Tiffany: *We developed this question as the basis of our work: What do you wear that makes you feel powerful? The way we formulated the question contributed to the ease with which women could become involved in* Trappings. *We wanted a discussion about power to surface, but did so by asking about clothing. To consider what their trappings of power were, women were open to discussing what power meant to them. In our project, clothing is a comfortable route to power—as power is to feminism.*

Mary: *What have you learned in this project that surprised you?*

Renee: *Perhaps what was surprising was the impact that those first few interview sessions had on us. I remember being in Tiffany's studio after the sessions, sitting on the floor with her mom, talking about how amazing our day had been. How much energy and thoughtfulness and emotion we had witnessed that day. We saw that the question we developed really touched women in a compelling way. We talked about how we should interview in other parts of the country. We just knew that we could not stop—did not want to stop. I am really grateful that Tiffany and I had the guts, stamina, and dedication to produce* Trappings. *It would have been a huge loss to me as a person and as an artist to have been aware of the power of the interview sessions and not to have taken the risk to continue after that first day, after that first exhibition.*

Tiffany: *What hasn't surprised me? I'm surprised how far geographically and emotionally it took Renee and me, and how long the project has continued. I'm thrilled with the success we achieved with the project. It's brought me closer to a fellow collaborator than I anticipated possible. I think Renee and I both began* Trappings *with ideas of grandeur. Why would we start a project with anything less? To fulfill those ideas has been terrific.*

Mary: *What advice do you have for other women who might have an idea or a dream they want to pursue?*

Renee: *That it is okay, and perhaps imperative, to forget about life balance for a period of time when you are doing something you completely believe in and are passionate about. Not having enough sleep or extra cash or time to attend every family event is worth the risk when you are doing something important to you. Just be sure to communicate with your family and friends so they can be in the loop, share your excitement, and encourage you.*

Mary: *What were some of the challenges you faced?*

Tiffany: *We could only have created a project like this in this day and age. The digital filmmaking, editing, and communication tools that exist today made this long-distance project possible. Our biggest challenge was financial. We began this project with our own credit cards as the primary backer. Over the years, by working with larger institutions, we were awarded grants and funding that allowed us to complete the interviews, the exhibition, the book, and the multiple installations of* Trappings.

Renee: *Tiffany and I have spoken a lot about how this project has made us more aware of our own prejudices. I have always considered myself open-minded, but this project made me aware of how much of a challenge it is to quiet any notions you may have about who a person is based on their appearance. Because of* Trappings, *I am more open than ever to give people the time and space to inform me about who they are. The project has certainly made me a more curious person.*

Women, Power, and Religion

Now let's see how two women responded to Renee and Tiffany's question: "What do you wear to feel powerful?" The first is the story of a young wife and mother who finds power in raising her family and through exploring her Native American roots. The second is the story of a young woman who is an Episcopalian priest. She talks about her struggle to find her place in Christianity and as an ordained priest. Their stories are part of the project *Trappings: Stories of Women, Power and Clothing* (Rutgers University Press, 2007).

Sunshine Howell

I'm thirty-one years old. I have three children. Three boys. They are eight, four, and two. I'm currently a student at the University of New Mexico and going part time. I'm actually in the Anderson School of Management for Accounting. I currently work here at the Indian Pueblo Cultural Center in the Accounting Department full time. I sell Avon on the side, and I'm gonna sell Tupperware on the side. My husband also works here. He's a banquet technician.

FIGURE 25. Sunshine Howell, Albuquerque, New Mexico, 2008.

I'm also a member of the Jemez Pueblo tribe. My dad's from Jemez Pueblo. His name's Stanley Wacue. And my mom's name's Gloria Seaberry. I recently moved here in August of 2003 to continue my education at UNM. I wanted to be surrounded more by Native American atmosphere, so I decided to move here with my family. I don't speak my native languages on both sides. I'm trying. My kids are learning from my dad, which I'm very grateful for. I didn't grow up with my dad. I grew up with my mom in Wyoming.

I feel I'm a survivor of three worlds. My tribe in Wyoming and my tribe down here, what you can do here, you can't do up there. Like, down here in Jemez, it's an honor when you kill a rabbit. In Wyoming, you don't do that. We have a ceremony called the Rabbit Lodge, so when you kill a rabbit, it's bad. To me, I think I'm living in the modern-day society, plus both of my tribes conflict. But I'm proud to be a member of both tribes. And I try to teach my kids when we're here you learn this, when you're there then you respect and honor what you're supposed to do there.

Power to me, well actually, I dress like this 'cause of chasing after my kids and being constantly on my feet. But at the same time, power to me means survival and self-esteem. 'Cause nobody can be powerful unless they believe in themselves and they're happy with themselves. When I say survival, it's from our ancestors. I'm here because of my ancestors. They survived so that we can be here to survive some more. My grandpa told me a lot of stories about forced assimilation, boarding schools, you know, all that.

When I was going to my anthropology class, we had to do something and we did it on boarding schools, forced assimilation, PowerPoint presentation. I did it on my grandpa and just stories that he shared. Some of it was actual information I found, resources, sites, everything. Some of the sources I found were Navajo people and Navajo tribe and just different nationalities that went through that. I even asked my dad, 'cause he doesn't go to church either. I'm like, if they ask you what religion what do you say? He said, I say Catholic. He doesn't practice it either. He's more traditional. He's a really important man of our tribe. He composes a lot of the songs for our tribe and he sings a lot of the songs.

When people ask me my religion, a lot of my family in Wyoming say Catholic. I participate in Native American church, but I don't really say I'm Catholic. Even with the Jemez Pueblo tribe, some of the history I'm learning is they forced you to pray. They forced this Catholic religion on you. And now on every pueblo there's a Catholic church. My grandma, she just recently passed away in November, her name was Corinna Wacue. She was a very faithful Catholic lady. And I said, Grandma, I said, they forced it on you a long time ago. They embedded it in you so bad. I said, now you have a right to decide to be traditional or Catholic.

I pray when I want. I pray with corn meal. My dad tells me stories, he's teaching me things. But, I can't understand. They forced people to cut their hair. They forced you not to talk your native language. So then for me to say I'm Catholic and to be proud, I can't because of the past part of it.

For me power is survival from the ancestors to come into here. Self-esteem. When I think of power, I think anybody can be as powerful as they want. I feel that I'm no better than anybody, even though I'm going to school. I'm just making a better choice to go to school. Anybody that's a doctor, a lawyer, they're no better than somebody that stays home and takes care of their kids. They just made a choice to go to school. We're all equal. We're all the same. So when I say self-esteem, I'm happy with who I am. When you're happy with who you are, you can do whatever you want. You won't care what anybody says to try to bring you down. As long as you're happy in here, then you can make your kids happy. You can provide for your family, you can be a friend, the best sister, the best employee. Whatever. So, when I think of power, that's what I think of.

Anne Fowler

I'm an Episcopal priest and rector of a parish in Jamaica Plain, which is part of Boston. The things that I wear that make me feel powerful are my vocational, my professional clothes.

Underneath what I'm wearing I have on a black shirt with a collar, which, as my parishioners would tell you, I very rarely wear because it's not my favorite fashion statement. But when I'm out in the world, doing political advocacy, which I do a fair amount, I do tend to wear my collar so that I'll be known to be a priest.

FIGURE 25. Anne Fowler, Boston, Massachusetts, October 2005.

What I'm wearing tonight that you can see, is called a chasuble and underneath a white alb. I wear the alb during every Sunday service that I do. The first part of the service, which we call the Service of the Word, consists of biblical readings and prayers and a sermon. For this, I wear a priestly stole, which is a sign of office. Ordinarily for the first part of the service, I'll wear another stole which is more interesting. We have the Peace after the Service of the Word; people greet one another and I make some announcements and there's some singing and then we go into the Service of the Eucharist. As we're doing the singing and during the break time, I don this chasuble, which is something that a priest may wear, and often does wear, to celebrate the Eucharist.

The power that I feel wearing these garments is mysterious and hard to describe, perhaps because it's a power that I feel transcends me. It becomes a very representative outfit, if you will. It becomes a symbol of my priesthood and my standing representing the people to God. And, I feel less confident saying the next thing, but certainly some people would say I'm representing God to the people. Anyway, I'm in an intermediary role which has a lot invested in it, certainly by the congregation, and by me because it is my calling. I feel a power that is sort of transcendent. It's not an ego trip; it's quite humbling, and I feel as if I'm taken out of myself. So it's an unusual kind of power, I think.

I grew up as an Episcopalian and I was taken to church by my grandmother, who was my namesake and whom I adored, so I have very good memories of church. The church had been built by an ancestor of mine, so there was a certain proprietary feeling in the family about the parish and I felt very much at home there as young child.

As a teenager, I was very active in the state of Maine in what was then called Episcopal Young Church Men, and I remember thinking at that time that it would be nice, it might be nice to be married to a priest. Women were not being ordained then, so it wasn't a sort of childhood or teenage dream of mine, because I think I was fairly realistic and a concrete thinker. And, you know, it wasn't possible.

When I went to college, I fell in love with 17th-century religious poetry and in particular with a poet named George Herbert, who was an English priest and poet. I went to graduate school, and wrote a doctoral thesis on George Herbert, and in the meanwhile, I got married and divorced twice in my twenties. By the end of my twenties, I was a single parent, which had not been in any game plan that I had.

I went back to church after that sort of tumultuous period, because I was lonely and wanted to meet people, and became gradually active in the parish. And the rector then, I think, saw in me some calling toward ordination, perhaps before I saw it myself. I was working on this doctoral thesis on George Herbert and not doing research in the way I thought of scholarly research, but going to the library and reading George Herbert poems and crying, and discovering, I think, that I had a spiritual life. Reading poems that were very volatile, and very honest toward God about different moods of anger and depression and defiance and reconciliation and hope, and a whole sort of rollercoaster of a spiritual life that never resolved itself. There was some reconciliation, and resolution would happen, and then the next day, you know, down in the dumps again.

So I thought this sounds plausible, and the minute that I finished my doctoral thesis on George Herbert I enrolled in a course in seminary. I was ordained a priest just two days before I turned forty, so it was a kind of mid-life, or young-mid-life, change or evolution of a vocation, I guess.

We have what's called the three-legged stool of theological understanding: scripture; tradition, which is the church and its teachings over time; and then reason, in which is included experience, feelings, and so forth.

I think that the Anglican church, which is the Episcopal tradition, has always valued reason and experience and our theology depends very strongly on the incarnation—that is the idea, you know, the concept of the embodied divinity in Jesus, and in the risen Christ, and finding the risen Christ in one another. I think that emphasis has forced people to recognize the full humanity of women and therefore our fitness to be priests and more and more, thank God, fully recognizing gay and lesbian people as fully human and also fitted to be ordained people and married people.

The first women were ordained in the Episcopal Church in what is now called an Irregular Ordination, in 1974. Eleven women decided that they could not wait any longer for the male church to decide it was okay to ordain women, so they found three bishops who would ordain them and got ordained after this general convention that I was talking about that meets every three years had denied women's ordination in 1973. In 1976, the convention met again and decided, whoa, it's a done deal. So, they voted to ordain women and regularize those Irregular Ordinations.

In my view, the first eleven women to be ordained were clearly all quite radical women and none of them ever felt a calling to parish ministry. I think they had been so damaged in their journey that it just wasn't gonna work. Some of them are seminary professors; they've done a bunch of different stuff.

And then after those eleven, the first women, it seemed to me there was a wave of women who got ordained who really were quite conservative, and they really were very male-identified. That was what they knew and that was what they saw and that was how they dressed.

And then, then it sort of opened up after it was not quite so new anymore. But I tell you, when I was in ordination process, I was told to get a new hairdo and new glasses. And I said: "Well, what's wrong with my hair? What's wrong with my glasses?" My advisor said: "I don't know, I don't know. You look kind of like a schoolteacher." And I said, "I am a schoolteacher. I think you want me to look like a nun." I was quite exercised by that comment and I didn't think that they would ever tell a man that.

I was complaining one day to one of my friends at lunch. We were in one of those downstairs restaurants on Newberry Street, and I said, "Can you imagine them ever telling a guy that?" My friend looked up out the window and a man was walking by with a Mohawk in rainbow colors and no shirt and chains all over his chest. She said, "That man, yes, that man they would tell to get a new hairdo." So, I was corrected.

Wrapping Things Up

Women may be reluctant to talk about power directly, but when it's wrapped in clothing, they've got plenty to say. This exciting project includes over 600 interviews with women all over the country talking about what they wear to feel powerful. The conversation goes deep below the surface and looks at women's relationship with power from many angles. This amazing project, developed by two equally amazing young women artists, is being archived at the Schlesinger Library of the Radcliffe Institute at Harvard University and will be studied for years to come. See the resources at the back of this book for Tiffany Ludwig and Renee Piechocki contact information and how to find *Trappings: Stories of Women, Power and Clothing.*

IN CONCLUSION

*I*n concluding this exploration of women's spirituality vis-à-vis power and grace, consider getting a group of women together and beginning your own discovery of the sacred—even writing your own theological statement. Women's spirituality is about recognizing the holiness in the ordinary events of life. It's not an activity, but a consciousness we bring into all our activities—and it is an organic part of who we are. It doesn't require formal education, special clothes, or cathedrals; it is everywhere, all encompassing, omnipresent. The only thing we need to do to effect the changes we want in our lives and in society is to own our awareness—validate it, refuse to be put down or be wronged—and do the next right thing. Spirit will guide the process.

BIBLIOGRAPHY

Ackerman, Susan. *Warrior, Dancer, Seductress, Queen: Women in Judges and Biblical Israel.* New Haven, CT: Yale University Press/ Anchor Bible, 1998.

Adler, Margot. *Drawing Down the Moon.* New York: Penguin, 1997. Rachel Adler, "In Your Blood, Live: Re-visions of a Theology of Purity," in *Tikkun* 8: 1 (January/February, 1993) 38–41.

Allen, Paula Gunn. *The Sacred Hoop: Recovering the Feminine in American Indian Traditions.* Boston: Beacon Press, 1992. Author, poet, speaking engagements, educational events. Contact: *www.paula-gunnallen.net.*

Binet, Noris. *Women on the Inner Journey.* Nashville: James C. Winston Publishing, 1994. Contact: see ORIGINS Educational Tours.

Birnbaum, Lucia Chiavola. *Dark Mother: African Origins and God-mothers.* Lincoln, NE: Authors Choice Press, 2001.

Bielecki, Tessa. *Teresa of Avila: Mystical Writings.* New York, NY: The Crossroad Publishing Company, 1994.

Bolen, Jean Shinoda. *Goddesses in Every Woman: A New Psychology for Women.* San Francisco: Harper & Row, 1985.

Borysenko, Joan. *A Woman's Book of Life: The Biology, Psychology, and Spirituality of the Feminine Life Cycle.* New York: Riverside Books, 1996. Contact: *www.joanborysenko.com.*

Bowie, Fiona. *Celtic Christian Spirituality.* London: Continuum, 1995.

Budapest, Zsuzsanna. *The Holy Book of Women's Mysteries*. Weiser Books: San Francisco, 2007. Contact: *www.zbudapest.com* for workshops, rituals, speaking, educational events.

Caldecott, Moyra. *Women in Celtic Mythology*. Rochester, VT: Destiny Books, 1988.

Carnes, Robin Deen, and Sally Craig. *Sacred Circles*. San Francisco: Harper San Francisco, 1998.

Chicago, Judy. *The Dinner Party*. New York, NY: Penguin, 1996.

Christ, Carol P., and Judith Plaskow. *Womanspirit Rising: A Feminist Reader in Religion*. San Francisco: Harper & Row, 1979. See Educational Tours and Goddess Trips.

Cole, Ronan, and Taussig. *Wisdom's Feast: Sophia in Study and Celebration*. Kansas City: Sheed & Ward, 1996.

Conway, Diane. *What Would You Do If You Had No Fear? Living Your Dreams While Quakin' in Your Boots*. Novato, CA: New World Library, 2004. Contact: *www.dianeconway.com* for retreats, comedy, speaking engagements.

Estes, Clarissa. *Women Who Run with the Wolves*. New York, NY: Ballantine Books, 1992.

Falk, Marcia. *The Book of Blessings: New Jewish Prayers for Daily Life, the Sabbath, and the New Moon Festival*. San Francisco: Harper Collins, 1996; paperback edition, Beacon Press, 1999.

———. *The Song of Songs: Love Lyrics from the Bible*. Boston: Brandeis University Press/University Press of New England, 1993.

Gilligan, Carol. *In a Different Voice: Psychological Theory and Women's Development*. Boston: Harvard University Press, 1993.

Gimbutas, Marija. *The Civilization of the Goddess: The World of Old Europe*. San Francisco: Harper San Francisco, 1991.

Henes, Donna. *The Queen of Myself*. Jackson, MS: Monarch, 2005. Contact: *www.engagements.donnahenes.net* for speaking engagements and workshops.

hooks, bell. *Ain't I a Woman*. Brooklyn, NY: South End Press, 1981.

Lerner, Gerda. *The Creation of Feminist Consciousness*. New York, NY: Oxford University Press, 1993.

Ludwig, Tiffany, and Renee Piechocki. *Trappings: Stories of Women, Power and Clothing.* New Brunswick, NJ: Rutgers University Press, 2007. Archived: Schlesinger Library of the Radcliffe Institute at Harvard University. Contact: *www.twogirlsworking.com.*

McFague, Sallie. *Life Abundant: Rethinking Theology and Economy for a Planet in Peril.* Minneapolis: Fortress Press, 2000.

Monaghan, Patricia. *The Goddess Companion.* Woodbury, MN: Llewellyn Worldwide, 1999. Contact: *www.patricia-monaghan.com* for publications, events, and newsletter.

Myss, Caroline. *Anatomy of the Spirit: The Seven Stages of Power and Healing.* New York: Three Rivers Press, 1997.

Plaskow, Judith. *Standing Again at Sinai: Judaism from a Feminist Perspective.* New York, NY: HarperCollins Publishers, 1990.

Reuther, Rosemary. *Gaia and God: An Ecofeminist Theology of Earth Healing.* San Francisco: Harper San Francisco, 1994.

Rich, Adrienne, "Transcendental Etude," *The Dream of a Common Language, Poems 1974–1977.* New York: W.W. Norton & Company, 1993.

Robinson, Dorothy Marie. *What Makes An Actor: A Director's View of Acting.* Nashville: Blue Ball Publishing, 2010. See Films for more information.

Ross, Carolyn Coker. *Healing Body, Mind and Spirit: An Integrative Medicine Approach to the Treatment of Eating Disorders.* Denver, CO: Outskirts Press, 2007.

Searles, Jo C. *Of a Like Mind*, XIV: 3, 25, Re-Formed Congregation of the Goddess International.

Sjöö, Monica, and Barbara Mor. *The Great Cosmic Mother: Rediscovering the Religion of the Earth.* San Francisco: Harper & Row, 1978.

Small, Jacquelyn. *Embodying Spirit: Coming Alive with Meaning and Purpose.* New York: HarperCollins Publishers, 1994.

Stanton, Elizabeth Cady. *The Woman's Bible.* Original printing 1895. Public Domain Books, February 1, 2006.

Spretnak, Charlene. *The Lost Goddesses of Early Greece.* Berkeley, CA: Moon Books, 1978.

Starhawk. *Spiral Dance, A Rebirth of the Ancient Religion of the Great Goddess.* San Francisco: Harper & Row, 1979. Contact *www.reclaiming.org* for speaking, workshops, teaching.

Teish, Luisah. *Jambalaya: The Natural Woman's Book of Personal Charms and Practical Rituals.* San Francisco: Harper & Row, 1985. Contact: *www.luisahteish.com* for teaching events, rituals.

Turner, Kay. *Beautiful Necessity: The Art and Meaning of Women's Altars.* New York: Thames & Hudson, 1999.

Wagner, Sally Roesch. *The Untold Story of the Iroquois Influence on Early Feminism.* Aberdeen, SD: Sky Carrier Press, 1996.

Walker, Alice. *In Search of Our Mothers' Gardens: Womanist Prose.* New York: Mariner Books, 1984.

Walker, Barbara G. *The Woman's Dictionary of Symbols and Sacred Objects.* New York: HarperOne, 1988.

Westfield, Lynne N. *Dear Sisters: A Womanist Practice of Hospitality.* Cleveland, OH: Pilgrim Press, 2001.

Woolger, Roger J., and Jennifer Barker Woolger. *The Goddess Within: A Guide to the Eternal Myths That Shape Women's Lives.* New York: Fawcett Columbine, 1987.

Ywhoo, Dhyani, Venerable. *Voices of Our Ancestors: Cherokee Teachings from the Wisdom Fire.* Boston, MA: Shambala Publications, 1987. Contact: Sunray Meditation Society, *www.sunray.org*.

Young, Serenity, ed. *Sacred Texts by and About Women.* New York: Crossroad, 1994.

ADDITIONAL RESOURCES

Retreats, Programs, Workshops

BENEDICTINE WOMEN RETREATS. A green retreat center, not for women only, but with deep feminist commitment: *www.benedictinewomen.org*

CONWAY, DIANE. Women's Retreats, Marin County, CA. *www.dianeconway.com*

COYOTE CAMP. PO Box 659. Occidental, CA 95465. *www.oceansong.org*. Environmental programs for children.

EMERICK, COREY. Integrative Life Center, a wellness program for addiction recovery. *www.integrativelifecenter.com* or (877) 334-6558.

LAUGHING WINDS. a spiritual community hosting classes and events for personal growth. *www. laughingwinds.com*. Call (615) 446-4594.

MARZONI, JANE. Soul Spring Retreat Center and life coaching, Sonoma County. *janemz@bellsouth.net*

RABUCK, DONNA FONTANAROSE, PH.D. Center for the Sacred Feminine, P.O. Box 86884, Tucson, AZ 85754. *drabuck@u.arizona. edu*; *www.centerforsacredfeminine.com*. Call (520) 743-4138.

RICH, CATHERINE ABBY. Combining Forces Natural Herbal Products, educational programs for adults and children. 201 Hawthorne Ave Larkspur, CA 94939. Call (415) 924-5961.

SEARLES, JO C., PH.D. Rise Up and Call Her Name Workshops. Contact (520) 626-0656.

STEWART, SARAH. Integrated Healing Arts Certification in Clinical Hypnotherapy, Guided Imagery, Deconstructing Trauma, Stress Reduction. West Coast call (707) 933-9374; East Coast call (615) 646-0040. *wwwintegratedhealingarts.com*

WEILAND, MARY. Star Prairie Retreats. Call (715) 248-3312.

Art, Blogs, Films, Jewelry, Music, Photography

FOWLER, KATHERINE. Artist, psychotherapist, dialoguing with archetypes. *www.kateye.com*

FRIENDSHIP BEADING COMPANY. Affirmation Beads and other personally designed jewelry. *lazypalms@aol.com*

HUNT, CARLENE, ED.D. Photograph of the SISTER Program. Call (615) 269-3283. *chgfocus@comcast.net*

JEFFERSON, JACQUELINE. Insoulful. CD. *tunecore.com* or *jackiejazz12@yahoo.com*

LEQUIRE, ALAN. Athena. Centennial Park, 2600 W. End Ave, Nashville, TN.

REICHMAN, SYDNEY. Franklin, TN. Call (615) 799-8094.

ROBINSON, DOROTHY MARIE. Alternative Routes. Nashville: Blue Ball Productions in association with Nashville Public Theatre. For presentation of film and discussion on women's issues and telling your story, contact *dotrob@yahoo.com* or *www.AlternateRoutesMovie.com*.

Academic programs

ASSOCIATION FOR THE STUDY OF WOMEN AND MYTHOLOGY (ASWM). The only academic organization devoted to goddess study. *www.womenandmyth.org.*

CALIFORNIA INSTITUTE OF INTEGRAL STUDIES: *www.ciis.edu*

INSTITUTE OF TRANSPERSONAL PSYCHOLOGY: *www.itp.edu*

WISDOM UNIVERSITY (not accredited): *www.wisdomuniversity.org*

Educational Tours and Goddess Trips

NORIS BINET, PH.D. ORIGINS. Traveling workshops to the sacred sites of Mexico, Costa Rica, the four corners of the Southwestern United States, and Alaska. Dr. Binet is available for seminars and lectures on creating cultural awareness. *nbindt@aol.com*

CAROL CHRIST. Goddess trips to Crete: *www.goddessariadne.org*

CHERYL STRAFFON. Cornwall: *www.goddess-tours-international.com*

Programs of Transformation

SISTER PROGRAM. Recovery for African American women and children. 1005 D. B. Todd Blvd., Nashville, TN 37208. Call (615) 327-6233.

THE ARK CROSSROADS COMMUNITY CAMPUS. *Istetar@prodigy.net*

Publications

GODDESS PAGES: *www.goddess-pages.co.uk*

OCHRE: *www.ochrejournal.org*

NEWSLETTER: *www.patricia-monaghan.com*

INDEX

ABOUT THE AUTHOR

Mary Faulkner holds a master's degree in religious education. She has published books in the fields of holistic healing, religion, and spirituality. In addition to writing, she is a psychotherapist, teacher, and workshop leader. Faulkner is on staff at the Integrative Life Center in Nashville, Tennessee.

Mary is the mother of three and grandmother of five.

Visit *maryfaulkner.com* and find out more.